Edward W. Blyden's Intellectual Transformations

Ruth Simms Hamilton

AFRICAN DIASPORA SERIES

The Ruth Simms Hamilton African Diaspora series at Michigan State University Press presents the past and contemporary experiences of African people throughout the world, written by emerging and established scholars in various fields in the social sciences and humanities in pursuit of a reconceptualization of the historical global movements of African peoples. This series pays tribute to the life and legacy of Dr. Ruth Simms Hamilton, a pioneer in African Diaspora Studies, and builds on her seminal work and conceptualization of the African diaspora.

The series editors are particularly interested in innovative book length manuscripts grounded in scholarly research and inquiry that challenge both preexisting and established notions of the African diaspora by engaging new regions, conceptualizations, and articulations of diaspora that move the field forward. In underscoring new frontiers and frameworks in the study of African descendants' lived experiences, the series presents new approaches to the production of knowledge on African diasporas. In keeping with the tradition of the field, the series is an interdisciplinary undertaking devoted to scholarship on the histories, political movements, institutions, cultures, intellectual discourse, ways of knowing, and identities of African and African descended peoples. Since the diaspora is based largely on movement, the transnational migrations of Africans throughout history and in contemporary times have complicated what it means to be black and/or African depending on the political, economic, religious, geographical, and cultural context Africans find themselves. As a result, scholars are forced to confront the evolving realities and constructions of blackness and Africanness in a changing world. While much of the scholarship in the diaspora continues to focus on the Americas due to the enduring legacy of the Middle Passage and trans-Atlantic slave trade, in addition to these areas the editors encourage manuscript submissions that bring greater visibility to less studied but nonetheless critical areas of the Africana world. This includes internal diasporas within the African continent and African diasporas of the Indian Ocean, Pacific and European regions.

The series highlights the global experiences and dynamic dimensions of peoples of African descent. It maps their historical and contemporary movements, speaks from their radical (unique) narratives and explores their critical relationships with one another. By exploring Afrodescendents within their particular and broader sociocultural, historical, political, and economic contexts, it contemplates similarities, difference, continuity and transformation.

Edward W. Blyden's Intellectual Transformations

AFROPUBLICANISM, PAN-AFRICANISM, ISLAM, AND THE INDIGENOUS WEST AFRICAN CHURCH

Harry N. K. Odamtten

MICHIGAN STATE UNIVERSITY PRESS | *East Lansing*

♾ The paper used in this publication meets the minimum requirements of ANSI/NISO Z39.48-1992 (R 1997) (Permanence of Paper).

Michigan State University Press
East Lansing, Michigan 48823-5245

Printed and bound in the United States of America.

29 28 27 25 24 23 22 21 20 19 1 2 3 4 5 6 7 8 9 10

LIBRARY OF CONGRESS CATALOGING-IN-PUBLICATION DATA
Names: Odamtten, Harry N. K., author.
Title: Edward W. Blyden's intellectual transformations : Afropublicanism, Pan-Africanism, Islam, and the indigenous West African church / Harry N. K. Odamtten.
Description: East Lansing, MI : Michigan State University Press, [2019] | Series: Ruth Simms Hamilton African Diaspora series | Includes bibliographical references and index.
Identifiers: LCCN 2018047548| ISBN 9781611863208 (pbk. : alk. paper) | ISBN 9781609175993 (pdf) | ISBN 9781628953657 (epub) | ISBN 9781628963663 (kindle)
Subjects: LCSH: Blyden, Edward Wilmot, 1832–1912. | Pan-Africanism. | Black nationalism. | Africa, West—Religion—19th century. | Intellectuals—Liberia—Biography. | Intellectuals—Africa, West—Biography. | African Americans—Intellectual life—19th century. | Free blacks—United States Virgin Islands—Saint Thomas—Biography. | Saint Thomas (United States Virgin Islands)—Biography. | Multilingual persons—Biography. | Liberia—Biography.
Classification: LCC DT634.3.B58 O33 2019 | DDC 320.54096—dc23
LC record available at https://lccn.loc.gov/2018047548

Book design by Charlie Sharp, Sharp DesIgns, East Lansing, MI
Cover design by Erin Kirk New
Cover photo: Dr. E. W. Blyden in 1894. New York Public Library, Digital Collections.

Michigan State University Press is a member of the Green Press Initiative and is committed to developing and encouraging ecologically responsible publishing practices. For more information about the Green Press Initiative and the use of recycled paper in book publishing, please visit *www.greenpressinitiative.org*.

Visit Michigan State University Press at *www.msupress.org*

Contents

Dedication

To my families of the blood, water, of the spirit, and of the past, present, and future. Especially to the memory of those who have gone before us: university distinguished professor Harriette Pipes McAdoo and state representative Rev. Dr. Michael C. Murphy. To the living, my aunt and uncle, Percel and Harriett Singleton of Grand Rapids; my godmother, Gwendolyn Taylor; Barbara Roberts Mason; and my entire Lansing family, as well as Christopher Dion Rooks and our family in Detroit, whose return journeys to Ghana intertwine with my academic pursuits and my making of a home away from our home in Ghana.

Introduction

The significance of Edward Wilmot Blyden's career as the most influential black intellectual of the nineteenth to early twentieth century is not only evinced by his books, such as *Christianity, Islam and the Negro Race* (1887) and *African Life and Customs* (1908), and in his writings in leading journals of the day, like *Nineteenth Century*, *Athenaeum*, *Southwestern Christian Advocate*, and *Royal African Society*, but also revealed by the streets and memorials that bear his name in different parts of the Atlantic world. A street in his birthplace, Charlotte Amalie, St. Thomas; a library in Norfolk, Virginia; a bust in Freetown, Sierra Leone—all serve to demonstrate Blyden's importance to various peoples of the Caribbean, North America, and West Africa.

This book examines the sequential development of Edward Wilmot Blyden's scholarly activities. It tracks key historic events and life experiences in Blyden's checkered career, which is to say the incidents that transformed him from a diasporic Ethiopianist to a purveyor of African life and customs. Through a close reading of sources culled from multiple archives, this intellectual biography of Blyden demonstrates that a chronological rather than a thematic analysis of his enduring ideas reveals his undervalued yet influential thinking on race, culture, Islam and Christianity in Africa and its American diaspora.

In contrast to scholarly examinations of Blyden's racial ideas, this book argues that Blyden did not uncritically receive racialist ideas from European interlocutors. Kwame Anthony Appiah claims that Blyden's ideas on race were a combination of the racialist views of Alexander Crummell, Queen Victoria, William Ewart Gladstone, Charles Dickens, and Charles Sumner.[1] The evolution of Blyden's ideas on race, however, were rooted in his travels across the Atlantic world and his association with diasporic communities, Victorian England, and Jewish intellectuals. His notions of race ideas began to crystallize in the Danish West Indies, where he witnessed the race-based Budoo rebellion, and further developed while in the United States as he grappled with the fear induced by the Fugitive Slave Act of 1850 as well as disappointment from rejection at three colleges on account of his race. His ideas on race continued to evolve with his failed marriage to Sarah Yates and interaction with mixed-race women like Anna Julia Cooper.

His views on race outside the Americas were shaped by his experiences in Liberia, where American-born Liberians who tended to be phenotypically lighter-skinned had established a political system that discriminated against indigenous Liberians, who were darker-complected, like himself and his second wife, Anna Erskine. Blyden blamed the failure of his first marriage to Yates on her association with the Americo-Liberian mixed race elite. Without these historical contexts, Blyden can be mistaken for an unrepentant racist—especially when his critique of the homogenization of African ethnic groups is not duly considered. Blyden knew the differences between the Fula, Asante, Yoruba, and Hausa.[2] The racialist ideas on which he based his Pan-African project were more about culture than about innate characteristics.

Blyden's views on ethnicity and ethnic differences have heretofore gone cursorily treated within the framework of his ideas on race. Investigating his claims of an Igbo identity affords a novel appreciation for Blyden as a seminal writer of Igbo identity. In many ways, he presaged Chinua Achebe, Adiele Afigbo, Kamene Okonjo, and others in the articulation of that ethnic identity. This investigation also explicates why many African American intellectuals maintained authentic African origins in order to stake their claims to black leadership positions.

While many authors have commented on Blyden's treatment of the "Jewish Question," none has meticulously engaged or researched his direct connections to the Jewish diaspora in the Caribbean, beginning in St. Eustatius through St. Thomas and to Venezuela. *Edward W. Blyden's Intellectual Transformations* illustrates Blyden's close connections to the Jewish community of St. Thomas, revealing that his examination of the Jewish Question and Zionism was more than just a perceived parallel with the Back-to-Africa movement.

This intellectual biography makes explicit Blyden's role as an African public intellectual and conceptualizes the spaces in which he operated as public spheres. In doing so, it features African cities like Accra, Freetown, and Lagos as cosmopolitan spaces in which Blyden's ideas proliferated. It also highlights his adoption and use of an Afro-positivist discourse in the public arenas of West Africa, Victorian England, and the United States, among others. Along the way, *Edward W. Blyden's Intellectual Transformations* traces the long history of Afro-positivist discursive practice among Africa-born Atlantic intellectuals and Africa-born plantation intellectuals. Notably, this book departs from a historiography that suggests that, at the time of his passing, West African Islam was the apex of Blyden's thinking. To this end, it shows in definitive ways that his final thoughts were about Africanized Christianity,[3] and further posits that Islam was, in fact, a bridge to his West African Ethiopianism. Through his involvement with West African Muslims, I posit, he was able to accept, engage, and articulate the epistemologies that defined African societies and cultural traditions.

By analyzing Blyden's lived experience in Africa, this book brings fresh scholarship to understanding his moments of cerebral metamorphosis; for example, his abandonment of a diasporic Ethiopianist attitude toward indigenous Africans following his cathartic connection with them while serving in the Liberian militia and his encounters with the African Muslim civilizations of Greater Senegambia. These events prompted his study of Arabic, original and conscientious research of Islamic manuscripts, and engagements with Islamic scholars and their communities.

This book argues, then, that Blyden was the first black African scholar in the modern era to be engrossed by the systematic and scientific study of Islam in West Africa, a claim yet to be made in scholarship on Blyden. I show how Blyden's methodical engagement with West African Islam prompted an increasing respect for African societies and cultures, leading to his final transformation—reflected in his last book, *African Life and Customs* as well as in the distinctive brand of West African Ethiopianism or Christianity he inspired. Ultimately, Blyden came to believe that Africa's regeneration was to come from within rather than from outside change.

Finally, I argue contrary to Blyden scholars Hollis Lynch and Thomas Livingston, who viewed Blyden as a failed leader with little organizing ability who possessed only a superficial understanding of African life and customs and truncated the development of education in Liberia.[4] Blyden influenced at least two generations of Pan-African scholars in the first half of the twentieth century, notably J. E. Casely Hayford and W. E. B. Du Bois, and Kwame Nkrumah and George Padmore in the second half. He influenced the emergence of West African Ethiopianism, founded newspapers to circulate his ideas in various public spheres, established literary and drama clubs, and developed working relationships with many groups and societies. Blyden had shortcomings, but those did not make him less than the most influential black intellectual of the late nineteenth and early twentieth centuries.

Biography and Historical Background

Unlike the progeny of the enslaved population in the Danish West Indies, Blyden was born to free black parents in St. Thomas on August 3, 1832.[5] At the age of ten, Blyden moved with his family briefly to Porto Cabello, Venezuela. They returned to St. Thomas in 1844 and resided at No. 2 Ananas Street.

Blyden, at this time, was a freeborn black, who lived in the mostly Jewish, English-speaking community of Charlotte Amalie and enjoyed a relatively peaceful upbringing. During his school years, his mother, father, and mentor J. P. Knox were influential. Earlier, in 1844, when the Blydens returned to St. Thomas, Eddie, as people in Charlotte Amalie knew Edward Blyden, was attending school in the morning while working as an apprentice in a tailoring shop that was likely owned by his father, Romeo Blyden. Blyden also studied privately with his mother, Judith Blyden (née Nicholson), a schoolteacher.[6]

It was, however, Reverend Knox of the Dutch Reformed Church of St. Thomas who would influence Blyden to travel to the United States in an attempt to attend theological college at Rutgers University.[7] Due to the prevailing racial climate, Blyden was unsuccessful in his bid to be educated in the United States. Rather than continue as a servant in a New York home while attending night school, Blyden became involved in the nineteenth century's Back-to-Africa movement. He immigrated to Monrovia, Liberia, to acquire an education that he could not get in the United States and to escape the Fugitive Slave Law, enacted in 1850.[8]

In Monrovia, Blyden attended Alexander High School, where he would later serve as principal.[9] From Liberia, Blyden would travel the world, articulating and confronting various concerns of black life. Between 1850 and 1912, Blyden traveled on more than fifty ships and steamboats with diverse names, including the *Accra*, *Athenian*, *Baltic*, *Cleopatra*, *Calabar*, *Denmark*, *Ethiopia*, *Istambul*, *Liberia Packet*, *Minnesota*, *Senegal*, SS *Biafra*, and *Tenerife*. The names of the ships reflect Blyden's cosmopolitanism—denoting various points of departure and destinations, and suggesting his familiarity with diverse cultural and intellectual communities.[10] Throughout his travels, Blyden was a voice of conscience and an agent of resistance for people of African descent throughout the world. Thus, from his base in Monrovia, Liberia, and later Freetown, Sierra Leone, Blyden loomed large as an African public intellectual in the scholarly and nationalist atmosphere of global black life in the nineteenth and early twentieth centuries.

"African public intellectual" refers here to the activities of African thinkers like Blyden who energetically engaged with numerous African issues—philosophical, literary, and cultural—that circulated in various public spheres. These African intellectuals formed or became part of various counterpublics in response to the Afro-pessimism of various travelers, scholars, litterateurs, and public figures who wrote negatively about African societies and peoples. *Edward W. Blyden's Intellectual Transformations: Afropublicanism, Pan-Africanism, Islam, and the Indigenous West African Church* is an intellectual biography of the Afropublican career, Pan-African activities, and Black Atlantic writings of Edward Wilmot Blyden.

In these pages, I use *Afropublican* as a portmanteau to describe African public intellectuals who utilize an Afro-positivist discourse and whose scholarly engagement with provincial, cosmopolitan, and global public spheres is undertaken from an African perspective. By African perspective, I mean homegrown viewpoints or ideas harnessed from a rootedness in the African historical experience. Gregory Mann defines *Afro-positivist* discourse as "a real, empirical and ethical commitment to perceiving African societies—and when possible and appropriate 'Africa' as such—as lived, by Africans, now."[11] Many African intellectuals may be described as Afropublican, but none more so than Edward Blyden. Before his eighteenth birthday, Blyden had already traveled throughout the Caribbean and the United States. At that same age, he traveled as a diasporic African to Liberia, West Africa. He became literate in Romance and African languages. He held conversations in person and print with African Muslims, Islamic scholars, Victorian royals and intellectuals, Jewish rabbis as well as Caribbean and African American thinkers.

Although Blyden was born in the Danish West Indies, this book treats him as an African intellectual because of an interrelated group of historical factors discussed throughout the various chapters. Briefly, they include Blyden's unquestionable African heritage, his literacy in multiple African languages as well as his claim to a specific ethnic-African heritage—Igbo. In addition, Blyden's Afro-positivist discourse originates from African epistemological foundations. A majority of the ideas Blyden shared with the global public emanated from his lived experience in Africa beginning at age eighteen, rather than from his Diasporic African experiences. Finally, Blyden not only became a citizen of the Republic of Liberia, West Africa, with his ideas spreading throughout the region and beyond, but also served Liberia in various civic capacities including Ambassador Extraordinary and *Plenipotentiary* to Great Britain.

Blyden was without a doubt informed by the major ideas, important personalities, and intellectual debates of his time, but he participated in the public discourses of his day from a unique experiential understanding of African histories and societies. To date, his unique constellation of experiences has not been satisfactorily studied. *Edward W. Blyden's Intellectual Transformations* seeks to elucidate these pivotal encounters. It will highlight Blyden's Afropublicanism—that is, his ascent to global public significance through his remarkable ability to lucidly articulate from an African perspective African histories, cultures, and social issues in multiple public spheres: cultural, religious, nationalist, social, and intellectual. A notable example is Blyden's formulation of the *African Personality*, an essential conceptual foundation around which later understandings of Pan-Africanism were developed. Blyden's African Personality celebrated a glorious African past and espoused ways in which that past—African social institutions, cultural practices, communalism, and humanism—could be nurtured. The fruits of this fostering would have been the regeneration of a modernized Africa and contemporaneous influence from Africans' encounter of with European imperialism.

Blyden's African Personality may, therefore, be described as Afro-positivist in that it sought to use critical observation methods to portray what Blyden thought was more truthful about African societies past and present. This approach counters previous European travelogue and literary tropes as well as negative images of Africa in the contemporary public sphere produced for the consumption of the Western public, which often reinforced perceptions of Africans as nonhistorical, contemptible brutes who occupy the lower rungs of a false racial hierarchy. I argue that Afro-positivist discourse is the approach Blyden and nineteenth-century West African intellectuals used to challenge European colonial and cultural policies.

Blyden wrote for his fellow African and African diasporan peers as well as the general African public, he also wrote for the benefit of European intellectuals and the European public. Taking into consideration the African, African diaspora, European, Islamic, and Jewish audiences that Blyden engaged through his Afro-positivist discourse, one may say that Blyden and others created new discursive spaces within the global public sphere. Blyden's importance to global public discourse as an Afropublican whose main concern was with Africa is demonstrated in the multiple public circles he participated in and influenced while debating various interlocutors—whether they were Afro-pessimist or sympathetic to Africa.

I coined the term *Afropublican* to help illumine the role of Blyden and other African intellectuals who were consumed by and concerned with the status of Africa and people of African descent in the world community. This reinterpretation of Blyden's intellectual career emphasizes his role as a public intellectual as well as his use of Afro-positivism as a discursive practice on behalf of Africa and African-descended peoples.

Blyden's various writings on specific and general histories of African peoples as well as his attempts at explaining African societies from an African perspective provide further evidence of the indigenous emergence of modern West African thought. I have chosen Blyden from an eminent list of equally significant nineteenth-century West African intellectuals; among them are Carl Christian Reindorf (1834–1917), who authored *The History of the Gold Coast and Asante: Based on Tradition and Historical Facts Comprising a Period of More than Three Centuries from about 1500–1860* in 1889; Bishop Samuel Ajayi Crowther (1809–1891), the first African bishop of the Anglican Church; James Africanus Beale Horton (1835–1883), who completed a treatise, *West African Countries and Peoples: A Vindication of the Negro Race*, in 1868; Joseph Ephraim Casely Hayford (1866–1930), who penned *Ethiopia Unbound: Studies in Race Emancipation* in 1911, and many other works.[12]

All of these writers made essential contributions to the history of ideas generated in West Africa. However, I have chosen Blyden not only because of his African and Danish West Indies background or because he was an ordained minister of the Presbyterian Church but also because of the evolution of his understanding of Africa. Blyden advanced from an attitude of condescension to one of respect, as found in his book *African Life and Customs* (1908). Over the course of this biographical arc, he derived the Pan-African concept of the African Personality. The foundational and burgeoning nature of Blyden's emblematic African-centered contributions to Pan-African historiography and the indigenous African nationalist movement in West Africa, combined with his strong personality, have resulted in conflicting interpretations of his life and writings. I will attempt to clarify various competing views about the meanings and central ideas of Blyden's writings.

Valentine Mudimbe's description of Blyden's ideas as "inconsistent," while compatible with a thematic analysis, is itself incompatible with a chronological examination and historical contextualization of Blyden's various ideas on race, nationalism, and history.[13] Also, most other writers' accusations of Blyden's "anti-mulatto" stance in Liberia are not tempered by an analysis of his fractious relationship with Sarah (Sally) Yates, a member of the mixed-race class or Blyden's prescient analysis of the racial gradations that those of partial white descent had constructed and imposed in Liberia.[14]

Indeed, in the aftermath of the recent Liberian civil wars—the first in 1989–1996; the second in 1999–2003—no one thanked Blyden for his wisdom. The ruling class of Liberia did not heed his advice about its mixed-race hegemony. Blyden, the race vindicator, might have felt vindicated if he were alive today, as his analysis of the Liberian polity was echoed by the Truth and Reconciliation Commission of Liberia in the twenty-first century. In 2008, the commission released a report to the country's national legislature and its first female president, Ellen Johnson Sirleaf. The report asserts that the cause of the civil strife that engulfed Liberia between 1944 and 1980 as well as 1989 to the present stemmed from the history of Liberia's founding. It elaborates: "President Tubman's authoritarian reign—though progressive in some instances—laid down the continuation of Americo-Liberian hegemony through oligarchy, for national chaos, state break down and violent conflict between 1979–2003."[15] The commission faulted not only the Americo-Liberian "settlers' hegemony" and their clashes over land with indigenes but also their suppression of indigenous Liberian participation in government.[16]

In the opinion of the commission, "The political contest between Tubman (Americo-Liberian) and Twe (indigene) symbolized the continuation of the age-old divide between settlers and natives to their children and was in a sense, a defining moment for Liberia."[17] Ironically, these supposedly defining moments had long been defined by Blyden in his voluminous writings penned over a century ago. From the grave, Blyden the Afropublican still speaks, and his influence in various public and intellectual circles endures.

This biographical analysis focuses on the various audiences Blyden sought to influence with his writing. It highlights his strengths and weaknesses as a scholar and examines his original contributions to modern African history and Pan-Africanism. More importantly, unlike previous biographical studies and theoretical engagement with Blyden's work, this book adopts a chronological approach in order to engage, on the one hand, Blyden's various transformations as a thinker. On the other hand, it seeks to track these changes in the various books he published. It argues that Blyden's final work, *African Life and Customs* (1908), is an ultimate reflection of the multiple ways he had successfully transcended a narrow Ethiopianist or a condescending view of indigenous Africa.

Ethiopianism was an Afro-Christian providential belief among some diaspora Africanists. This movement sometimes manifested in African diaspora discourse as a sense of superiority over indigenous African cultures and peoples because of the former's experience of Western civilization. Some African diaspora intellectuals and leaders believed that diasporic Africans were divinely ordained to civilize and Christianize their "native" brethren. While Blyden initially held this view, his direct encounters with African people, societies, and intellectuals led him to formulate the first systematic and philosophical articulation of a Pan-African concept—the so-called African Personality.

Following the widespread acclaim for *African Life and Customs*, as well as other writings, Blyden became the first intellectual theoretician of Pan-Africanism. On the basis of the subsequent literature produced on Blyden's early formulation of the African Personality, the present book defines Pan-Africanism as the conceptualization that people of African descent—no matter their geographic location—share kinship and historical, sociological, and cultural connections that transcend their physical separations.

This book, therefore, contributes to the field of political theory by tracing the ways in which West Africans, including Blyden, participated in the growth of Pan-Africanism, as both an idea and a social movement. It contends that Pan-Africanism developed distinctively in different locations of the Atlantic world and shows the particular ways in which West African scholars thought of themselves as part of a worldwide African kin group. This is particularly important because an erroneous perception has developed in Pan-African historiography: that because West Africans comprise different ethnicities, they were incapable of or less committed to Pan-African ideas. Most scholars, therefore, perceive Pan-Africanism as an idea introduced to continental Africans by diasporic African intellectuals.

This external origin thesis of Pan-African intellectualism has been the source of narrow conceptual and geographic emphases in scholarly contributions to the field of Black Atlantic studies. These previous efforts have mostly focused on cultural manifestations of African descendants resident in Europe and the Americas.[18] Discussions of African intellectuals highlight or treat their ideas as extrinsic to their organic development in Africa. An excellent example of this is Paul Gilroy's treatment of Blyden's work. Gilroy sees Blyden's writing as a critique of European Enlightenment thought; however, he excises Blyden's writings from the African contexts in which they were developed.[19] This silencing of African contributions to the intellectual exchanges of the Atlantic world has been extremely troubling. In reviewing and reenvisioning the literature on the Black Atlantic, I interrogate this "import thesis" and correct its imbalance.[20]

Further, an examination of Pan-Africanism is inadequate if the mutual exchange of ideas on both sides of the Atlantic is glossed over. Initially, Pan-African ideas and activities occurred among and between people of African heritage who lived in locations near the Atlantic Ocean—localities conceptually referred to as the *Black Atlantic* that comprise a multiplicity of black actors and their activities, texts, and textual flows. Given the preponderance of literature on European, North American, and Caribbean spaces of the Black Atlantic, this study is mainly centered on West Africa but still traverses the four geographic regions.

The analytic insights of Robert Farris Thompson and Gilroy on the Black Atlantic are relevant to this book's position on Blyden's place in the array of Black Atlantic scholars. Thompson, the intellectual progenitor of the term *Black Atlantic*, situates Africa at the center of his analyses of black cultures of the Americas.[21] Gilroy relegates Africa to a distant past in his examination of the cultural and intellectual world of the "Black Atlantic"; in his estimation, the *Black Atlantic* encompasses only blacks in the West.[22]

While this book builds on both scholars' work, its explication of an *Afropublican* intellectual class in West Africa adopts Thompson's original position. It introduces Blyden and his West African peers as not from the distant past but rather as nineteenth-century intellectuals in a "global" Africa. Global Africa, as theorized by Ruth Simms Hamilton, refers to Africa and its multiple African diasporas—an important conceptual framework that allows scholars to grapple with the complexities, similarities, and differences of older, current, and newly emerging African diasporas. My concerns are more with Blyden and the nineteenth-century interactions between African societies and their Atlantic diaspora.[23]

Even as I focus on Anglophone West Africa, the idea of Pan-Africanism and the life of Edward Blyden as its intellectual forerunner offer the unique opportunity to treat the Atlantic as a single body of analysis. Throughout this book, I make connections between Pan-African intellectuals in West Africa and the African diaspora. With this methodological intent, this work demonstrates that ideas about the Black Atlantic not only circulated in Europe and the Americas but were also distinctively developing in West Africa.

Historical knowledge of Pan-Africanism in West Africa is scant. This book seeks to fill this gap by highlighting how West African thinkers such as Blyden proposed agendas that emphasized an enhancement of indigenous African sociopolitical and cultural practices. I further contend that Blyden's insistence that relevant European ideas be domesticated to the African Personality was a distinctly Africa-derived idea. These Afro-positivistic conceptions became the basis on which West African intellectuals exchanged thoughts with their black kin in other parts of the world, including the Black Atlantic, as defined by both Gilroy and Thompson.[24]

Blyden and other African scholars were able to participate in these discourses because they lived during an innovative period in world history. Blyden made frequent use of the steamship, the press, and other technological advances of his era. As a trained man of the cloth, he utilized newspapers, journals, and efficient means of transportation to circulate his contestations and exchange knowledge with intellectuals in the western hemisphere.

Keeping a central focus on Blyden, this work highlights West African and African diasporan intellectuals' joint participation in the formation of the Pan-African social movement. In so doing, it contends with scholars who negate Africa's relationship with the African diaspora and simplistically describe Pan-Africanism as a racialist ideology or exclude Africa from the Black Atlantic.[25] By embedding Blyden in a broader conception of the Black Atlantic, it links the less-written-about Danish West Indies region of the Caribbean with Danish spheres of influence in West Africa during the Atlantic age (1450–1890).

Blyden's unique biographical history and intellectual career allows for an intermeshing of various historiographies and intellectual trends in Black Atlantic studies, African historiography, Western intellectual history, and

Danish participation in the Atlantic trade. I place particular attention on Denmark's Atlantic relationship with Ghana and the U.S. Virgin Islands. While a great deal of material has been generated about the Black Atlantic in the last decade, very little of that literature deals with Scandinavian involvement in the Atlantic, specifically the Danish presence among black populations in the Atlantic.[26]

Expounding on the life of Danish West Indies–born Blyden, I crisscross black localities in the Atlantic while still focusing on West Africa, and bringing the less-known Danish sphere of influence into Atlantic history. Through this approach, I illuminate the endogenous development of a West African intellectual canon of ideas. I do this in contrast to scholarship that claims an unbridled external influence in the emergence of modern African thought. This canon of philosophies in West African thought, seen through the intellectual and social biography of Blyden, contributes to the intellectual and social history of the Atlantic age.

In focusing on Blyden's intellectual transformations, this book necessarily relies on his voluminous published writings as well on such published primary sources as Edith Holden's *Blyden of Liberia* and Hollis Lynch's *Selected Letters*. These works are supported by unpublished archival documents collected in Ghana, St. Thomas, the United States, and England, and include the Furley Collection at the Balme Library of the University of Ghana, which are utilized in this introduction and chapter 1.

Chapter 1 opens in St. Thomas and explains how specific events in the Danish West Indies led to the quasi-freedom that allowed Blyden to crisscross the Atlantic. It continues with three main sections: Blyden and Afropublicanism; Blyden, the Danish West Indies, and the Gold Coast/Volta Basin Diaspora; and Atlantic Age Commons. Each division lays out the significance of key events or ideas that shaped Blyden's development as an African public intellectual.

The section on Afropublicanism takes its cue from the conceptual issues outlined in the introduction, drawing upon Blyden's life and itineraries as evidence of the continued connection between Africa and the African diaspora. It shows how Blyden used an Afropositivist discourse and problematizes the exclusion of African cities (public) as equally sophisticated human centers. In doing this, it justifies why Blyden and other African scholars qualify treatment as public intellectuals. It also establishes what distinguished Blyden from his colleagues in the global black intellectual struggle. The second part of the chapter utilizes data from the Trans-Atlantic Slave Trade Database to highlight the Gold Coast/Volta Basin diaspora in the Danish West Indies as a crucial stepping stone for Blyden's Afropositivist discourse. Finally, the section closes by centering Blyden within specific Atlantic ideas and happenings: technological advancements and publishing, post-Enlightenment thought, colonialism, Euro-Christian missionary activity, and literacy.

The second chapter combines issues of *The Crisis: A Record of the Darker Races* with published correspondence between W. E. B. Du Bois and Blyden from the Special Collections of the University of Massachusetts at Amherst. Chapter 3 makes use of the contemporaneous published translations of C. G. A. Oldendorp's firsthand accounts of life in the Danish West Indies in *History of the Mission*, and Protten's *Description of His Admission to the Evangelical Moravian Brethren's Congregation*. Chapter 4 explores personal interviews conducted in St. Thomas with Rabbi Shimon Moch and Mr. Myron Jackson, as well as scarcely used nineteenth-century newspapers in the Danish West Indies: *Sanct. Thomae Tidende*, *St. Croix Avis*, and *Royal Danish American Gazette*. These publications were accessed at the Von Scholten Collection of the Enid M. Baa Public Library in St. Thomas, Virgin Islands (formerly Danish West Indies). Chapter 5 consults archival documents of the Church Missionary Society (CMS) as well as British Colonial Office (CO) correspondence at the National Archives, Kew Gardens. The final chapter combines the CO correspondence with archival information from the University of Central Arkansas's Special Collection on the American Colonization Society (ACS) and the ACS's *African Repository*.

Chapter 2 is divided into two sections. The first part engages with representations of Blyden among his peers, reviews of his books, and his esteem in various Atlantic public spheres. It begins with W. E. B. Du Bois's representation of Blyden in the *Crisis* and shows Blyden articulating his Africa-centered ideas to a global public sphere of African intellectuals, Victorian elites, Enlightenment scholars, African America intellectuals in the United States, and Jewish Intellectuals, when he addresses the "Jewish Question." The second part covers Blyden's formative stages in the Danish West Indies and addresses why he left the United States for Liberia in 1851. It shows the gradual shift in his thinking between 1851 and 1856 after immigrating to Liberia as a teenager. Thus, it first explains the cultural "baggage" of Ethiopianism that accompanied Blyden to Liberia and then shows the very first important transformation in Blyden's thinking as he began to discard his condescension toward indigenous Africans. The chapter shows how this change in Blyden's thought led to his constant critique of the Americo-Liberian oligarchy in Liberia and adds that this intellectual conversion in Blyden's perspective—from pledging to a civilizing mission to adopting an indigenous African viewpoint—would characterize his later writings.

The third chapter provides a comprehensive definition and analysis of the history of Pan-Africanism with emphasis on West African contributions. It first examines the various Afro-positivist practices of enslaved Africans throughout the Americas, as they articulated Africa-based philosophies and ideologies in reaction to the dehumanization of Africa-based ways of life, including religion, social organization, aesthetics, and polity. This is followed by an examination of West African–born intellectuals like Olaudah Equiano, Christian Protten, and Ottobah Cugoano, who lived as public intellectuals in Europe and the Americas but still made Africa the center of their writing. The chapter then shows that Blyden inherited this Africa-based literary and philosophical perspectives from enslaved Africans and his eighteenth-century predecessors. It concludes by arguing that, from early enslaved Africans in the Americas to Africa-born intellectuals in Europe and the Americas and then to Edward Blyden's nineteenth-century cohort, West African intellectuals made unheralded contributions to the development of

Pan-Africanism as an idea as well as to the fountain of ideas circulating in the Black Atlantic world.

The fourth chapter uses oral history, contemporary newspapers, and slave trade statistics as well as current literature on the Igbo in the Atlantic world to discuss Blyden's diasporic Igbo, Afro-Danish, and Jewish identities. This chapter offers an alternative approach to the binary discourse on the African and Jewish diasporas by showing the confluence of Igbo, Afro-Danish, Jewish, and Iberian histories on the Danish West Indies island of St. Thomas. It concludes that Blyden's biography—and his connections to these histories—reveals layers of his cultural and racial identity that do not fit a neat narrative. The intersections of the Jewish and African diasporas in the Atlantic era show that we cannot definitively confine each Atlantic diaspora, culture, or ethnic or cultural group into a homogeneous conception of biology, race, culture, or religion as the processes and cultural contacts of the Atlantic world were not only varied but intertwined.

Chapter 5 goes beyond the popular understanding of Blyden's association with Islam to examine his pioneering role in the systematic study of Islam in West Africa. Utilizing an Atlantic framework inspired by Farris-Thompson's work on the Black Atlantic and Gomez's Diasporic Africa, it explores the reciprocal relationships that developed between Blyden and the Muslim communities and intellectuals of the Greater Senegambia region of West Africa.[27] Further, it shows the symbiotic relationship that developed between Blyden and the Muslim peoples of the region as well as his careful study of Arabic and other West African languages. Chapter 5 takes account for his various travels in the interior of the Greater Senegambia as he collected and historicized original manuscripts written by West African Muslims. Blyden, a trained Presbyterian minister, pioneered the study of Islam and Islamic societies in Africa. Through this commitment, he recognized and articulated the indigenization of Islam in West Africa—and yet has not been given due recognition for his contributions to the academic study of Islam. The chapter also shows Blyden's interaction with Islamic leaders and institutions and how they held him in high regard for his "Oriental" scholarship and his interest in accurately depicting Africa as experienced by African peoples.[28] It further argues that this stage of Blyden's intellectual career influenced his eventual transformation from a believer in the civilization of Africa by outside forces (African diaspora and Euro-American) to an African intellectual who advocated African agency.

The sixth chapter makes the claim that, based on the available literature, Blyden can be described as the nineteenth century's most popular and influential black scholar. It shows this by first documenting how Blyden became an inspiration for several people in the American South—to the extent that he was impersonated by con men who swindled some rural blacks as they sought to leave the United States in the face of Southern Redemption. It then reviews Blyden's influence on several generations of African and Pan-Africanist intellectuals like Joseph Casely Hayford. Unlike previous examinations that stop at the influence of Muslim societies on Blyden and his esteem for Islam, this chapter strives to evidence that Blyden evolved into an Africanized Christian and not a crypto-Muslim.[29] It shows that following Blyden's encounter with Africanized Islam, he was inspired to a new form of Ethiopianism in West Africa, which involved the establishment of West African churches whose leadership encouraged African music, dance, fashion, and personnel. This view contrasted with the Ethiopianism that Blyden initially held upon arriving in West Africa. It closes with an overview of Blyden's place as a revisionist historian, especially his views on race and slavery. This chapter ultimately serves to counter earlier historiographical analyses by both Lynch and Livingston that portray Blyden as a failure whose poor organizing skills led to his inability to remain committed to one idea. On the contrary, this book concludes that Blyden's writings on the African Personality made him an intellectual progenitor of Pan-Africanism. In addition, he pioneered the establishment of Arabic/English schools for Muslim communities in Liberia and Sierra Leone as well as of indigenous African-led Christian churches. Blyden's influence in many public spheres is truly unparalleled by any black intellectual of his time.

Edward W. Blyden's Intellectual Transformations closes with a short epilogue, which places all the histories highlighted in the preceding chapters within the contemporary circulation of ideas, aesthetics, music, and public culture in general. It specifically examines the cyberpolitan circulation of Pan-African ideas in African public culture.

Afropublican Commons: Conceptual Groundings

> Edward Wilmot Blyden has sought for more than a quarter of a century to reveal everywhere the African unto himself; to fix his attention upon original ideas and conceptions as to his place in the economy of the world; to point out to him his work as a race among the races of men; lastly and most importantly of all, to lead him back unto self-respect.
>
> —Joseph Casely Hayford, *Ethiopia Unbound*

Blyden's birthplace was the island of St. Thomas, now a part of the U.S. Virgin Islands. He was, however, born during the period when the island was a part of the Danish crown's colonies. His rights as a free person under the Danish Crown were therefore enshrined in a document promulgated by King Frederick V of Denmark in 1755. The "Reglement for Slaverne" referred to the emancipation of the Danish West Indies' enslaved Africans, stating that "the freed are to enjoy all rights on par with the free-born and are to be esteemed and respected in all regards equally with the free-born subjects of the crown." Frederick V's successor, Christian VII, also enacted a "local and émigré" ordinance in 1776, which further protected

Blyden's rights as a freeborn person, particularly the immigrant standing of his parents, who had come to the island from St. Eustatius.[1]

By 1830, two years before Blyden's birth, a population of freed men and women in the Danish West Indies forced the governor of the islands, Peter von Scholten, to draft a report that granted free blacks full equality before the law.[2] Blyden was, therefore, born as an Afro-Danish subject.[3] Blyden eventually became a citizen of Liberia, an English-speaking West African country with a considerable black American immigrant population with cultural and political influence. Blyden thus transitioned from an Afro-Danish subject to a West African in a nation of Anglo-American persuasion. Blyden's crisscrossing of these various African and African diasporic communities is evidence of the dynamic connection between Africa and the African diaspora. Blyden's influence in these global circuits of blackness was the catalyst to his becoming a globally acclaimed black intellectual.

Blyden and Afropublicanism

The use of *Afropublican* and *Afropublicanism* in this work is a reconceptualization of ideas in contemporary discourse on African globalization. It draws mainly on the ideas of global Africa and diasporic Africa. Ruth Simms Hamilton defines global Africa as "the geographically and socio-culturally diverse people of Africa and its Diaspora . . . linked through complex networks of social relationships and processes."[4] Michael Gomez similarly defines diasporic Africa as the inextricable link between the "histories, cultures, and communities of Africa" and its diaspora.[5] Blyden's embodiment of Afropublicanism emerged in these "complex networks" as he navigated several public spheres of global Africa: Afro-Islam, the Mediterranean, Black Atlantic, West Africa, and the West Indies.

Afropublicanism is, therefore, to be viewed as an analytic practice or paradigm used by Blyden and the African cadre of nineteenth-century West African intellectuals to challenge Afro-pessimistic discourse and to pursue

Pan-African schemes. As such, their engagement of various spheres in the global public arena was *centered* on or *rooted* in the African experience.

This book's central emphasis is therefore on Blyden's public intellectualism and his rootedness in the African historical experience. Less a social biography than an intellectual biography, it highlights the specific historical circumstances that influenced the scholarship he produced about the black world. It stresses the importance of Blyden's lived experience in Africa as one of the transformative stages of his career. While noting his initial Ethiopianist sense of superiority over indigenous African peoples and how this attitude eventually evolved to a greater appreciation for African customs and traditions, I focus on his Afropublicanism, centered on the African experience, and his articulation of an Afro-positivist perspective to advance a Pan-African agenda.[6] Blyden was very clear about an experiential and observed understanding of Africa. As will be shown in more detail later, Blyden critiqued his friend and interlocutor Herbert Spencer for his secondhand accounts of Africa and reliance on European travelogues.[7]

Blyden's Afropublican career evolved while he traversed the cosmopolitan and "local" worlds of the Middle East, Europe, and West Africa arguing for an observation-based and ethical approach to the study of African aesthetics, history, and religions. As a result, another consideration of this text is its view of a cosmopolitan African way of life lived abroad—that is, outside of Africa. It does not view cosmopolitanism in Africa or African cosmopolitanism abroad as novel because an African-centered cosmopolitanism is evinced in the rhetorical practices of African intellectuals as they traveled and exchanged ideas across the globe in the eighteenth and nineteenth centuries.

For example, the Igbo-born Olaudah Equiano (1745–1797) spent much of his life in the Americas and Europe, and yet the center of all of his known writing was his empirically lived experience in Africa, Igboland, and Esaka. This is also evident in Blyden's globetrotting and politicking from West Africa, the Caribbean, and the southern United States. Even as Blyden advocated a return to Africa for diasporan Africans and engaged with several cultural publics, the center of his analysis was West Africa. The tradition of engaging negative discourse about Africa begins with enslaved Africans who formed African-inspired maroon communities. Their actions are paralleled by Africa-born Atlantic intellectuals like Equiano and Danish West African scholar Christian Protten (1715–1769). Blyden and his peers continued this tradition in the nineteenth century.

Besides, while the idea of a cosmopolitan city is well established in the literature, at its core, it is a Western understanding of a global phenomenon. A cosmopolitan city such as New York or London is conceptualized as not only the locus of global interactions but also the dominion of global enterprise and political power. Cosmopolitanism is consequently conceptualized as only situated in Euro-American global cities. Cities or towns that are not European-American, by definition, fail to meet the test for cosmopolitanism.

On the contrary, Blyden's cosmopolitanism was not restricted to the Atlantic West, and his firsthand understanding of Africa did not arrive exclusively from his experience of cosmopolitan Freetown, Sierra Leone. Freetown comprised descendants of black West Indians, black Americans, European missionaries and colonialists, Muslim intellectuals, and Jewish merchants. On the contrary, his knowledge of Africa also emerged in the simple but equally cosmopolitan towns and cities of Liberia and Sierra Leone's interior, where Blyden's final intellectual transformation occurred.

This book's use of Afropublicanism, therefore, challenges the singularity of cosmopolitan notions as it reconceptualizes our understanding of different historical epochs and notions of "area studies." This complexity is personified in Blyden, who, compared to his contemporaries, was comfortable in both advanced and modest societies and groups. As a result, Blyden had the rare gift of articulating the concerns of these communities to each other. It comes as no surprise, then, that he was able through his direct experiences and studies to appreciate and argue for the integrity of the histories of both the sophisticated and simple societies of Africa. By mapping the unique trajectories, particularities, and historical context of Blyden's ideas, I examine him as representative of a West African intellectual class who also participated in generating the wealth of ideas in the Black Atlantic.

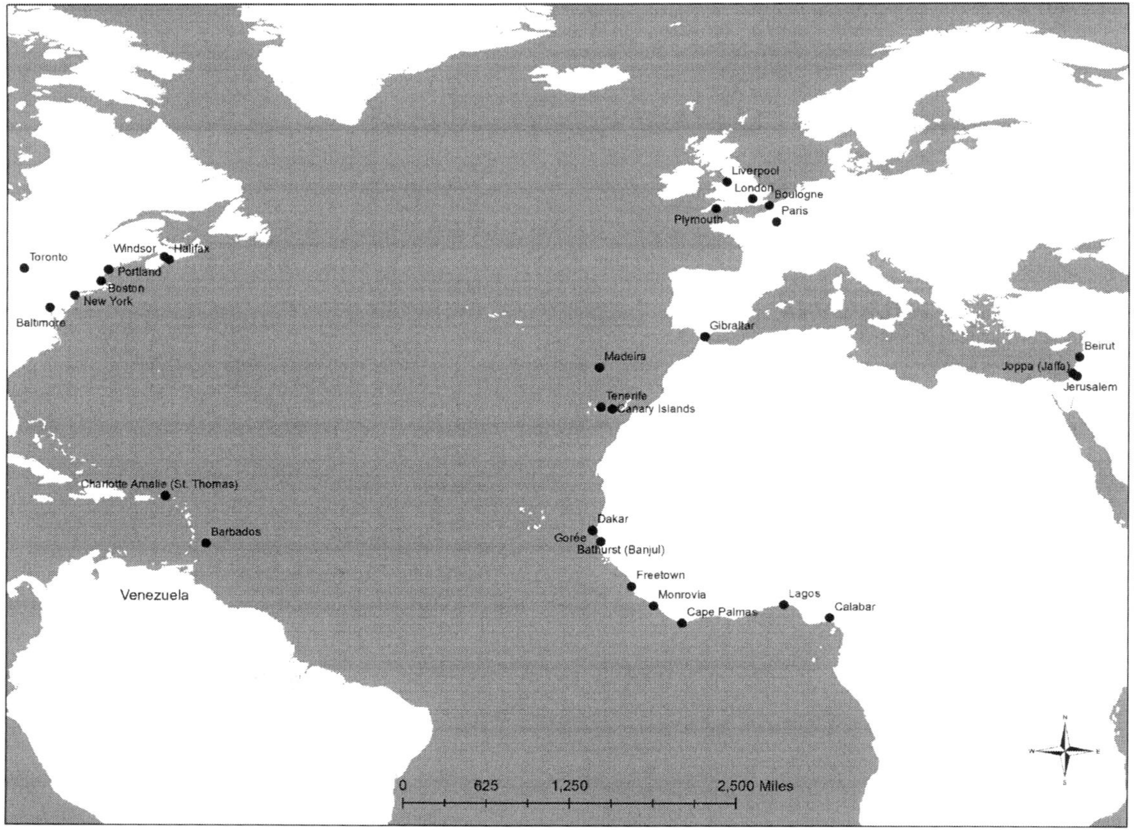

MAP BY CHARLES YORKE

MAP 1. Blyden's global influence. This map shows the major Atlantic and Mediterranean cities through which Blyden travelled, stayed, or lectured during his checkered intellectual career in the nineteenth century.

Before we proceed, two terms need further elaboration to contextualize the public sphere terms of reference under which I bring the varied discursive fields and works of Blyden and other African intellectuals: *African public intellectuals* and *public culture*. *African public intellectuals* is used here to describe Africans whose scholarly works were not just present in the nineteenth-century academic sphere (public) but who, through their interaction with other publics, as individuals and as intellectuals, disseminated and debated their ideas on issues concerning Africa. This book defines *public culture*, inclusive of its literary, political, mass and social media as well as cosmopolitan contexts, as the metadiscursive realm within which global cultural flows occur. These spheres of global intellection include ideas/intellectual culture, institutions, practices, popular arts/entertainment, and public performances (whether religious or secular processes of a public or social kind) in which public opinions and ideas are contested, negotiated, deliberated, and formed. This definition of public culture is not limited to Jurgen Habermas's *Public Sphere*.[8] It also takes cues from Mary Kupiec Cayton's discussion of public culture in the context of cultural theory, as well as theoretical insights from the seminal contributions of Arjun Appadurai and others in the journal *Public Culture*.[9]

Few nineteenth-century African intellectuals like Blyden and James Africanus Beale Horton (1835–1883) have, for example, been specifically discussed as public intellectuals. Yet, several of the thematic or disciplinary areas—Islamic, Atlantic, nationalism, cultural theory—fall within the rubric of African intellectual history, while others do not directly address their African subjects as public intellectuals. However, many of these African intellectuals—be they Islamic; or Atlantic scholars like Blyden; or West African nationalist like Casely Hayford, who founded the National Congress of British West Africa (NCBWA)—were a part of African social and public spheres. They developed intellectual traditions that evaluated the economic, social, political, and technological development of the various African publics with which they were engaged.

Blyden and other African thinkers of the nineteenth and early twentieth centuries such as Horton and Hayford, like intellectuals elsewhere, could be described as public intellectuals because their scholarly assessments occurred through processes of a public kind wherein their ideas were disputed, exchanged, or shaped. The *public* herewith used corresponds with public/political gatherings, newspaper articles, historical writings, and social media. The intentional act of writing, which African thinkers like Blyden engaged in on multiple occasions as well as their attempts to influence colonial policy and African cultural practices, to critique Afro-pessimism, and to debate other pertinent issues are all very public actions.

Further, the activities of these thinkers in the various discursive traditions could easily fall under Michael Warner's concept of *counterpublics*.[10] In contrast to an accepting-without-questioning dominant public, Warner describes counterpublics as "spaces of circulation in which it is hoped that the poesies of scene-making will be transformative, not replicative merely."[11] Texts produced by Blyden and West Africa's cohort of intellectuals were not replicas of false racialist theories, or mimicry of their Western training, as is evident in Appiah's *In My Father's House* and V. Y. Mudimbe's *Invention of Africa*.[12] Like these works, this book accounts for the tension between the African identity and the Western training of these African intellectuals but also moves beyond the tensions to address the transformative elements of their thinking as representatives of a counterpublic.

Blyden's advocacy for the indigenous West African church movement following his study of African Islam is a clear example of transformative discourse—that is, an escape from the culture of mimicking European culture. Likewise, the writing of Reindorf, another Danish West African and Blyden's contemporary, who authored *G.C.A. Histories*, the first historical book of its kind by an African author in the nineteenth century, can be equated to Appadurai's definition of culture-making activities in the public domain. Appadurai writes that "culture making activity includes the conscious writing of national histories, the construction of national and folk symbols and rituals, and the revitalization of various traditional identities."[13] I have argued elsewhere that in his *G. C. A. Histories*, Reindorf constructs real, imagined, and symbolic histories of various Gold Coast and West African polities.[14] As Cayton further explains:

> Counterpublics may form around a variety of foci. If they develop agency in relation to the state, they can be said to be political movements. They may coalesce around texts, codes, styles, or behaviors centered on race, gender, ethnicity, sexuality, or any number of categories. These become identity publics. Nothing in one's essence or social location determines membership in such an identity public. Rather, it's one's participation in publics defined by identity-inflected discourse that does so.[15]

As this applies to Blyden and African intellectual history, all of the various nationalisms that arose in Africa in opposition to colonial rule can be described as counterpublics of a political kind. Specific organizations reflecting various ethnic-nationalist movements in Africa, protomodern nationalist or anticolonial movements, such as the Aborigines Rights Protectorate Society in the Gold Coast as well as the NCBWA and the Afropublican intellectuals that constituted them can be described as not only counterpublics of a political kind but also of an identity kind.

While African intellectuals were excluded from the emergent public sphere in European discourse, Blyden as well as other Afro-Danish intellectuals such as Protten in the eighteenth and Reindorf in the nineteenth century had access to various media through which they debated and disseminated their views on a variety of subjects, including European descriptions of African history and culture. Blyden was distinguished from his peers because he was not merely a public intellectual whose work was available to "local" and cosmopolitan Africans but also a Pan-Africanist whose works engaged African, African diaspora, European, Mediterranean, Islamic, and Jewish public spheres. Deploying the term Afropublicanism, therefore, allows one to critically parse Africa's engagement with the world through a subject like Blyden, whose multisitedness in many "local" and cosmopolitan locations in Africa, the Middle East, the Caribbean, Victorian England, and North

America makes him unique. Afropublicanism also allows us to focus on a transcendent humanistic discourse articulated by West African intellectuals like Blyden rather than on an ethnocentric nativism that is falsely perceived of as Pan-Africanism.

Ultimately, Blyden, as an Afropublican scholar-activist, was part of a global intellectual struggle, emerging in the nineteenth century to vindicate African peoples' contribution to humanity. Blyden was also at the vanguard of critiques of the Eurocentric ideas of African inferiority generated by some European Enlightenment thinkers of the previous epoch. Blyden and his West African peers were also part of what Robert July has called the indigenous African nationalist movement, which produced early historical writing on West Africa.[16] This indigenous African nationalist movement encompassed the late-eighteenth-century writings of black personalities like Protten and Equiano and ended with the activities of the NCBWA in the 1920s.[17] Blyden came to scholarly attention in the latter half of this era, and his writings offer significant social and historical glimpses into the philosophical underpinnings of West African intellectual life.

The discursive fields of African philosophical thought, African Islamic intellectual traditions, modern African thought, African literary and cultural criticism, African religious thought, and African political thought all fall within the general scope of African intellectual history.[18] Due to diverse methodological approaches and disciplinary leanings, these different media of African intellection often appear to be exclusive, when they are often mutually inclusive. In treating Blyden as a public intellectual, this work provides an umbrella under which all the complex subfields of African intellectual history can be treated as one. One can, therefore, examine most of the African intellectuals under any of the named subfields as public intellectuals. Thus, rather than having scattered categories of public intellectualism, we are able to utilize a canon of African public intellection.

Blyden, the Danish West Indies, and the Gold Coast/ Volta Basin Diaspora

While Blyden claimed to be of Igbo, and therefore Bight of Biafra, origins, the Danish West Indies where he was born was at its foundation a Gold Coast/Volta Basin Diaspora. Focusing on Blyden, therefore, helps to highlight the participation of the Danish West India Company, established by charter in 1671 by King Christian V of Denmark, in the Atlantic slave trade from the Gold Coast. A majority of the trade in human beings conducted from the Gold Coast to the Danish West Indies encouraged and exploited warfare between various ethnic polities—Ga-Adangbe, Akwamu, Akyem, Fante, Ewe, and Asante—in West Africa.[19] The connection between Denmark's West African establishments, specifically the Gold Coast and its West Indian islands, is captured in the name of the slave-trading syndicate Danish West India and Guinea Company. The company's name combines the West Indies and Guinea (West Africa), reflecting a clear intent to link the Danish West India Company to the Danish settlements on the Gold Coast, West Africa.

The first Danish settlement on the Gold Coast was established at Fetu in 1657.[20] With the influence of high-ranking Danish nobility, particularly Jens Juel, diplomat and first director of the new company, Christian V established the Danish West India and Guinea Company to complete the triangular trade among Denmark, Guinea, and the West Indies, and to give Denmark a share in the fledgling transatlantic slave trade. The connection between the two Atlantic locations is also seen in the names given to the company's ships. There were Danish names such as the *Christianus Qvintus*, *Prinsesse Sophia Magdelena*, *Postillionen*, *Cron Printzens Onske*, and *Laarbug Galiei*, and Gold Coast–derived names like *Rio Volta* (River Volta), *Acra* (Accra), *Ningo*, *Ada*, and *Kongen of Ashanti* (King of Ashanti).[21] These ships carried thousands of enslaved Africans from Danish forts and castles on the Gold Coast to the Danish West Indies islands of St. Thomas, St. John, and St. Croix, where they were forced to work on plantations belonging to the company and to individual Danish and Dutch families.[22] These points of embarkation included Fredricksberg/Fredricksborg, built at Fetu in 1657; Fredrensborg, at Ningo in 1737; Konegesteen, at Ada in 1783–1784; Prisensten/Prindsensten, at Keta in 1784; Augastaborg, at Teshie in 1787; and Issaegram, at Kpone in 1787. The data in graphs 1–4 highlight this Atlantic connection between the Gold Coast and the Danish West Indies.

Against this historical background, I argue that a Volta Basin diaspora was established and institutionalized in the Danish West Indies by the Danish West India and Guinea Company as a result of its exportation of ethnic clusters of people from the Gold Coast and the Bight of Benin.[23] Ethnic peoples of Volta Basin heritage in West Africa include the Akan, Ewe, Ga, and Adangme peoples of the Gold Coast and the Gbe-speaking groups of the Bight of Benin. The latter include the Fon and Aja as well as the Yoruba-speaking Anago and the Mina (all of whom comprise various Akan, Ga, Adangbe, and Ewe diasporas—essentially a Gold Coast diaspora in the Bight of Benin). It is therefore essential to understand that while the Danish West Indies did receive enslaved Africans from the Bight of Biafra, Blyden grew up in an African Diasporic community that was a predominantly Gold Coast Diaspora. It was from the Afropositivist practices of these Gold Coasters that Blyden began to develop his Afropositivist discourse.

This book builds on the earlier scholarship on cultural areas and ethnic zones in Africa, taking into consideration their various limitations and some of the debates that have ensued.[24] In addition, while adapting the new and burgeoning scholarship on ethnic diasporas, transatlantic ethnicity, ethnic clusters, and transformations in African identities, I argue that the Afro-Danish culture of the late seventeenth and eighteenth centuries in the Danish West Indies received enslaved Africans from all over Africa but were heavily influenced by the Volta Basin cultures of the Gold Coast and the Bight of Benin.[25] These Gold Coast groups were collectively responsible for the several rebellions in the Danish West Indies. Examples of such revolts include the St. John rebellion of 1733, the Antigua slave rebellion of 1736, and

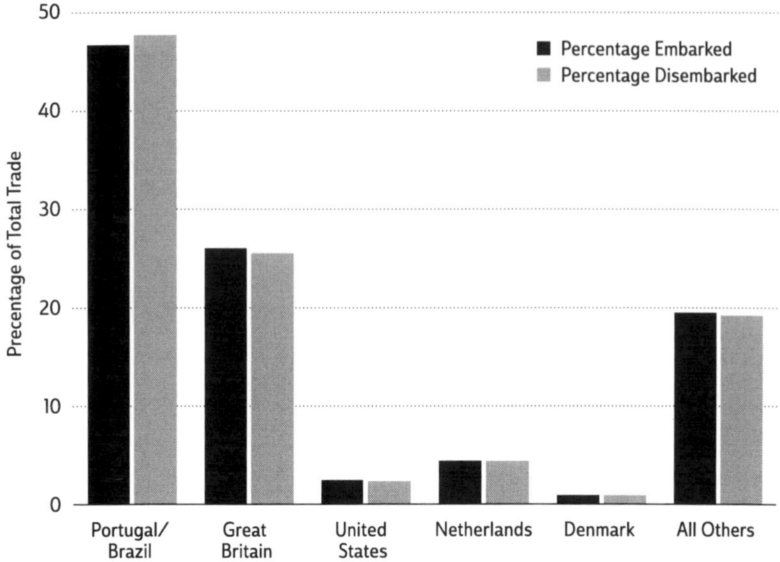

GRAPH 1. Total from all African regions to all regions of the transatlantic slave trade.

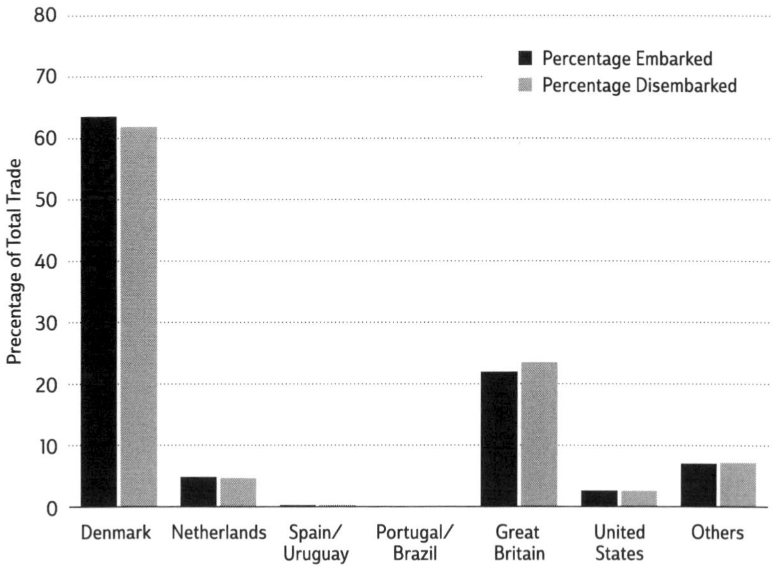

GRAPH 2. Percentage from all African regions to the Danish West Indies.

ALL DATA FROM THE TRANS-ATLANTIC SLAVE TRADE DATABASE, HTTP://WWW.SLAVEVOYAGES.ORG

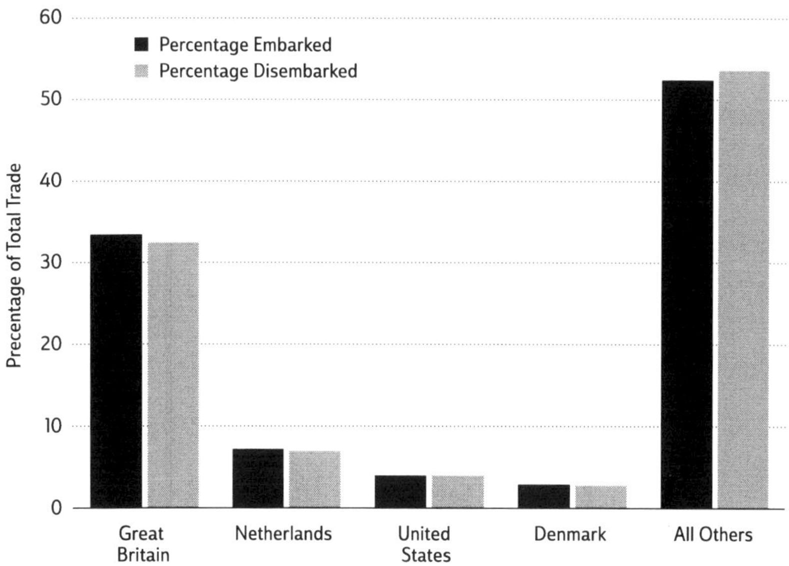

GRAPH 3. Percentage from Volta Basin to all regions.

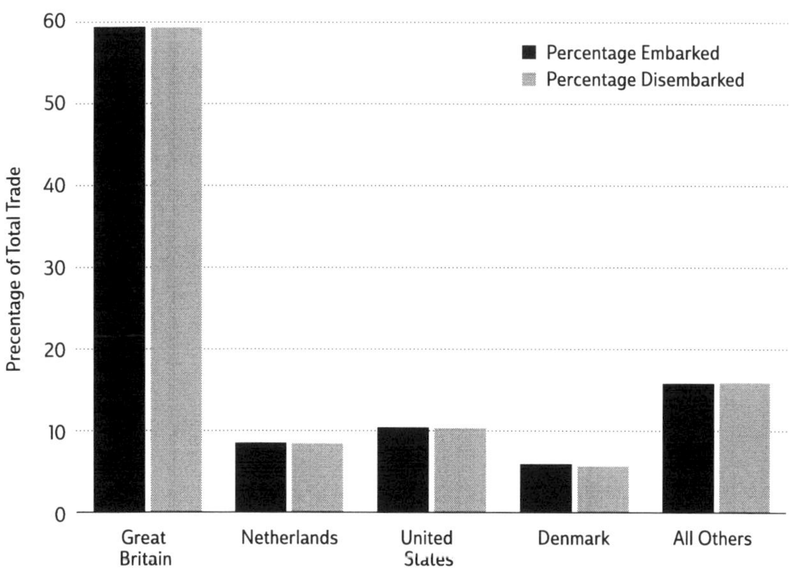

GRAPH 4. Percentage from Gold Coast to all regions.

ALL DATA FROM THE TRANS-ATLANTIC SLAVE TRADE DATABASE, HTTP://WWW.SLAVEVOYAGES.ORG

uprising in St Croix in 1759.[26] The African cosmological and ideological ideas that underpinned the rebellions as a critique of plantation slavery became instructive for Blyden's intellectual career.

Atlantic Age Commons

Events of world-historical significance that preceded Blyden's lifetime radically transformed social existence throughout the Atlantic world in which his writings circulated. The triangular trade in goods and enslaved Africans was part of the historical framework that produced the racially hierarchical social orders in the Americas and by extension the presence of Blyden's ancestors in the Caribbean. In the early modern period, major technological developments occurred such as the building of the Portuguese caravel in the fifteenth century, which coincided with Prince Henry the Navigator's commissioned exploration of the West African coast and the Canary Islands.[27] This encouraged European navigation of the Atlantic Ocean, thereby increasing contact among different geographic regions of the world.

The dynamic repercussions of these contacts ultimately led to the forced dispersion of peoples of African descent and their social stock of knowledge into various locations of the Atlantic world. Voluntary movements of Europeans and forced migrations of Africans also contributed to cross-cultural exchange and the contestation of ideas and worldviews between the peoples of the various landmasses bordering the Atlantic. A significant result of this process for African-descended people was the proliferation of the African experience in the Atlantic world.

Though these formative processes are important, my focus is on interactions in the nineteenth century because of the acceleration in the circulation of people and in the dissemination of information due to major advances in technology during this time. The numerous technological inventions of this epoch included the steamship, a more efficient printing press as well as the electrical and wireless telegraph.[28] Then, as now, African intellectuals and cultural carriers were able to travel and share their African experience.

Inevitably, nineteenth-century technological advances accentuated and enhanced the various webs of dynamic rapport among diasporic African communities, and these productive and energizing transmissions, I argue, are exemplified in the life and career of Edward Blyden. The advent of the caravel may have aided the enslavement of Blyden's ancestors, but the steamboat and schooners that were later developed in Blyden's generation allowed him to travel from St. Thomas to the United States, and from there to Liberia. From Liberia, Blyden also visited various Diasporic African locations in the United States as well as Antigua, Lagos, Cairo, and elsewhere.[29]

The spread of printing also opened up an avenue for the participation of other West African intellectuals in global discourse addressing such issues as West African nationalism, Black Atlantic debates, and Pan-Africanism. J. Lorand Matory in *Black Atlantic Religion* discusses the transatlantic dimensions of the Lagosian cultural renaissance in the cosmopolitan West African city.[30] Lagos's nineteenth-century newspapers, the *Lagos Times* and the *Lagos Weekly Record*, were the literary media for the Black Atlantic exchange and deliberation of issues such as return migrations to Africa and religious and cultural dimensions of Pan-Africanist thinking.[31]

Another conduit of such discourse across the Atlantic was Blyden's friend and peer John Edward Bruce (1856–1924), an African American journalist and historian who, in 1911, cofounded the Negro Society for Historical Research with Puerto Rican–born bibliophile Arthur Schomburg (1874–1938). Like other literate African Americans, Bruce subscribed to African newspapers like the *Lagos Weekly Record*, *Sierra Leone Weekly News*, *Gold Coast Aborigines*, *African Times*, and *Orient Review*. Bruce reprinted the newspapers and made references to them in his weekly editorials in the United States.[32]

Enlightenment scholarship played a vital role in shaping Blyden's intellectual life. This was crucial because, for thinkers of the European Enlightenment, African societies and peoples had not reached the lofty heights of civilization Europeans had. This belief is evident in Georg Wilhelm Friedrich

Hegel's *The Philosophy of History*, in which he states "Africa proper, as far as History goes back, has remained-for all purposes of connection with the rest of the World-shut up; it is the Gold-land compressed within itself-the land of childhood, which lying beyond the day of history, is enveloped in the dark mantle of Night. Its isolated character originates, not merely in its tropical nature, but essentially in its geographical condition."[33] The social manifestation of Enlightenment thinking is reflected in Europeans' compulsion to impose their cultural ideals on Africans.[34] It is from this historical context of European imperial and cultural expansionism that Hugh Trevor-Roper delivered his infamous comments that Africa had no history and that "there is only the history of Europeans in Africa. The rest is darkness."[35] It is also such notions of progress and modernity that Immanuel Geiss brought to bear on his interpretation of the Pan-African movement as constituting traditionalists and modernists. Geiss's analysis is that the former was likely to give way to the African modernists, who were perceived as having imbued European modernity and thus were more in harmony with the progress of world history.[36] Blyden confronted this Enlightenment scholarship in his various writings and public engagements.

Other than his acquaintance with Enlightenment scholarship and its cultural imperialism, Blyden witnessed significant episodes of black life in the nineteenth and early twentieth centuries. Critical to this era was a variety of acts of self-determination taken by black individuals and communities to assert their humanity. About three decades before Blyden's birth, for example, Haiti, the first independent black republic, had gained its independence from France; and two years before, David Walker's (1785–1830) famous *Appeal to the Colored Citizens of the World*, a text considered to have anticipated the idea of Pan-Africanism, was published.[37]

Although Western European countries and the United States abolished the slave trade by the second decade of the nineteenth century, plantation slavery continued in the Americas, including the Danish West Indies.[38] As a result, Blyden became aware of some of the century's slave rebellions and legal struggles that ended slavery in Europe and the Americas. As noted earlier, for Blyden, racial discrimination and the fear of false enslavement under the U.S. Fugitive Slave Law convinced him to emigrate to Liberia in 1851.

While in Liberia, Blyden witnessed the scramble for African colonies by European imperialists supported by the 1884–1885 Berlin Conference that "legalized" European partitioning of African territories. By the time of the Berlin Conference, Blyden was well into his intellectual advocacy for Africa. He therefore sought to use his influence through various reports of his travels in West Africa to effect whichever European power colonized West African territories. Interestingly, he preferred British colonialism—a disquieting loyalty given that there were no Africans at the table during the European parceling of Africa. How could African scholars like Blyden, who may have made a difference at the table, have assented to colonialism? Why did he support British colonialism, in particular? At the time of partitioning, the French were colonizing areas around Liberia and threatening its sovereignty. This, coupled with Blyden's frustration with the American-Liberian authorities, made him prefer that Liberia become a protectorate of Britain.

However, this explanation is in itself not a satisfactory answer for why Blyden preferred Britain or gave assent to European colonialism. On the surface, Blyden's choice of Britain is at odds with his African nationalism and undermines his work and importance as an Afropublican intellectual. At a deeper level, however, the contradiction between Blyden's Afropublicanism and his support for European colonialism is resolved on the altar of his providential understanding of history. That is, while Blyden moved gradually from a providential interpretation of history throughout his career, he continued to use it to resolve contradictions in his mind about various issues. This final transformation is reflected in his advocacy and support for the establishment of an indigenous African church in his last publication, *African Life and Customs*.

Blyden saw European colonialism—with its attendant technology, trade, and so-called humanitarianism—as a means of achieving the African modernity he desired. However, Blyden warned, perhaps naively, that "the sudden and wholesale imposition of European ideas and methods upon Africans has been like the investing of David in Saul's armour. He is falling before the Goliath of progress." In pursuing an African nationalism, Blyden advised European colonizers to "encourage the development of the natives along the lines of their own idiosyncrasies as revealed in their institutions . . . to give to the African taken under British rule all the advantages, in their spirit and effect. . . . Do not deprive them of rights an advantages which they valued and enjoyed before you came."[39]

Nonetheless, Blyden was critical of the administration and operations of European colonialism. He wrote poignantly and understood that "it is not the business of imperialism to make men but create subjects, not to save souls but to rule bodies."[40] Blyden lamented that European colonization "looks upon the possible destruction of individuals as no serious evil; as possible for their own good and for the advancement of the cause. . . . The native, is as a rule, simply the victim of an unsympathetic apparatus of political and commercial machinery."[41]

Blyden resolves these contradictions and anxieties about European colonization in *African Life and Customs* after his encounter with Africanized Islam. In this work, Blyden reckons that the violence and alienation of European colonization should be resisted through African culture, religion, family, and social structures. It was in the pursuit of the maintenance of these African social institutions that Blyden advanced a critique of European Christian missions and sought for the establishment of an indigenous West African Christian church that reflected African idiosyncrasies in fashion, language, liturgy, music, and worship.

It is important to reiterate that Blyden immigrated to Liberia, one of only two independent African nation states in the nineteenth century.[42] He had, in essence, become a "noncolonial" subject, a citizen of "independent" Liberia, which was formed under the influence of the American Colonization Society (ACS). Thus, Blyden the Afro-Danish subject by virtue of emigrating to Liberia became of Anglo-American persuasion. This transformation in

FIGURE 1. Edward Wilmot Blyden.

identity and sociocultural space substantially influenced Blyden's writing and shaped his various ideas on the future direction of Africa.

Until his resignation in 1886 to become a "minister of truth," Blyden was an ordained Presbyterian minister. In many ways, he owed his involvement with Western education to the Euro-American Christian establishment. Blyden's parents were members of the Dutch Reformed Church on the Island of St. Thomas. It was through their membership in these Christian circles that Blyden came under the "benevolent" influence of the Dutch Reformed Church minister Rev. Knox.[43] It was, in fact, Knox, who initially sent the young Blyden to the United States, where he was rejected at three theological colleges on racial grounds.[44]

Another way Christians contributed to his education was that Blyden's arrival in Liberia was part of the African American church's own Ethiopianist, or civilizing, project in Africa, which was to be achieved through the

Christianizing of their African brethren. An underlying premise of such Christian proselytizing was that there was something wrong with African culture that Christianity would help correct. Blyden, however, after years of living in West Africa, began to distance himself from such "civilizing" discourse, raising questions about Christianity as practiced by Europeans. *Edward Blyden's Intellectual Transformations* shows that such a fundamental turnaround was important to the Africa-centered critiques that Blyden advanced against the Eurocentric mischaracterization of African peoples. Blyden's introspection and reflection on these commitments in his Christian faith are evidence of his struggle with aspects of his Christian training that demeaned African culture. The book explores Blyden's posture toward Euro-Christian thought as he dealt with the alienating role and ideological underpinnings of Christian missionary education in Africa.

Blyden was also a polyglot.[45] For nearly two decades of Blyden's early life in St. Thomas, he spoke Dutch, which was the lingua franca, even though Danish was the official language.[46] Blyden may also have been one of the last speakers of the now extinct "Negerhollands, also called Negro Dutch, or Dutch Creole," the language of enslaved blacks on St. John and St. Thomas.[47] Later, Blyden learned English, probably under the guidance of his mother and Rev. Knox, who was Anglo-American. During the Blyden family's two-year relocation (1842–1844) to Venezuela, Blyden learned to speak Spanish.[48] In Liberia and Sierra Leone, Blyden spoke the West African–based English Creole and Fula. He also studied Latin and Greek in high school and taught himself Hebrew and Arabic later in life.[49] Moreover, he was appointed the minister of the interior by the Liberian government under President J. J. Roberts. In this capacity, Blyden dealt with many local societies on behalf of Liberia because he possessed conversational skills in the languages spoken in the interior.[50] These literate and multilingual abilities gave Blyden access to various speech communities, which influenced his thinking and writing and ultimately helped shape his Afropublicanism—his peculiar discursive approach as an African public intellectual who produced scholarship in order to combat objectionable ideas about Africa in multiple public spheres around the world.

Conclusion

West Indian scholar and poet Kamau Brathwaite describes his scholarship upon returning to the West Indies after a long sojourn in Africa as follows:

> My absence [from the West Indies] and travels . . . had given me a sense of movement, and restlessness-rootlessness. It was, I recognized, particularly the condition of the Negro in the West Indies and the New World. . . . My verse until 1965 had no real center. The center is connected to my return to the West Indies after twelve years' absence. . . . I had at the moment of return, completed the triangular trade of my historical origins.[51]

This work is not about rootlessness but about an individual and collective movement of African-descended people.[52] I hope that the link between West Africa and the Danish West Indies, through Edward Wilmot Blyden, will make rootlessness a place of belonging for contemporary "Afropolitans" as it became for Brathwaite during his West African sojourn. Brathwaite writes that "West Africa gave me a sense of place, of belonging; and that place and belonging, I knew was the West Indies."[53]

Representations of the Father of Pan-Africanism

Negro Africa has suffered irreparable loss in the death of Dr. Blyden, and the world is poorer for the disappearance of we fear—the only pure blooded Negro who was capable of applying his knowledge of Europe and white civilization to the needs of Negro Africa and the African civilization. More fully versed in the literature and ethics of Europe than any other Negro, *Blyden's studies only made him more of an African—more passionately the upholder of an African soul, an African culture, an Africa of clearly demarcated and peculiar racial needs* [emphasis mine].

—*African Mail*, February 16, 1912

The January 1912 issue of the *Crisis*, edited by the inimitable W. E. B. Du Bois, announced, in celebration, the approaching eightieth birthday of Edward Wilmot Blyden (1832–1912). This edition of the world-renowned magazine described Blyden as "the leading representative of his race in West Africa."[1] The description of Blyden as West African helps establish that Blyden's numerous ideas about Africa and black people worldwide were nurtured through his engagement with the West African intellectuals, peoples, cultures, and societies he had encountered.

Commenting on Blyden's work in West Africa, Rev. Dr. Mark C. Hayford, a Gold Coast intellectual, remarked during a banquet held by African residents in London for Blyden at the Holburn Restaurant on August 15, 1903:

> It has for some time been the desire of the Natives of West Africa to give expression, not only to their high appreciation of the long and able services which Dr. Blyden has rendered to the African race, but also to endorse certain phases of his teaching as to the work and destiny of his countrymen.[2]

However, the characterization of Blyden as the "leading representative of his race in West Africa" by the *Crisis*, if not disingenuous, does not fully capture Blyden's significance beyond West Africa to the diverse intellectual and social worlds throughout the Atlantic Basin by the beginning of the twentieth century. Blyden's myriad ideas were developed in Africa, but they reached far beyond the continent. Apart from the roads and monuments named after him in different parts of the world, evaluations of Blyden's published writings are found in an expansive list of nineteenth-century newspapers from around the world. They include *Nineteenth Century*, *Southern Recorder*, *Literary World*, *Athenaeum*, *Sierra Leone Weekly News*, and *African World*, among many others.[3] Journals like the *Royal African Society* (published in London), the *African Repository*, the *Southwestern Christian Advocate* (New Orleans), and the *Methodist Review* all ran excerpts of Blyden's work in their pages.[4] Other information gleaned about Blyden, his contributions to the literary world, and his advocacy for the black world are found in writings by his contemporaries and friends.

In the estimation of a reviewer for *A. M. E. Church Review*, "The one Negro of standing in the English world of recognized scholarship is Dr. Blyden," and in the same year an evaluation of the republication of Blyden's *Christianity, Islam and the Negro Race* by the *Interior* (Chicago) reads:

NEW YORK PUBLIC LIBRARY, DIGITAL COLLECTIONS.

FIGURE 2. E. W. Blyden.

> Dr. Blyden has spent his entire life on the West coast of Africa. In the use of terse, vigorous and pure English, he is scarcely second to Macaulay. Anything upon the subjects indicated and coming from the head and pen of such a man, who has been twice sent by the British Government upon diplomatic missions to the powerful chiefs in the interior of Africa, should at least be carefully read and pondered.[5]

Blyden was also well known in Orientalist intellectual and political circles. He received a medal of honor from the sultan of Turkey, and West African Muslims referred to him as Mukhtar (the Chosen One). More of his appraisals are also found in the statements and writings of some of the leading public figures of the African, black, and literary worlds. On the basis of this evidence, I characterize Blyden as an autodidact whose public sphere of influence embraced not only West Africa, the West Indies, and the northern U.S. black intellectual scene, but also working-class blacks from the American South who wrote him letters expressing the desire to emigrate to Liberia.

If Du Bois was the leading black intellectual of the twentieth century, he took that mantle from the leading black intellectual of the nineteenth century, Edward Wilmot Blyden. A review of Blyden's stature and influence among various global communities of thought, including Victorian England, the Jewish diaspora, and black Americans, demonstrates this assertion.

Blyden and Victorian England

Blyden was already a recognized figure in Victorian England before he arrived there. This was on account of his own autodidactic pursuit of self-professionalization while educating himself on the available literature and discourse of his era. An illustration of this attempt at scholarly proficiency is seen in a letter he wrote in 1860 when he was still principal of Alexander High School, in Monrovia. The letter was addressed to W. E. Gladstone, Britain's Chancellor of the Exchequer, a well-known classicist and later prime minister. Blyden's letter was received in Britain as coming from someone in the "honorable office of teaching, and his quotations from Latin and Greek showed that he had, as he represented, devoted himself to the study of the ancient in addition to the modern languages."[6]

In Blyden's communication, he told Gladstone:

> I am a youth endeavoring to obtain an education, my taste and predilections—strange as it may seem for one in my circumstances—are for classical literature. The love of languages is my predominating passion. . . . I have acquired some knowledge of the Greek, Latin, and Hebrew languages. Of modern languages I read write and speak the French somewhat, the Spanish I read a little. I have read some of the principal Latin, and portions of two of the Greek authors—the Anabasis of Xenophon and a part of Homers Iliad.[7]

Blyden went on to describe the limited resources available for pursuing his interests and pointed out that he knew he belonged "to a race which for centuries had been despoiled by other races"; he felt his race had "been made to subserve the commercial and agricultural interests of the American continent, for no other reward, than physical deterioration and mental brutalization."[8] He then asked Gladstone for the classical studies curriculum he had used and also requested that the Londoner "forward to [him], if convenient, a small library composed" of Oxford and Cambridge University examination papers and works by classical, Victorian, and contemporary English writers. These included Herodotus, Shakespeare, Milton, Coleridge, and J. C. Hare.[9]

In response to Blyden's request, Gladstone magnanimously offered him a scholarship to a British university. But Blyden turned it down on the grounds that his work for the race prevented him from being able to "hold converses with the muses in England." He added, "I should not now be in this country, were it not that I have been sent by my fellow citizens to endeavor to interest, if possible the friends of Africa in the literary advancement of Liberia."[10]

Blyden, however, did continue his independent scholarship. At Alexander High School, Blyden was described as an A student, scoring excellent marks in "Scripture, Latin, Greek, Arithmetic, Behavior, and Industry" and recording no absences in his first term, which ended June 12, 1852.[11] By 1858, Blyden was teaching Latin, Greek, math, and vocal music, and later became principal of his alma mater.[12] In the same year, he became a candidate for ordination in the Presbyterian Church. For three days, October 25–27, 1858, the presbytery examined Blyden. He passed and was to be ordained on January 3, 1860.[13] By 1861, while still in charge of the high school, Blyden had put out a number of inquiries to determine whether his treatise on "Missions in Liberia" and other writings for literary periodicals could earn him "a B.A. or M.A."[14] It is not clear what became of these ambitions, but Blyden was mostly a self-taught and independent scholar. According to Blyden's high school teacher, Rev. Wilson, Blyden became a better Greek scholar than himself. He explained that Blyden also studied Hebrew and Fula, and that he read the scriptures in the ancient original languages.[15]

When the Liberia College was first built in 1861, Blyden was appointed professor of Greek, Latin Languages, and Literature.[16] This was after Blyden had been interviewed by the Trustees of Donations for Education in Liberia, based in Boston. The secretary of the trustees, one Rev. Dr. Joseph Tracy, in appointing Blyden as a professor, indicated that he had "no academical degree," yet was "worthy of the degree of Master of Arts." He then forwarded Blyden's writings and sermons for an award of a master's degree from Middlebury College.[17] It is uncertain whether this graduate degree was ever granted to Blyden, but he went on to study briefly at Cambridge University in 1862 and at the Syrian Protestant College in Lebanon in the summer of 1866.[18] Eventually, Blyden became James Fulton (endowed) Professor, and later, president, of Liberia College, in 1881.[19] Blyden thus became what may be described as a trained theologian. He also earned two honorary M.A. degrees from Hamilton College, New York, and Lafayette College, Pennsylvania. He received LL.D. and D.D. degrees from Lincoln University, Pennsylvania.[20]

The fact that Blyden eventually served in a variety of positions in education—as principal of his high school, professor of Classics and Languages as well as president of Liberia College—is a testament to his self-made qualities. His self-actualization and correspondence with the future British prime minister is also a reflection of how Blyden inserted himself into countless public spaces—in this case, Victorian England.

It, therefore, should come as no surprise that Blyden also had the privilege of being in the company of the British monarchy, as well as its government, statesmen, and leading intellectuals. In 1878, for example, a committee including Herbert Spencer and Lord Carnarvon elected Blyden an "honorable member" of the Athenaeum Club of London with "full privileges of the club."[21] Blyden dined and held court with Victorian England's best. He even was invited to an audience with Queen Victoria. Some of Blyden's other English acquaintances include "remarkable literary men of his day . . . Lord Brougham, Mr. Gladstone, Dean Stanley, Charles Dickens, [and] Charles Sumner." Some of these Englishmen were also his fellow members in the Athenaeum Club of London.[22]

Blyden's relationship with Gladstone is the subject matter of several short essays and a number of journal articles that began to appear on the pages of some of the leading black journals of the day, including the *Journal of Negro History*. The earliest article appeared in 1850 and was entitled "Edward W. Blyden—a correspondent of William Ewart Gladstone."[23] This article and a subsequent one were very specific in their treatment of his correspondence with Gladstone, the British statesman.[24] They focused on Gladstone's and Blyden's views on the American Civil War, Britain's position on the war, Blyden's trepidation about being mistaken for a slave, and his prejudiced treatment in the United States during a visit in 1861.[25]

Aside from his relationship with Gladstone, Blyden addressed many business chambers and societies in England, including the African Society of London, an organization that made him an honorary vice president when it was founded.[26] Finally, British writer and explorer Mary Kingsley, who corresponded with Blyden and was a staunch advocate of traditional African social systems, described Blyden as "a great Arabic scholar and an educated man of the first class, perfectly typical Negro."[27] Blyden's acclaim in Victorian England may have influenced Tracy Flemming, on the basis of Simon Gikandi's work on colonialism and Englishness, to erroneously characterize him as an African Victorian.[28] But Blyden was not always comfortable among the English. He describes the English middle class as particularly racist and in his own words, as a people "among whom the caste feeling is more deeply seated." At the same time, he describes them as a "class of men whom it is less interesting and agreeable to meet in traveling." He also decried the fact that they, "more than any other people," were being sent "into various portions of the globe" to impose "pure religion undefiled upon the remotest tribes" under the guise of philanthropy and a false "Christian idea of universal brotherhood."[29]

Thus, Blyden was an African public intellectual who had successfully inserted himself into the Victorian public community on behalf of Africa. Blyden enjoyed the company of his English friends and was well versed in European literature, as this chapter's epigraph culled from the *African Mail* attests. Blyden's dialogue with his Victorian friends about Africa was, however, Africa centered and not Victorian derived. This commitment is especially evident in his scholarly sparring with Herbert Spencer. In the article "African and Africans," published in *Fraser's Magazine*, Blyden questioned Spencer's attempt at producing an:

> African Sociology, in the shape of a classified compilation of materials taken from the works of writers on Africa. But as his facts have been drawn from second-hand sources and from the writings of travelers whose observations were confined to very small localities, and made under the disturbing influence of disease, we cannot expect the work, when completed, though it will be one of considerable merit and a monument of industry, will be a trustworthy guide. The author will have relied, to a very large extent, upon isolated cases and *ex-parte* statements.[30]

Hence, Blyden, the African public intellectual utilizing an Afro-positivist discourse, questioned the empirical basis of Spencer's account of Africa in the Victorian public arena. Blyden's discursive thrust in this review was classic Afropublican discourse. While acting on behalf of Africa as an Afropublican thinker in the English public sphere, he confronted the rigor of Spencer's scholarship because it was devoid of the standards of Afro-positivism. Afro-positivism required not only thoroughness but also an experiential and conscientious approach to the study of African peoples and their societies. Spencer was his friend, but he had still fallen short of Blyden's requirements for an ethical and empirical way of portraying Africa as lived by Africans. Blyden, therefore, did not hesitate to point out Spencer's armchair approach to the study of Africa and the Afro-pessimism that lurked in accounts of the European travelers on which Spencer relied.[31]

Blyden and the Jewish Question

Victorian England was not the only public sphere in which Blyden would engage outside of Africa. In a speech on Zionism and the "Jewish Question" delivered in Liverpool in 1898, Blyden expediently states that he was born on the Danish island of St. Thomas and that he grew up with several Jewish families in his neighborhood.[32] This neighborhood included the family of Judah P. Benjamin, who is described variously as "America's first openly Jewish Senator," "the brains of the Confederacy," the U.S. Senate's quick-witted "Gentleman from Louisiana," and a gifted orator—the most prominent American Jew of the nineteenth century."[33] After the Civil War, Benjamin left the United States for London, where he lived a life of luxury, having established a successful legal practice.

Blyden's engagement with the Jewish public sphere on the so-called Jewish Question a year after the World Zionist Conference again reflects his global importance and acclaim as a public intellectual. The Jewish Question entailed the status, conditions, and immigration of diasporic Jewish communities from around the world to their ancient homeland. As Michael Echeruo notes, Blyden's *Jewish Question* was an important intervention by "one of the most respected of his generation–with what from the middle of the 19th century, was a major issue of public disputation among European intellectuals, namely, the fate not only of persecuted Jews in various European countries, especially Russia and the Balkans, but also (more generally) of all the Jews in the Diaspora."[34]

Blyden was respected because, just as he had taught himself other languages, he now embarked on an even more rigorous study of Hebrew in an attempt to read ancient Jewish religious texts after having earlier visited "Jerusalem and Mount Zion, the joy of the whole earth."[35] The question of the Jews' return to their homeland and their status in multiple European countries dominated the works of the nineteenth century's prominent European and Euro-Jewish intellectuals.

Interestingly, the author of "On the Jewish Question, 1843," Karl Marx (1818–1883), a German Jew, addressed the topic with his German interlocutor Bruno Bauer (1809–1882). Bauer had published *The Jewish Question, Braunschweig* in 1843.[36] Bauer's and Marx's analyses of the Jewish question centered more on the political and religious rights of Jews in Germany and France.

Marx disagreed with Bauer's total secularization as a solution to the problem. Using the United States as an example, Marx opined that total secularization would not offer complete freedom since a secular state presumes freedom of religion. Marx, therefore, argued that human emancipation that includes emancipation from religion (whether Judaism or Christianity) was a better solution to the Jewish question.

Blyden and Jewish intellectuals, pro-Zionist and non-Zionist alike, joined the debate much later in the century, arguing with each other in the pages of the *Nineteenth Century*, a British literary magazine founded in 1877. As mentioned earlier, Blyden's own writing had received a favorable appraisal in *Nineteenth Century*. He was also an avid reader of the magazine. This is evident in his contribution to the subject, *The Jewish Question*, in which he cites articles published in the magazine, and other publications by Jewish intellectuals on both sides of the debate. These included James Darmesteter, Herbert Bentwich, Oswald John Simon, Israel Zangwill, Herman Adler, Theodore Herzl, Isidor Kalish, and Abraham Kuenen.[37]

Blyden mostly straddled the middle of the two Jewish positions concerning the return to Palestine. He was, however, emphatic in his theological opinion that such a return was more of a spiritual return than a physical one. What is more significant, though, is that Blyden joined the debate, as he put it, "from an African standpoint," or from an Africa-centered perspective.[38] Here again, we see Blyden, the Presbyterian-trained Christian minister and self-trained African Orientalist, inserting himself into European and Jewish public domains on behalf of Africa.

From Blyden's African standpoint on the Jewish question, he saw similarities in the history of the Jewish peoples and peoples of African descent in the Atlantic world. He saw the oppression and persecution of both groups as having some divine or providential design that would benefit mankind in the long run. He also likened the Jewish spiritual return to Palestine to his quest for diasporan Africans to return or repatriate to the African continent. Thus, Blyden, the African public intellectual, used his familiarity and knowledge of the leading magazines and articles, biblical scholarship, and knowledge of the Hebrew language and Jewish history to assert African humanity, history, and place in God's divine will, including to promote his Pan-African strategy of repatriation to Africa. Blyden hence used what I will explain later as an Africa-centered Orientalist discourse to promote his Pan-African agenda in European and Jewish public spheres.[39]

Blyden and Black Intellectuals in the United States

Blyden also expressed his Pan-African agenda through his engagement with black intellectuals, institutions, and cultural movements in the United States. Blyden was well regarded by his peers in America, and his writing also earned reviews in African American journals like the *African Methodist Episcopal Church Review* and newspapers like the *Southwestern Christian Advocate,* which printed the following in 1890: "No book on Africa that has come to our hands has been found so full of thoughtful description of the Negro in the native land.... Dr. Blyden is an able writer, and his book will take rank as an authority, no doubt, on the subjects of which it treats."[40]

Blyden's presence in the pages of the *Crisis* magazine under the section "Important Men" is in itself a reflection of his prominence in the circuits of black intellectual and social life. For example, Blyden, while traveling in the United States, joined the "Saturday Circle," a reading group in Washington, DC, that included well-known black intellectuals and clergy like Anna Julia Cooper, Francis Grimké, Fannie Smythe, and Ella Somerville.[41] Blyden comments about his involvement with this reading group in his serialized newspaper columns and editorials, which were distributed throughout West Africa. In addition, he corresponded with some U.S. newspapers and embarked on several lecture and preaching tours, including an address to the Bethel Literary and Historical Society in the U.S. capital, during his travels in 1874, 1889–1890, and 1895.[42]

Blyden was additionally befriended, corresponded with, and met some of the period's most noted white American statesmen, including William

Coppinger, who supported his emigration proposals, and black intellectuals or clergy, including Frederick Douglass, Henry McNeal Turner, and Henry Highland Garnet. Blyden became a corresponding member of the American Negro Academy (ANA) when it was founded in 1898. He was also an honorary president of the Negro Society for Historical Research in 1911, an organization cofounded by his friend John Edward Bruce (1856–1924), with Puerto Rican–born bibliophile Arthur (Arturo) Schomburg (1874–1938).[43]

Blyden also cofounded the Athenaeum Club of Monrovia, Liberia, with Du Bois's mentor and cofounder of the ANA, Alexander Crummell. Compendiums of African and black scholarly greats commented on Blyden's place among black intellectuals in works such as *Masterpieces of Negro Eloquence*, *Sons of Africa*, *The Native Problem in Africa*, and "Great Sons of Africa."[44] Most of these writings, as their titles suggest, thought highly of Blyden. Alice Dunbar-Nelson's extract on him, for example, describes him as "one of the greatest scholars of the race."[45]

Further, Du Bois's personal correspondence with Blyden reveals the latter as a colossus in the black world. In a letter addressed to Edith Holden, Du Bois notes that he "never met Dr. Blyden, but I know of him and have greatly admired his work."[46] Indeed, in a 1909 letter addressed to Blyden, Du Bois told Blyden he knew him "by reputation" and was seeking his help with the publication of a "Negro Encyclopedia." Du Bois asked Blyden to serve on the editorial board of the encyclopedia and also requested his recommendations of other black scholars and white benefactors who could help fund the project.[47] Blyden's pamphlet *The Arabic Bible: A Plea for Transliteration* was also reviewed posthumously in the *Crisis*.[48] It is therefore curious why the *Crisis* and Du Bois, well aware of Blyden's international reputation, relegated his influence to just West Africa.

To be fair to the *Crisis*, the magazine also mentioned that Blyden was born in the Danish West Indies and lived in the United States for a while before emigrating to West Africa. In Liberia, "he held many positions of honor and trust, being secretary of state, secretary of interior and minister to England." The *Crisis* informed its readers that Blyden's book *Christianity,*

Islam and the Negro Race had earned him a great deal of fame and that Blyden believed in the idea of "Africa for the Africans."[49] What the *Crisis* failed to mention was that he had indeed originated the public use of the slogan "Africa for the Africans." It was a phrase that Marcus Garvey, a twentieth-century rival of Du Bois, would later popularize through his Universal Negro Improvement Association (UNIA), believed to be the largest black-led movement in history.[50]

Nonetheless, despite the *Crisis*'s own elucidation of Blyden's international credentials throughout Africa and the African diaspora, the magazine and its editor continued to characterize him as just "Blyden the African." In spite of the *Crisis* limiting Blyden's influence to Africa, his involvement with women like Cooper and Somerville in the Washington reading group, the Saturday Circle, and his presentations to literary organizations, such as the Bethel Literary Society, signals two important things. First, that Blyden was an important contributor to yet another public sphere: the beginning of the New Negro Movement in Washington, DC, a cultural and literary movement that Wilson J. Moses argues preceded the Harlem Renaissance.[51]

Secondly, it was in these circles that Blyden pioneered the capitalization of *Negro*. Blyden thought *Negro* should be used in preference over *Colored*. He began capitalizing *Negro* in his 1869 publication, "The Negro in Ancient History," believed to be the first article by a person of African descent to appear in an academic quarterly.[52] In 1872, he also founded the weekly newspaper *The Negro*, in Freetown, Sierra Leone.[53] In subsequent and separate publications in 1875 and 1883, he challenged his friend, Bosworth Smith, and Oliver Johnson for not capitalizing *Negro* when describing "one of the great families of man" while capitalizing *Indian* and *Mandingo*.[54] Blyden offered the same challenge to another friend, Bishop Benjamin Tanner of the African Methodist Episcopal (AME) Church in 1872.[55]

Through his participation with Cooper, Charlotte Forten, and Somerville in literary associations and clubs in Washington, DC, and as an ally, Blyden influenced the eventual emergence of women's club organizations in the 1890s, including the formation of the National Association of Colored

Women and the National Council of Negro Women. Ultimately, Blyden played a part, even if a small one, in the development of black women's political activism and discourse on race and gender that emerged at the turn of the twentieth century.

The Memorization of Blyden in the Global Public Sphere

Not long after the *Crisis*'s earlier announcement of Blyden's impending birthday, he passed away. When Blyden went to rest with his ancestors on the morning of February 7, 1912, in Freetown, his merit as a statesman of Africa and its diasporan world was immediately evident. Several newspapers announced Blyden's passing before the next issue of the *Crisis* was published. His death was announced on February 8 in the *New York Daily Tribune* and the *New York Times*, as well as in Monrovia, Liberia, where "seventeen gun shots were fired on the hill in respect of his official rank and service to country."[56] Announcements of Blyden's passing was also later circulated in Lagos, Nigeria, and obituaries were carried in the *Sierra Leone Weekly News* and the *African World*, plus the *London Times*, which read: "On February 7 occurred the death of Dr. E. W. Blyden, an old and well-known resident of Sierra Leone, at the age of 80. Dr. Blyden was the author of several books on the Negro question, he himself being a staunch respected member of that race."[57]

In this manner, Blyden was remembered around the world as an authority on black issues and a "race man" or "race vindicator."[58] These were the exact sentiments of the Hon. Samuel Lewis, a barrister and member of the legislative council of Liberia, who wrote the introduction to Blyden's 1887 edition of *Christianity, Islam, and the Negro Race*. In this piece, Lewis describes Blyden as having "a central idea [race]," which is "not only the sentiments of a careful observer and diligent student, but they are the exponent of a purpose—the patriotic purpose of a lover of his race."[59]

J. E. Casely-Hayford, a Gold Coast African, lawyer, and nationalist of the late nineteenth and twentieth centuries, and perhaps Blyden's most ardent advocate, wrote about his status in the black world. Casely-Hayford, who became an acquaintance of Blyden, preferred the Pan-African ideas of Blyden to those of Du Bois and Booker T. Washington. In his much-acclaimed 1903 work, *Ethiopia Unbound*, Casely-Hayford considered Washington's and Du Bois's work for the race as "provincial" but assessed Blyden's as "universal, covering the entire race and the entire race problem." In Casely-Hayford's opinion, "Afro-Americans must bring themselves into touch with some of the general traditions and institutions of their ancestors, and though sojourning in a strange land endeavor to conserve the characteristics of the race," a point Blyden sought to explicate in his lifetime. Casely-Hayford believed Blyden was one who had come to understand the cultural characteristics of his African forebears. He therefore considered him "a leader among leaders of African aboriginal thought" or, as this book highlights, Africa-centered ideas.[60]

Nonetheless, when the March 1912 issue of the *Crisis* was released following Blyden's death, it acknowledged the various scholarly degrees that Blyden had acquired during his lifetime and the intellectual societies and social clubs to which he belonged as well as his reputation as a scholar, yet continued to refer to Blyden as the "'Grand Old Man' of West Africa."[61] Years later, when Blyden's first wife, Sarah Yates, died, the *Crisis* chose to announce her passing by stating that "Mrs. Edward Blyden, widow of the noted African, is dead at the age of 83 years," irrespective of the fact that Blyden had been separated from Yates for years after a very fractious relationship.[62] Thus, the magazine still limited Blyden's scholarship and activism to Africa, much less to West Africa.

On the one hand, the various descriptors for Blyden—a noted African, a grand old man of West Africa, and a leader of the race in West Africa—help us understand the significance of Africa to the development of his Pan-African ideas. It also helps us confront recent work that has extricated Blyden's ideas from their African contexts and placed them in the general context of external influences on African thought. On the other hand, Blyden's Danish West Indies origins, his familiarity with Western and Orientalist scholarship, and his association with African American intellectuals have led to a completely different representation of him by recent scholarship.

It is consequently important to point out that Abiola Irele does not attribute all of Blyden's ideas to European intellectuals. Rather, he notes that Blyden was familiar with the writings of Giuseppe Mazzini and Johann Gottfried von Herder, whom he claims influenced Blyden's ideas about African nationalism.[63] Tracy Flemming, in referring to Blyden as a "complex diasporic intellectual," is also of the view that "while Blyden lived most of his life in Africa, he was a product of the Atlantic, not of Africa."[64]

This perception is also echoed in Paul Gilroy's treatment of Blyden in *The Black Atlantic: Modernity and Double Consciousness*. Gilroy examines the cultural and intellectual works of descendants of enslaved African Americans. Interestingly, he excludes the African pasts of the African American or Euro-African on one hand, and the contemporaneous African in the said Black Atlantic on the other. The primary premise of Gilroy's book is that the Black Atlantic is a transcultural formation and a critique of ethnic and national absolutism. He further argues that the cultural formulation of the Black Atlantic, while originating with blacks, ceases to be their exclusive property; the Black Atlantic is a counterculture to modernity.[65]

Gilroy describes transcultural formation by claiming that the Black Atlantic is a product of the intercultural exchange between the black populations of the Caribbean, Europe, and North America *excluding Africa* (thus, logically, Blyden's interactions in Africa would not be considered as part of such exchanges). As a result of these Atlantic exchanges, a reworking, or a reconfiguration, of these multivalent cultures into an organic whole, called the Black Atlantic, occurs.

Gilroy also analyzes individuals, including Blyden, in the Black Atlantic or diaspora populations whose writings reveal an engagement with modernity; he describes them as a product of the West or as influenced by European modernity.[66] Accordingly, the intellectual labor of the Black Atlantic world, he argues, was aimed to variously critique Enlightenment scholarship and provide an alternative modernity for the West.[67] Gilroy claims this alternative modernity for the whole of the Atlantic "West," signaling his aversion for ethnically absolutist approaches—both Eurocentric and Afrocentric.[68]

Gilroy's framework, in essence, rests on the idea that the Black Atlantic is a hybrid configuration that has nonetheless been formed in the heart of Western modernity. It is with this background that Gilroy treats Blyden by disengaging him from his lived realities on the African continent since the age of eighteen. Blyden's ideas are treated as extrinsic to the African presence in which they were formulated. While Gilroy acknowledges his influence on African nationalist thinking, he ascribes Blyden's ideas to European romantic nationalism through influences of such thinkers as Herder, Fichte, Mazzini, and Dostoevsky, and to Jewish Zionism.[69] Blyden's Africa-centered Pan-Africanism is therefore reduced to the strictures of Gilroy's Black Atlantic—sans Africa.

Needless to say, Gilroy's assessment of Blyden is contrary to the view of Casely Hayford. Casely Hayford, who was also a member of the ANA, as noted, pays tribute to Blyden's race work when he writes about the global influence of his writings: "The Claim of Edward Wilmot Blyden to the esteem and regard of all thinking Africans rests *not so much upon the special work he has done for any particular people of the African race, as upon the general work he has done for the race as a whole.*"[70]

And to distinguish Blyden's global recognition in contrast to his peers, Casely Hayford describes Blyden's intellectual influence on the black world in the following manner:

> The work of men like Booker T. Washington and W. E. Burghardt Du Bois is *exclusive and provincial. The work of Edward Blyden is universal, covering the entire race and the entire race problem.* What do I mean? I mean this: that while Booker T. Washington seeks to promote the material advancement of the black man in the United States, and W. E. Burghardt Du Bois his social enfranchisement amid surroundings and in atmosphere

> uncongenial to racial development, Edward Wilmot Blyden has sought for more than a quarter of a century to reveal everywhere the African unto himself; to fix his attention upon original ideas and conceptions as to his place in the economy of the world; to point out to him his work as a race among the races of men; lastly, and most important of all, to lead him to self respect. He has been the voice of one crying in the wilderness all these years.[71]

Casely-Hayford may have been biased in his analysis, given his little to no experiential knowledge of black life in the United States. In addition, he had a close association with Blyden in the last decade of the nineteenth century. However, Casely-Hayford was no intellectual lightweight, and he must have been aware of the ideas in circulation among blacks in the late nineteenth and early twentieth centuries. Founder of the NCBWA, Casely-Hayford had an almost unbridled regard for Blyden, which is a testament to Blyden's influence on his era. Nonetheless, it is important that Blyden's work be seen as important not only to his African contemporaries or mentees like Hayford but also to his diasporan colleagues, along with European intellectuals of the post-Enlightenment age with whom he came into contact.

Blyden, an advocate for the black world, was also a conduit for the exchange of ideas between African scholars and their African American counterparts. He reprinted or commented on several articles and columns in African American newspapers, writing for *Fraser's Magazine*, the *Liberian Herald*, and the *Negro*, which he edited while living in Sierra Leone. Blyden's essays appeared in journals like the *North American Review*, *Royal Geographical Society of London*, and the *Journal of the Royal African Society* for the benefit of his global audience.[72]

As a member of the ANA himself, Blyden was personal friends and corresponded with several founding members of the ANA including Bruce, Alexander Crummell, Francis Grimke, and John Cromwell. During the ANA's early years, Blyden and Sierra Leonean Sir Samuel Lewis (1843–1903) were its only African members.[73] Later, Egyptian author and editor of the *African*

Times and Orient Review Duse Mohammed (1866–1945), Gold Coaster James Kwegir Aggrey (1875–1927), and Casely Hayford were elected corresponding members. But prior to this, Blyden took it upon himself to recommend other African thinkers to be inducted into the ANA.[74] Even though his recommendations were not always taken, as in the case of J. J. Dosen, vice president of Liberia, Blyden is arguably the originator of the term *vindicationist* as it was used by the ANA. He wrote an essay in 1857 titled "A Vindication of the Negro Race."[75] The original essay included an introductory essay by ANA cofounder Crummell.[76] Blyden may, therefore, be said to have influenced the ANA's formative stages through his close relationship with some of its founding members.

In his capacity as a bridge between African scholars and African American intellectuals, Blyden joined and influenced several black collectives while he traveled in the United States. One of these, as mentioned earlier, was the Saturday Circle women's reading group.[77] He is thereby fully deserving of the moniker "prophet of the renaissance of the Negro race," as Du Bois quietly acknowledged later in 1915, three years after Blyden's death.[78]

Do Blyden's citizenship as a Liberian and his residence in Liberia and Sierra Leone as well as his wide popularity in West Africa brand him as the "leader of the race in West Africa"? This book takes the position that Blyden's Africanity is not singularly derived from his lived experience in West Africa but is rather a contributory factor among other dynamics. Does his birth in the Danish West Indies make him less of an African, or does it make him Afro-Danish—an African-descended person born in a colony controlled by Denmark? Was Blyden's public sphere limited to West Africa, or did it include the Caribbean, where he was born, and Europe, with whose intellectual history he was intimately familiar? Does his familiarity with contemporaneous Western scholars put him in the Western intellectual tradition, or does his self-training and subsequent studies at the Syrian Protestant College in Orientalist scholarship reduce his life's work to Orientalism? These are some of the questions that Blyden's peers, like Du Bois, or recent scholars, like Gilroy, raise.

In tackling these questions, I offer the perspective that Blyden's Afropublicanism was not restricted to any of the domains that Du Bois, Gilroy, or others have assigned to him. Rather, his Afropublicanism is evidenced not just in his various mentions in the *Crisis*, or in his correspondence with its astute editor, Du Bois. In addition, his ubiquity in West African intellectual and cultural circles, Victorian England, and African American public culture of the nineteenth century shows that his preeminent standing in global discourse was a result of his concern with the standing of Africa and people of African descent in world affairs. Blyden, the Afropublican, used his standing in these various domains of culture and intellection to influence discourse about Africa.

If W. E. B. Du Bois is perceived as shaping the Pan-African struggle in the twentieth century, Blyden is the doyen of the Pan-African intellectual, political, economic, and social milieu of the nineteenth century. Blyden was an Afropublican intellectual of Afro-Danish heritage who, over the course of his studious life, produced an Africa-centered scholarship that was Pan-African and Afro-positivist. That discourse engaged a Pan-African network of scholars that ranged from Africa, the Caribbean, the United States, and European as well as Orientalist and Jewish intellectuals. Put another way, Blyden articulated his perspective, based on his lived experience in metropolitan and provincial communities of Africa, to a public field of African intellectuals, Victorian elites, Enlightenment scholars, black intellectuals in the United States and the Caribbean, and Jewish intellectuals.

I use an intellectual biographical approach to trace moments in Blyden's life that help us understand how his thinking was first shaped by his birth in the Danish West Indies, why he immigrated to the United States, and why he left to go to Liberia. I describe the cultural "baggage" and skills he took with him and the exact moments when he realigned his thinking to an Africa-centered paradigm following encounters with indigenous Africans and West African Muslims. These encounters resulted in the publication of two of his most acclaimed texts: *Christianity, Islam, and the Negro Race* (1887) and *African Life and Customs* (1908). On this basis, I argue that his pioneering contributions to Pan-Africanism were therefore Africa derived. Hence, my treatment of him as an *African* intellectual, notwithstanding his varied geographic connections and his earlier strand of patronizing Ethiopianist attitude toward African societies.

Blyden, Ethiopianisms, and Liberia

Fleeing the United States because of the Fugitive Slave Law, Blyden left for West Africa in 1851. Nonetheless, when the *Liberia Packet* sailed from the Chesapeake Bay, en route to Grand Bassa, Liberia, Blyden was not consumed by fear. If not fear, what was the state of mind of the *Liberia Packet*'s eighteen-year-old passenger? Ethiopianism, a feeling that had permeated the hearts of many African diasporans over centuries, dominated Blyden's mind. The historical record shows that Blyden was brimming with Ethiopianism.

Ethiopianism can generally be described as the Afro-Christian belief or sentiment among African diasporans, especially blacks in the United States, that their enslavement in the Americas was God's providential plan for Africa to experience a renaissance. This reawakening in industrial technology, business, and world affairs was to be organized and led by African American returnees to Africa (conceptualized from the book of psalms as Zion) who, having experienced Western culture, had been divinely ordained to civilize and Christianize their native kin. It was a providential theology that placed American blacks at the center of African/black political liberation and spiritual regeneration.[79] Such sentiments can be traced from the eighteenth-century poetry of Phillis Wheatley through the activities of Marcus Garvey and the UNIA in the nineteenth and early twentieth centuries to the contemporary beliefs of Rastafarians, who believe in both a physical and a spiritual return to Zion/Africa.[80]

Proponents of Ethiopianist doctrine cite ancient Ethiopia and its classical connections to Israel and Christendom, together with Bible verses (Psa. 68:31; Psa. 87:4; Isa. 19:19–21; Isa. 45:14; Zeph. 3:10; Acts 8:27) that mention

Ethiopia and Egypt, to prove their conviction. Most notable among these verses is Psa. 68:31, “Princes shall come out of Egypt, Ethiopia shall soon stretch out her hands unto God.” For Afro-Jamaican Rastafarians with some inspiration from Garvey as well as other Ethiopianists, Ethiopia’s success against the Italian army in the 1896 Battle of Adwa and the coronation of Haile Selassie (1892–1975) as emperor of Ethiopia in 1930 confirmed that Ethiopia (representing Africa as a whole) had finally stretched her hands unto God. Africa was therefore not only an ancestral home, but also the biblical Zion, a place of final redemption.[81]

For the purpose of understanding Blyden’s connection to Ethiopianism, it is imperative to delineate historically four forms of Ethiopianism because Blyden was influenced by two of the four forms and inspired the fourth and final Ethiopianist tradition. These four forms are Black American Ethiopianism, Euro-American Ethiopianism, Southern and Central African Ethiopianism, and West African Ethiopianism, which Blyden spearheaded. I will explain the first three and offer an explanation for the distinctiveness of West African Ethiopianism as a religious, cultural, and political movement led by West Africans against colonialism and Europeanized Christianity in particular.

Euro-American (or white) Ethiopianism itself had an assortment of strands. The earliest strand can be found in the preaching and writings of Samuel Hopkins, a Newport, Rhode Island, preacher who criticized Americans and Rhode Islanders in particular for participating in the slave trade and building their state economy on slavery. Hopkins believed that a superior divine good could emerge from this American original sin if the sinners chose to atone for their wrongs. Atonement for Hopkins meant returning black Americans to Africa, where they would, in turn, spread the Christian gospel to Africans.[82]

Another strand of Euro-American Ethiopianism came out of the Revolutionary War in Britain’s North American colonies and the abolitionist movement in England, which led to the need for Britain to resettle its Black

Loyalists. Black Loyalists were blacks who fought alongside the British against the American revolutionaries in exchange for their freedom.

Later, the British establishment's desire for a more "legitimate" trade with Africa led to the 1787 formation of the Sierra Leone colony by leading abolitionist Granville Sharp (1735–1813) and the Committee for the Black Poor in London. The colony was thus first settled by the blacks from London; and then, in 1792 and 1800, respectively, 1,200 Black Loyalists from Nova Scotia and 550 Jamaican Maroons were "returned" to Sierra Leone. The returnees to Sierra Leone also included recaptives, Africans who had been freed from illegal slaving ships by the British Naval Squadron following the abolition of slavery.[83] These returnees, having experienced Western culture and having been Christianized by the activities of England's Church Missionary Society (CMS), were to be the vanguard of Britain's cultural, economic, and colonial onslaught on African societies.

In the United States, another strand of Ethiopianism arose as a result of the activities of nineteenth-century Quakers, evangelistic revivalists, and various abolition societies like the Pennsylvania Abolition Society, which culminated in the establishment of the American Colonization Society in 1816. James Campbell described the ACS board of directors as "a who's who of the nation's leaders," including Supreme Court Justice Bushrod Washington, George Washington's nephew and heir, Speaker of the House Henry Clay, General Andrew Jackson, Secretary of the Treasury William Crawford, and Francis Scott Key, composer of "The Star-Spangled Banner."[84] Like its British counterparts, the ACS established a colony, Liberia, and named its capital Monrovia after sitting president James Monroe, who funded a shipload of colonists to build houses for the returnees.

The ACS, however, had ulterior motives that became a source of disengagement with the Black Ethiopianist tradition. House Speaker Clay and Virginia congressman John Randolph made these designs public by arguing that sending free blacks to Africa would secure slavery in the United States. This scheme drew the ire of black clergymen and intellectuals across the country who vowed to "never separate [themselves] voluntarily from the slave population of the country." The response to the lawmakers was spearheaded by leaders of the independent black church movement, such as Bishop Richard Allen, founder of the AME Church, and James Forten, "a wealthy sailmaker who had outfitted [Paul] Cuffe's *Traveller* for its inaugural visit to Sierra Leone."[85]

Ethiopianism accordingly also represents the historical breakaway of black churches from a racialist and white-dominated church and the institutional creation of independent black churches in the United States, Southern and Central Africa, and West Africa from about 1860 to 1910.[86] The origins of the Black Ethiopianist tradition, in the United States in particular, can be traced to early black associations, such as the Free African Union Society (1780) of Newport, Massachusetts, and to individuals like black mariner Paul Cuffe (1759–1817) and fugitive slave, abolitionist, and cofounder of the AME Church Daniel Coker (aka Isaac Wright, 1780–1846), who led various colonization missions to West Africa in the early nineteenth century.

As Shepperson explains, the idea of Ethiopianism signaled the creation of independent African and African American churches.[87] Expressions of Ethiopianism in the black tradition include the creation of the African Methodist Episcopal Church, which separated from the (white) Methodist Church. This project took place with Coker's founding of black Methodist churches in Baltimore in 1807, in Philadelphia in 1816, and later throughout the Eastern Seaboard, under the leadership of Richard Allen and Absalom Jones (1746–1818).[88]

In the case of Southern and Central African Ethiopianism, the ideology was found in African churches that asserted their independence from white institutional control but "which often [found] their origins in the missionary efforts of similar American groups white and Negro."[89] Shared among these groups, both white and black, was the intention to civilize Africans, who were in need of the Christian gospel. In Southern Africa, examples of Ethiopianist churches include the independent Tembu Church, which broke away from the Wesleyan Church under the guidance of Nehemiah Tile in

1884.[90] Southern and Central African Ethiopianism was, however, distinctive in its millenarian and apocalyptic theologies.

Implicit in Ethiopianist ideologies were the Back-to-Africa movements of the nineteenth century, which involved all kinds of emigration schemes.[91] When white abolitionists and missionaries began recruiting northern blacks for emigration to Africa, black American leaders and intellectuals like Martin Delany pursued alternative colonization and emigration arrangements. They did this in distinction from and opposition to the white-dominated American Colonization Society.[92] In the process, two traditions, which occasionally worked together, emerged: one predominantly white and the other black.[93]

Blyden was influenced by these U.S. emigration currents; but in institutional terms, he came under the influence of the white-dominated ACS and the Board of Foreign Missions of the Presbyterian Church, USA.[94] And even though at the age of eighteen he was aware of the perception of ACS among some American blacks as the "twin-sister of slavery," he was confident that the civilizing mission would succeed because it was "human and Christian."[95] As a result, before he arrived in Liberia, Blyden had unfortunately bought into the civilizing missionary ideas among U.S. whites and blacks who "believe[d] that God in his large providence [had] been preparing the American Negro to assume a hand in the evangelization of Africa."[96]

Blyden's Civilizing Mission: Epiphany in the Making of an Afropublican Intellectual

Consequently, when the *Liberia Packet* landed at Grand Bassa County, Liberia on January 25, 1851, one young man aboard the vessel, Edward Blyden, was filled with Ethiopianist rhetoric and wont to versify:

> About twelve o'clock we were riding safely at anchor, opposite the "beautiful bluff" that screens the town of Monrovia. You can easily imagine the delight with which I gazed upon the land of Cyprian and Tertullian, ancient fathers

> of the Christian Church; of Hannibal and Henry Diaz; yes and the land of my forefathers. On top of the elevation that intercepted the town from our view, was seen, waving gloriously the lone star.[97]

In this short quote, Blyden praises the supposed African fathers of Christendom, valorizes the land of his ancestors, and declares his patriotism for the second independent country in Africa, Liberia. It was Ethiopianism, Back to Africa, and the dawn of African nationalism all rolled into one. Blyden's missionary zeal was balanced by a sense of nationalism. He captured his nationalistic and Back-to-Africa sentiments in a poem he published in the *New York Colonization Journal*:

> Liberia, happy land! to thee
> The oppressed colored man may flee;
> Thy pleasant, thy delightful shore
> To him true freedom will restore!
> Ye Colored men who freedom want,
> Why stay in other lands and pant,
> When in Liberia's pleasant land
> You may as men, as freedmen stand?
> You who for genuine freedom crave,
> Who will not be the white man's slave,
> Come to Liberia's pleasant land;
> Here is the freedom you demand
> Why be reduced to poverty
> For want of genuine liberty,
> When on Liberia's pleasant ground
> Alone your liberty may be found.[98]

Thus, at a young age and early period of his life in Liberia, he was given to expressing passion and pathos in a prosaic nationalism to inspire the Back-to-Africa movement.

However, accompanying these notions of Ethiopianism, Back-to-Africa sentimentality, and nationalism among diasporan blacks was an aloofness and condescension about native African ways of life. Such arrogance is immediately evident in Blyden's narration of his arrival in Africa. He writes while on board the *Liberian Packet* that "in a few minutes the deck was thronged by natives—large, robust, intelligent-looking men, with no other clothing than a rag tied around their waist. Many of them had a tolerable smattering of the English language."[99] Blyden would, as a result of his diasporic Ethiopianist background, quickly join in American immigrants' fight against and disdain for the natives of Liberia. In a letter written to his mentor J. P. Knox, Blyden records:

> Three hundred citizens who some time ago started from here under the command of President Roberts to fight a tribe of Kroomen who sometime previously murdered several citizens of Bassa Cove, and attacked the settlements with the intention of taking it, have returned with the loss of but 4 men, having conquered and subdued more than two thousand of the enemy. Surely God is on our side. His name be praised. Ye sir there has been war here, and is yet, as the chiefs of those insubordinate tribes have not been apprehended, but we hope soon to have them. Though I was unable to accompany the men to war, I kept guard in turns at night which was necessary to prevent the tribes in our vicinity from taking advantage.[100]

Blyden's expression of the cavalier attitude that had been adopted by the American settlers (Americo-Liberians) toward the native peoples of Liberia epitomized the struggle against the different ethnic groups already living in Liberian territory. If Blyden was ready to go to war on behalf of the Americo-Liberian immigrants, he got his chance in 1853: when the Liberian government embarked on an expedition to Little Cape Mount to arrest Chief Boombo of the Vai ethnic group.[101] Blyden remembers having "suffered considerably from fatigue [and] still feel[ing] [him]self amply repaid—by the scenes which [he] witnessed—and the experience [he] gained

FIGURES 3–6.
Indigenous Liberians.

in the wearisome route."[102] Blyden's opinion of indigenous Liberians was not limited to the military field. In an 1852 letter, he opines:

> The influence of Liberia upon the surrounding tribes is very happily manifesting itself. Even the Krooman who, some years ago, proud of the customs and habits of his ancestors, disdained all imitation of civilized life, and rigorously persecuted his neighbor . . . The native mind is undergoing a complete revolution. There exists among many of them the belief that some great day is approaching for Africa—some year of golden harvests.[103]

However, at some point in his stay in Liberia, Blyden would abandon the "civilizing mission" against the habits and customs of the Kroomen's ancestors. This change in his attitude began around the presidency of Stephen Allen Benson (1856–1864). In 1856, Blyden was once again part of a military expedition and a captain in the militia as aide-de-camp to the general. Blyden records his experience of the expedition:

> Mr. Benson succeeding to Roberts' disastrous aboriginal policy . . . to enter upon an expensive war—carrying two thousand men into the field—with the kroo tribes. . . . We traversed nearly the whole of Sinou country and destroyed scores of town—but though merely a boy then I regretted the waste of men and material to subdue and humble a people who only claimed to live as men in their own country. But this was Benson's inheritance from Roberts' rule.[104]

This change in Blyden's way of thinking about indigenous Africans would eventually lead him to author his landmark book, *African Life and Customs*, and his several writings on Islam among the ethnic groups in the interior of Liberia and Sierra Leone. These writings were the result of his several missions to cities such as Boporo, Musardu, and other places.[105] His travels would also lead to his constant critique of the Americo-Liberian oligarchy.

The fundamental modification of Blyden's perspective from a civilizing mission to an indigenous African viewpoint would characterize his subsequent writings. And although there still remained strands of the superior attitude toward indigenous African ways in his writing, Blyden successfully deculturalized some of his Ethiopianist positions compared to some of his diaspora counterparts. Together with Alexander Crummell and John Henry Smyth, the second black American to be appointed U.S. representative to Liberia, Blyden challenged thc Liberian leadership's discriminatory policies toward indigenous Liberians.[106]

His so-called anti-mulatto stance, as some have portrayed it, appears to have been more the result of his disdain for the Americo-Liberian establishment. It is on this account that I have previously called Blyden an iconoclast because he was willing to challenge his Americo-Liberian friends' contempt and separation from native Africans. Blyden not only persistently evolved in his thinking but continually spoke truth to power—as he often did in Liberia, to no avail.

From the foregoing, one can clearly see that although Blyden was imbued with the writings of Western scholarship, he also acquired his tertiary education in West Africa. Africa, where he lived primarily, and global Africa were at the center of his thinking. The change in Blyden's assessment of Africa and Africans and his writings on global African subjects and places were determined by his lived experience on the African continent. Unquestionably, his thoughts were cultivated in West Africa. His Black Atlantic writings, even if limited to his native St. Thomas and his adopted Liberia, did not exclude the rest of Africa. Gilroy's exclusion of Africa from the Black Atlantic while characterizing Blyden as a Black Atlantic scholar appears not only anachronistic but also Ethiopianist and devalues the African dimensions of Blyden's thinking and writing.[107]

Blyden was deeply conscious of the relationship between the African continent and its vast diaspora, as reflected in the several essays and addresses he delivered in Africa and on twelve separate lecture tours in the United States, including his tour of the States when he urged blacks to emigrate to Liberia. He undertook this circuit during his tenure as commissioner of colonization for Liberia.[108] For Blyden, connections between Africa and blacks abroad required emigration back to Africa. Although others, like Delany and Crummel, may have wavered, recanted, or amended their positions on emigration, Blyden, like his friend Bishop Henry McNeal Turner, was steadfast.

Delany, for example, pursued emigration plans in both Africa and the Americas. In contrast to Blyden, he was initially opposed to emigration to Africa, particularly Liberia, where the white-led ACS held sway. Delany disliked the ACS because he considered it "the most arrant enem[y] of the colored man, ever seeking to discomfit him, and envying him of every privilege that he may enjoy."[109]

In the midst of this mistrust, Delany—on different speaking as well as writing platforms—looked to the East African coast, Central America, and the West Indies as possible destinations.[110] Unlike Blyden, Delany, therefore pursued multiple strategies as alternatives to emigration to Africa. Delany later formally pursued emigration plans to Africa as a member of the two-man Niger Valley Exploration Party in 1859, but he again abandoned such plans during the American Civil War when blacks were being freed, and he enlisted in the Union army.[111]

In contrast to Delany, Blyden never reneged on the issue; he embarked on many journeys to the United States, St. Thomas, and other parts of the Caribbean, urging repatriation to Africa. Blyden considered the question of emigration inevitable because he believed that in the United States "there can never occur . . . equality, social or political, between whites and blacks."

This was the main thrust of the speeches he delivered as Liberian emigration commissioner when he visited the eastern United States in 1862. Blyden's extended association with the ACS may be called into question, given that black nationalists like Delany viewed it with scorn. Then again, Blyden, who was on occasion likewise critical of the ACS, also believed that "an African nationality is [Africans'] great need and God tells [them] by his providence that he has set the land before [them], and bids [them] go and possess it."[112]

In this fashion, even after the perceived gains of the American Civil War,

Blyden, like Turner, continued to champion emigration to Africa as late as 1887. Blyden wrote on the prospects of Liberia in the worldwide community of peoples:

> The nation now being reared in Africa by the returning exiles from this country will not be a reproduction of the American. The restoration of the Negro to the land of his fathers will be the restoration of a race to its original integrity, to itself; and working by itself, for itself and from itself, it will discover the methods of its own development and they will not be the same as the Anglo-Saxon methods.[113]

This statement demonstrates the transformation in Blyden's thinking concerning an African cultural and intellectual renaissance on the world stage.

Blyden arrived in Liberia in 1851 filled with Black and Euro-American Ethiopianist rhetoric. By 1887, however, after several years of living in Africa and studying its peoples and cultures, Blyden began to strike a different tone. Like the early plantation intellectuals, he continued to champion a physical return to Africa; he, however, no longer believed that the émigrés would be responsible for Africa's transformation. He believed that Africa's regeneration would come from within and not without. He was of the viewpoint that diasporic Africans would experience a reconnection with African peoples as well as a collective resurgence on the world stage as a result of their domicile and lived experience in Africa—as had happened to him. Here we see that Africa had moved to the center from the periphery of Blyden's thought.

This momentous shift was the first conceptual metamorphosis in Blyden's intellectual journey. In order to appreciate Blyden's public intellectual career, his entrenchment in African experience as well as his confrontation of Afro-pessimistic ideas that led him to the apex of his intellectual life, we must begin with events in the Danish West Indies that laid the framework for his identity formation and embrace of Pan-Africanism.

The Afro-Positivist Foundations of Pan-Africanism: Plantation Intellectuals and Africa's Atlantic Scholars

Mij dodte mij loppe in myn lande. [When I die, I shall return to my own (African) land.]

—Recorded belief of enslaved Africans on the Danish West Indies islands, March 1734

I have defined Blyden as a global African iconoclastic scholar; that is, an iconic intellectual whose transcendent and timeless scholarship, activism, politics, and social development activities defy easy categorization into a particular school of thought and impacts people of African descent globally.[1] Specifically, I address this complexity in two ways. In the first instance, I have adopted the more expansive term *Afropublicanism* to capture Blyden's various discursive practices and therefore employ it to encompass Blyden's public intellectualism, iconoclasm, Afro-positivist discourse, vindicationist scholarship, distinctive theology, emphasis on education, and insistence on understanding African languages as a means to understanding African cultures and societies.

In the second instance, I use two distinctive generations of Africans; that is, Africa-born captives in the Americas and Western-trained African intellectuals to cast light on the full scope of Blyden's life and scholarship while showing the debt he owed to the preceding generations in his methodical delineation of early Pan-African ideas. To this end, I explore three central themes. The first is an analysis of the influence that enslaved Africans whom I have classified as *plantation intellectuals* living on plantation societies had on Blyden's Afro-positivism and ideational Pan-Africanism. The second is the influence that eighteenth-century Africa-born Atlantic scholars had on Blyden as an African public intellectual.

Implicit in these two themes is the third thematic focus of the chapter, which argues that a distinction between early Pan-African ideas and the Pan-African movements of the twentieth century onwards is useful. This segmentation leads to proper acknowledgment of the distinctive contributions of West Africans to Pan-African ideas and intellectual currents in the Black Atlantic. Thus, both Africa-born plantation intellectuals and Africa-born academic intellectuals are vital for understanding West Africa's unique contributions to Pan-Africanism as well as the foundations on which Blyden emerges as the most outstanding black intellectual of the nineteenth and early twentieth centuries. Two of these Africa-born intellectuals are Anton Wilhelm Amo and Christian Protten, who were trained in Western academe and became African public intellectuals in Europe.

Afro-Positivist Foundations

In March 1737, Christian Protten, a Gold Coast–born intellectual, received a letter from Count Zinzendorf, leader of the Moravian church. In this correspondence, Zinzendorf urged Protten to leave his "africanisch wild [African savage] and maurisch [Moorish] habits in Amsterdam" before leaving Europe to return to the Gold Coast as a Christian missionary. Zinzendorf was referencing Protten's rumored "presumptuousness and high opinion of himself" as an Afropublican or African public intellectual responding to negative portrayals of Africa in European Christian and intellectual circles.[2]

Such negative representations of Africans also include Zinzendorf's belief that the enslavement of Africans was a divine curse because they were a proud people.[3] Zinzendorf, like Protten a few years later, visited Edward Blyden's birth island of St. Thomas between January 29 and February 16, 1739. While on the island, he heard about the slave rebellion on St. John, which had occurred six years prior to his arrival.[4] In learning about the agitations and very public protests of enslaved Africans on St. John and also writing to Protten about his pride in an African cultural identity, Zinzendorf inadvertently captures how Africa-born thinkers in American plantation societies helped establish an Afro-positivist foundation or tradition of valorizing Africa as part of a wellspring of ideas that shaped what eventually became known as Pan-Africanism.

Both of these historical events allude to an early expression of the Afro-positivist sentiments that Zinzendorf heard while on the island and that is encapsulated in the Afro-Creole Dutch expression "Mij dodte mij loppe in myn lande," meaning "When I die, I shall return to my own [African] land."[5] These words were spoken by enslaved Africans, who, with a "high presumption" of their African cultural backgrounds, participated in the St. John's rebellion. Three years before Zinzendorf's letter to Protten, these Gold Coast–born Africans on St. John, as plantation intellectuals, expressed their critique of plantation slavery as a socioeconomic system through their physical protestation. Their criticism, derived from African understandings of what it means to be human, drove them to engage in open rebellion against their slave masters. The rebellion was both an assault on the diminution of Africa and a rejection of the unequal racial, social, and economic hierarchy of the Danish West Indian slave plantation system.

Plantation intellectuals are Africa-born enslaved thinkers who actively participated in public discourse concerning the plantation system in which they had become ensnared, inclusive of the public culture in plantations as both volitive and imposed.[6] With few exceptions, examinations of slave societies in general and slave rebellions in particular have focused on cultural processes.[7] In addition, the use of "rebellion, conspiracy, and insurrection" tends to conjure only specters of violence and therefore obfuscates the intellectual practices the enslaved Africans undertook as part of their fight against slavery and plantation society. Plantation intellectuals or scholars, therefore, best represent the reflective and philosophical dimensions of African knowledge production, systematic thinking, and critical public culture in plantation societies.

In examining the underlying philosophical and intellectual deliberations that influenced the enslaved to engage in maroonage, rebellion, insurrection, conspiracies, or to run away, I argue that the plantation scholar's critique of plantation hierarchies, caste systems, concepts of race, plantation economy and polity, abstracted as Afro-positivism, is the anvil on which Blyden's Pan-Africanism was shaped. Their advocacy of alternative systems for human societies—that is, cultural pluralism—and their creation of maroon societies throughout the Atlantic world is material evidence of this earliest form of Pan-Africanism. At the height of his intellectual prowess, Blyden, like these plantation intellectuals, raised similar questions about global systems of racial oppression.

The epigraph—by plantation intellectuals in Blyden's Danish West Indies and Zinzendorf's statement concerning Protten, an eighteenth-century Afro-Danish intellectual—frame the original Afro-positivist highlighting of Africa as a stepping stone to the emergence of Pan-African discourse and social movement in the late nineteenth and early twentieth centuries. The emphasis here is that the idea of Africa as a homeland or a common place of origin, and an example of a place where African-descended peoples had thrived, is a central tenet of Pan-Africanism.

Africa as a mythologized homeland and a place of imagined or physical return is an enduring Afro-positivist tradition. We have already witnessed how, faced with the overt racism of the Fugitive Slave Law and the systematic racism at Rutgers, where when he was refused entry on account of his race, Blyden chose to return to Africa. The idea of returns to Africa is, however, part of a discursive approach that has been expressed, albeit distinctively, by a variety of African and African diasporic historical actors and Pan-Africanists, including Edward Blyden. The first to articulate it, however, are the Africans who arrived in the Americas to work on the racially hierarchical systems of the Atlantic world. Implicit in the dehumanization of these enslaved Africans was a denigration of their African past. Conversely, inherent in the enslaved Africans' critique of the plantation system was an understanding that, before their enslavement, Africans lived in complex societies that were imperial, centralized, small scale, or densely populated villages. These societies—with varying degrees of social, religious, political, and philosophical complexity, culinary and artistic expression—were for enslaved Africans in the Americas more successful spaces of human habitation and organization. Africans who resisted, rebelled, or marooned, therefore, either sought to restore, recreate, or return to a known African past.

Thus, While Blyden is undoubtedly the intellectual progenitor of the idea of Pan-Africanism by systematically delineating its essential parts, his views were built on the fundamental notions of Afro-positive valorization of African homeland by Africa-born plantation dwellers. West African–born plantation intellectuals, therefore, sowed the conceptual ideas that Blyden would develop in his Pan-African agenda in the late nineteenth and early twentieth centuries.

Nonetheless, their contributions have often been glossed over by historians of Pan-Africanism because historiography often conflates Pan-African thinking and the Pan-African social movement. This conflation is evinced in Joseph Adjaye's definition of Pan-Africanism as "an idea, a movement, and an ideology . . . a set of ideas, emotions, and ideologies that espouses unity among Africans living on the continent and those of African descent in the diaspora."[8] In this definition, Adjaye integrates the several distinct phases of Pan-Africanism. The complexity associated with accurately defining Pan-Africanism correspondingly rests on the unexplored distinction between Pan-African thought and the Pan-African social movement. An enhanced understanding of Pan-African thought as an intellectual enterprise provides innovative ways of appreciating and interpreting the Pan-African social movement and the unique ideologies it engendered. It additionally offers insights into original African contributions to Pan-Africanism through the Afro-positivist ideas of enslaved West Africans and Africa-born intellectuals in Europe—fundamentally, the antecedent Afropublican intellectual generations.

It is important to distinguish my interpretation of Pan-Africanism as an intellectual enterprise from the Pan-African movement, with its numerous congresses of the twentieth century. The intellectual tradition of Pan-African thought involves analytical considerations about attaining racial equality, advocating unity, and enhancing the social conditions of African-descended communities globally. Blyden made critical contributions to this analytical tradition. Pan-African thought is, however, distinct from Pan-Africanism as an institutionalized international social and political movement, in which Blyden played a minimal role, if any. While it is clear that a social movement requires a corpus of foundational thinking, the synthesis of the two (Pan-African thought and the Pan-African movement) has often led to the exclusion of West Africans whose ideas later influenced later Pan-African intellectuals. Notably omitted are plantation intellectuals who longed—and made many attempts—to return to Africa. Also excluded, as will be shown later, are Africa-born Atlantic intellectuals like Protten, who set the stage for a transcendent intellectual like Blyden to develop unique Afro-positivist reflections.

A distinction between the intellectual articulations of Pan-African ideas and the Pan-African sociopolitical movements as evidenced by the series of conferences and congresses organized at the dawn of the twentieth century allows for a clearer understanding of these West African intellectuals' poignant contributions to the idea of Pan-Africanism and the different phases of Pan-African sociopolitical movements. For example, Blyden's Afro-positivist elucidation of the African Personality should be included in the body of Pan-African ideas preceding the social movements of the 1900s, which were organized by the likes of Marcus Garvey, Henry Sylvester Williams, and W. E. B. Du Bois. Blyden's ideas emphasizing a return to the integrity of African ways of life parallels the actions and writings of people born in Africa who found themselves in Europe and the Americas either as enslaved laborers or as intellectuals in Euro-American public spheres.

It must be emphasized that these postulations are not an attempt to link all of the variegated and dynamic histories of people of African descent to one idea—Afro-positivist valorization of Africa. Nonetheless, where the links and continuities are palpable and indivisible, this book strives to show their historicity and demonstrate the connections with firsthand evidence. For example, in 1830, David Walker published his *Appeal to the Colored Citizens of the World*. Wilson Armistead, writing in 1848, and using a title similar to Walker's, includes Anton Wilhelm Amo in an extended list of black folks whom he felt vindicated the moral, intellectual, and religious capabilities of the "colored portion of mankind, with particular reference to the African race."[9]

Almost a decade later, in 1856, Blyden includes Amo and some of the same people Armistead had written about in his own list of twenty-seven renowned intellectuals of African descent. In the following year, Blyden, like Armistead, uses the term *vindicationist* in an essay titled "A Brief Examination of the Arguments of African Inferiority: A Vindication of the African Race."[10] The shared analytic purpose of these African-descended writers was to "vindicate" or cast people of African descent in a positive light.

The use of titles and analytic content show empirically verifiable connections between different generations of scholars of African heritage. One of the threads that bind plantation intellectuals, eighteenth-century Africa-born intellectuals, and Blyden together is the notion of Afro-positivism. I trace the foundations of this Afro-positivist tradition, chronologically and systematically, to the ideational contributions of plantation intellectuals or West Africa–born enslaved Africans as well as Western-trained Africa-born intellectuals. Further, I demonstrate the various means by which ideas first espoused through the beliefs and actions of Africa-born plantation intellectuals in Blyden's Danish West Indies left a legacy of an African homeland that was so central to the imaginations of Blyden and other scholars of African descent in Africa and the African diaspora.

Pan-African Beginnings: The Plantation Intellectuals and Afro-Positivist Discourse

Between May 4 and June 15, 1734, countless leaders of and participants in the St. John rebellion, numbering about "three hundred," sat in a circle "on a hill near Brismbay" and took their own lives by shooting one another. They committed this apparent act of "mass suicide" rather than face capture by the Danish colonial and slave plantation network.[11] In taking their own lives, these enslaved Africans from West Africa's Gold Coast avoided being sent back into the execrable conditions of plantation slavery. Also known as the "Amina" in the Danish colonial records, these Gold Coast–born Africans, through self-extermination, avoided the fate suffered by others who were eventually captured alive. If seized, rebellious slaves in the Danish West Indies and throughout the Americas were often tortured through burning or impaling at the stake and frequently ended up decapitated.[12]

Nonetheless, the shocking "mass suicide" should be understood more deeply than shallowly conceived as a fear of cruelty and suffering at the hands of their Danish or Dutch slave masters. The enslaved Africans' actions cannot be explained simply as suicide, as they took their lives on the basis of an African ontological belief: that when they die they will return to their own lands in Africa or Guinea.[13] In addition, the 1733 St. John rebellion was itself politically aimed at *restoring* autonomous African homeland–styled polities to the Danish West Indian islands and the island of Tortola in opposition to the racially hierarchical colonial slave polities of the Americas.[14] West Africans' deliberate destruction of their bodies was therefore not only an expression, but correspondingly an insistence on the validity of an African homeland or an African-derived way of human social organization.

Blyden came to epitomize this burning desire to return to Africa. He returned and lived in Africa as well as advocated the return to Africa of African descended peoples in the Americas through his writings and by embarking on recruitment tours. Blyden, in his later scholarship, came to the same validation of African ways of life beginning with his encounter with "Africanized Islam" in the Greater Senegambia region. This encounter with Islam in West Africa and his engagement with West African Muslim scholars resulted in his most celebrated book, *Christianity, Islam, and the Negro Race*. Following this experience, he began to research and explicate African families, political, and social organization, ultimately validating them in his final publication, *African Life and Customs*. Still the Christian theologian, Blyden's final advocacy of African customs and traditions like his Danish West Indies ancestors was his active encouragement for the adoption of African dressing, music, languages, and culture in the West African church.

Such autonomy in language, songs, and ethos was what plantation intellectuals throughout the Americas initially sought. Like other enslaved Africans throughout the Americas, especially in Jamaica, Cuba, Brazil, and the Gullah of the American Southeast, those on St. John had been successful in forming autonomous African-inspired communities on the peripheries of plantation slave societies. These zones of liberation came to be known as Maroon societies. In the Danish West Indian islands and throughout the Americas, Africa-born slaves consistently sought to practice African-derived ways of life. C. G. A. Oldendorp, another European missionary, witnessed, during his late-eighteenth-century domicile on the Danish West Indies, several Africans in the islands who, in the face of almost-certain death, refused to be subjugated to plantation slavery.[15] In other words, as African intellectuals (reflective thinkers) within the public realm of the plantation complex who endured the throes of slavery as a public realm, they reasoned, interpreted, and rejected the undesirable depiction of Africa and African peoples via the racially hierarchical societies of the Americas, which without exception dehumanized Africans through enslavement.

Similar rejections of plantation society culture can be found among seventeenth-century enslaved Africans taken from West Africa to the Caribbean island of Hispaniola (Haiti) and parts of mainland North America. West Africans from the Bight of Benin, the Gold Coast, and the Bight of Biafra who found themselves in Haiti proclaimed that they were "neg Ginin" (Black from Guinea) and longed to return either physically or spiritually to Guinea, their African homeland.[16] In North America and throughout the Caribbean, enslaved Africans from the Bight of Biafra, especially the Igbo, who found enslavement "worse than death," were noted for their purported transmigration or sudden flight to Africa by simply disappearing, "flying," or running away. As it is recorded in the U.S. Sea Islands, the Igbos either turned into birds and "fl[ew] right back to Africa" or "committed collective suicide by marching into the river and drowning themselves."[17]

Thus, although unable to physically return to Africa as Blyden later did, through maroonage, rebellion, self-destruction, or spiritual returns to Africa, enslaved Africans chose what they considered to be a more realistic and fitting alternative to their treatment as slaves and denounced the inaccurate depiction of Africa and African-descended peoples by Europeans as less than human. They were committed to portraying African societies and their human social institutions as lived by Africans, rather than accepting the interpretation of Africa as the land of darkness. Through their attachment to Africa and its cultural ideations, they legitimized and valorized Africa's past—its societies and institutions—for later generations of African-descended peoples in the Americas like Blyden who came to be full of pride in an Igbo-West African heritage.

Some African captives, like those from the Gold Coast and the Bight of Biafra, risked their lives to take over transatlantic slave ships. Others contributed to the establishment of autonomous maroon communities modeled on African societies, while many others participated in rebellions in a bid to go back to Africa physically or spiritually. They consequently laid the foundations for an Afro-positivist tradition paralleled in the Western intellectual arena by eighteenth-century West African–born scholars like

Protten. These Western-trained African scholars also asserted their African heritage and expressed ideational Pan-African sentiments in their writing.[18]

On this basis, I argue that the legitimization and centralization of Africa as a shared homeland and as a discursive practice was a decisive stage in the promotion of Pan-African sentiment. This tradition can be traced from the sixteenth-century Africans who found themselves enslaved in the Americas, through to eighteenth-century Africa-born intellectuals who were educated and lived in Europe, and finally to Blyden's generation. Protten and others, in turn, passed on this tradition to the nineteenth- and twentieth-centuries' intellectuals, who, through the Pan-African movements, made Africa a vital part of their conceptualizations of liberation; these include Edward Blyden of St. Thomas and Liberia, Chief Alfred Sam of the Gold Coast, and Marcus Garvey of Jamaica. These luminaries, like their West African ancestors, advocated a physical return of diasporic Africans to the African continent. Blyden's own return to West Africa as well as publications like *The Call of Providence to the Descendants of Africa in America* and *The Origin and Purpose of African Colonization* reflect such advocacy.

Some of the Africa-born Atlantic scholars—Equiano, or Gustavus Vassa, *the African*; his friend Ottobah Cugoano, whose narrative, *A Native of Africa* dates to 1757; James Albert Ukawsaw Gronniosaw, who wrote *An African Prince as Related by Himself*; and John Jea, author of *An African Preacher*—became popular in certain intellectual circles and have been described as "pioneering black Anglophone" Atlantic writers.[19] Yet there are others who were often non-Anglophone but polyglot, like the Danish- and German-trained Protten and the Dutch- and German-trained philosopher Anton Wilhelm Amo (Gold Coast, 1703–ca. 1759), among others, who deserve further investigation and acclaim as not only Black Atlantic pioneers but also, notably, as Afro-positivists.[20]

Their birth and experiences in Africa, self-identification as African, and the thrust of their writings outstrip the conventional definitions of a Black Atlantic that excludes Africa.[21] Thus, one profound characteristic that these pioneers shared was an insistence on adding African to their names, making

Africa the center of their writings and a celebration of their African cultural identities. For the purposes of this book, I single out two non-Anglophone speakers in this cadre of eighteenth-century scholars for discussion. They are Anton Wilhelm Amo *Afer* and Christian Jacob Protten *Africanus*, both of whom were born on the Gold Coast and lived their adult lives as public intellectuals in Denmark, the Netherlands, and Germany. These two scholars eulogized Africa in a variety of writings and signed their names on books and official documents with the imprimatur–*The African*. In addition, their Afro-positivist public intellectualism laid the foundation for Blyden to also influence various public spheres.

Like the work of these predecessors, a glance of Blyden's published writings and letters reveals his preoccupation with Africa, Africans, and Africanness. Most of his essays and books either have Africa or "Negro" in the title. A few examples here should suffice, *Christianity, Islam and the Negro Race, African Colonization*, "The Negro in Ancient History," *A Voice from Bleeding Africa, Hope for Africa, The People of Africa*, and *The African Problem, and Other Discourses*. These titles and the subjects about Africa they address illustrate that Blyden always found a way to make Africa the center of his intellectual deliberations. This Afro-positivist practice of valorizing Africa and its human organizations as well as making Africa the focal point of one's intellectual discourse within Western intellectual corridors, however, begins with Blyden's eighteenth-century predecessors.

Eighteenth-Century Afropublican Forerunners: Anton W. Amo, the Moor, (c. 1703–1759)

Anton Wilhelm Amo's role as an Afro-positivist thinker is evident in his choice of name and his imprints on official papers. Amo, on several occasions and in his own words, made sure that various public spheres he engaged with knew he was born in Africa. For instance, Amo often designated in his publications and on formal documents "Ab Aximo in Guinea Africa," meaning that he was born in Axim, West Africa, in the western region of modern Ghana. Around 1706, when Amo was only three years old, at the recommendation of local Dutch missionary Johannes van der Star, he was taken to the Netherlands and to Brunswick-Wolfenbüttel the following year. Here he was entrusted into the care of Duke Anton Ulrich and his successor, Wilhelm August. The original purpose of Amo's residence in Europe was to be "baptized, educated, and trained as a predicant."[22]

As fate would have it, much like Blyden's abandonment of the civilizing premise of the ACS as well as the theological conservatism of the Presbyterian Church, Amo would fulfill more than the original ecclesiastical intentions of his European sojourn and became a celebrated African intellectual in Europe.[23] Amo's elevation in Europe was primarily because of his genius and partially because of the patronage of his European benefactors, who became his official godparents when he was baptized at their Saltzthal Castle Chapel on July 29, 1708. Amo was christened after both of his godparents, hence the name Anton Wilhelm. Later, in 1721, when the church confirmed him, Amo's status as an African domiciled in Europe became more prominent. He was confirmed with the name Anton Wilhelm Rudolphe Mohre (Moor), the latter name meaning African or black.[24]

Notwithstanding Amo's African background, his royal patrons ensured that he received a regular stipend for his upkeep. This took care of his general subsistence while he was at the court and ensured that he was equipped with general knowledge through preparation at the Ritter Academy of Wolfenbüttel. From there, Amo attended the Helmstedt University and later the University of Halle in 1727.[25] It is believed that Amo obtained a bachelor's degree from Helmstedt and a master of philosophy and the liberal arts in 1730, which was later renamed a PhD at the University of Halle.[26] From this period, Amo, who later obtained postgraduate degrees in philosophy and medicine, went on to become a legal luminary, physician, and philosopher who was fluent in Latin, Greek, Hebrew, and three European languages: German, Dutch, and French.[27] It must be emphasized that these accomplishments were in themselves a vindication of African intellectual ability. As previously established, Blyden himself obtained such fluency in the same languages and distinguished himself as an African public intellectual on the histories and cultures of Africa among Euro-American as well as African equals. Blyden became a fellow of the American Philological Association, principal of Alexander High School, and a professor of languages and classics at Liberia College.[28]

Compared to Blyden's extensive experience in Africa beginning from his eighteenth birthday until his death in 1812, Amo had minimal domestic experience in Africa, having left as a three year old. Amo received a heavy induction into Enlightenment scholarship just as Blyden became sophisticated in European discourse. All the same, early in his exceptional academic career, Amo devised a way to make Africa the center of his learning and to self-fashion as an African public intellectual. He did this by repeatedly mentioning his African birth, identifying himself as an African, and continually seeking to cast a positive light on Africa in his assortment of publications. More importantly, Amo's European peers and interlocutors manifestly acknowledged and recognized his scholarship as evidence of his African background.

At the end of a poem written in 1737, which was attached to his comments on a doctoral dissertation he supervised, Amo signed as "Anton Wilhelm Amo, from Guinea, in Africa, Magister and University Lecturer in Philosophy and the Liberal Arts."[29] Amo succeeded in making his African birth public knowledge to the extent that all public pronouncements about him mentioned it. The *Halle Weekly* and university records address him respectively as "Magister Amo of Africa, and there born in Guinea, a genuine Negro" and "Anton William Amo, Master of Philosophy and the Liberal Arts, born in Guinea and a coastal province of Africa." The rector of the University of Wittenberg, in a public address to him, mentions Amo as "born in a very distant recess of Africa, where it faces the rising sun."[30]

While Amo and the European public's numerous nods to his African birth explicitly convey his African identity, Amo took significant pains to overtly indicate his pride in that identity. For instance, he celebrated his

African identity in a letter addressed to the faculty of the Department of Philosophy at the University of Jenna, in which he appeals for approval to give public lectures as a university lecturer. In this letter, Amo signs off in Latin as "Antonius Guilielmus Amo Afer," meaning Antonius Guilielmus Amo, the African.[31]

Amo's self-identification as an African is likewise found in a publication by his friend and colleague Gottfried Achenwall, one of the inventors of statistics in Germany. The compendium celebrated people "who had attained eminence in science and learning." Amo wrote in this publication on May 5, 1740, citing the Greek philosopher Epictetus: "He who can accommodate himself to necessity is wise and has an inkling of things divine." Amo signs off by writing, "These words Anthony William Amo, an African, Master and University Lecturer in Philosophy and the Liberal Arts, has put down in everlasting memory of himself."[32] This irrefutably signals that Amo adamantly desired to be remembered as not just born in Africa but as an African by self-identification. Such pride in African heritage is also evidenced in Blyden's discourse. Blyden insisted on the capitalization of the "N" in Negro, which was not the convention at the time.[33] It is therefore not surprising that, in the legacy of Amo's celebration of African heritage and identification, Blyden asserted his "pure Negro" parentage as a means of emphasizing his Africanness.

Very early in his career, Amo determinedly turned his academic lens onto the problems Africans faced in the West, especially slavery and popular Afro-pessimistic or negative perceptions of Africa and African peoples. He likewise sought to represent Africa in a progressive and constructive light. This Afro-positivist approach is profoundly evident in Amo's arguments against the enslavement of Africans. His 1729 dissertation, written at the University of Halle, was titled "De jure Maurorum in Europa" (About the Rights of Africans in Europe).[34] Here, Amo argues for the legal rights of Africans under Roman law, basing his argument on European legal precedent, specifically Justinian's Laws. Amo avers that because various parts of Africa had historically been under Roman rule, Africans were to be accorded the same rights as others subjected to the authority of Roman law. He supported this claim with evidence of the patent granted by the Romans and Emperor Justinian, which recognized African kings. Correspondingly, in arguing against the transatlantic trade in enslaved Africans, Amo concluded that the buying and selling of Africans was not only illegal but also against Christian morality.[35] This contention resonates with Blyden's public intellectualism, as he also sought solutions to African problems in education, development, and colonialism and slavery. Blyden published essays like "A Chapter in the History of the African Slave Trade" and "The Aims and Methods of A Liberal Education for Africans" and delivered addresses like *Some Problems of West Africa* to the African Society in London in a bid to find solutions to African issues.

Unquestionably, Amo was extremely successful in countering and disabusing the Afro-pessimism of some of the intellectuals of his day. His European peers not only acknowledged his erudition but also strove to point out his public intellection on behalf of Africa, which offered extensive glowing accounts about Africa and African peoples. His status as an African public spokesperson is evinced in this notice for his dissertation published in the University of Halle's newspaper: "Here resided for some time an African called Antonius Wilhelmus Amo. . . . he has very diligently and with great success studied here with the School of Private Law. In consequence he became accomplished in that field."[36] Clearly, Amo was viewed as a representative of Africa at the University of Halle.

Beyond this, Amo was successful in facilitating the academic community's acceptance that Africa had a distinguished past and inspired its respect for Africa's intellectuals. This triumph is evidenced in another address by the rector and public assembly of the University of Wittenberg following Amo's successful defense in a Master of Science dissertation titled "Of the apatheia of the human mind, namely the absence of sensation and the faculty of sense in the human mind, and their presence in our organic and living body." The dissertation was a critique of Rene Descartes's philosophy of mind.[37] The address to Amo reads: "Great once was the dignity of Africa . . . for she has given birth to several men of the greatest pre-eminence by whose talents and efforts the whole of human knowledge has been built up." Ironically, the same African theologians Blyden revered in his poem written on his first arrival in Liberia are mentioned in this address. The statement proceeds to mention a number of Latin writers of North African heritage such as Terence the Carthaginian, Apuleius the Madasrensian, Tertullian, Cyprian, Arnobius, Optatus, Milevitanus, and Augustine as representatives of Africa's distinguished intellectual heritage.

The proclamation subsequently mentions Africa's contributions to Iberian civilizations through the activities of the Almoravids and Almohads. It concludes by celebrating Amo as an African public intellectual for their European generation: "But though in our own time that part of the world is reported to be more prolific in other things than in learning, nevertheless, that it is by no means exhausted of genius, Anthony William Amo here, that Most Distinguished Master of Science and Liberal Arts, would teach by his example."[38]

As a final point, the chair of Amo's philosophy dissertation committee at Wittenberg, Gothelf Loescher, wrote an address that captures not only Amo's public scholarly status and erudition, but furthermore, how successful Amo had been in convincing European intellectuals of Africa's renown. Loescher writes:

> We proclaim Africa and its region of Guinea planted apart at a very great distance from us, formerly the golden coast, so called by Europeans on account of its abundant and copious gold, but known by us as your fatherland, in which you first saw the light of day, the mother not only of many good things and treasures of nature but also of the most auspicious minds, we proclaim her quite deservedly. Among those auspicious minds your genius stands out particularly, most noble and distinguished Sir. . . . I return to you still complete and absolutely unchanged in any respect that which you have worked out with proper contentiousness in an elegant manner supported with erudition. . . . It now only remains for me to congratulate you wholeheartedly on this singular example of your refined scholarship, and, with a more abundant feeling of heart than words can convey.[39]

Amo's Afro-positivist activities yielded great results for him and for Africa within his sphere of influence. Highly esteemed by his European supervisors, peers, and students, he was recognized as a representative of Africa. Through his scholarship and insistence on his African provenance, he succeeded in convincing some European academics of Africans' humanity and capability for intellectual sophistication and their creation of complex societies, not to mention their contributions to Christianity. Later, Amo's scholarship would elicit mentions in, and even inspire, the antislavery texts of European writers like French abolitionist Abbé Henri Grégoire, black English author Wilson Armistead, and several generations of black scholars and Pan-Africanists including Du Bois and Blyden.[40]

Much like Amo, Blyden, through his Afro-positivist discourse, came to be respected as a representative of Africa in Euro-American intellectual, political, and social circles. As shown earlier , he enjoyed the plaudits of his black, European, and American peers. Through his Afro-positivist posturing, he was able to earn the respect of his contemporaries like Herbert Spencer, Charles Dickens, Bosworth Smith, and King Leopold's nemesis, E. D. Morel, who described Blyden in the aftermath of his passing as follows:

> Negro Africa has suffered irreparable loss in the death of Dr. Blyden, and the world is poorer for the disappearance of—we fear- the only pure-blooded Negro *who was capable of applying his knowledge of Europe and White Civilization to the needs of Negro Africa and African civilization.* [Emphasis Mine] . . . His preaching and teaching were ever directed to the same end; that Negro Africa, while taking all in that was useful to her from Europe in material things, should, in so taking them, remain African and mould them to her own requirements, retaining her own spiritual life.[41]

Like Amo, Blyden captivated audiences with his erudition, delivering lectures about Africa to Europeans and Americans in banquet halls and churches in Liverpool, London, Edinburgh, New York, and Maine. Lady Ellinor Flora

Bosworth Smith Grogan, the daughter of Bosworth Smith, remembers Blyden as a child in this way:

> More awe-inspiring from the children's point of view but not less likeable was Dr. Blyden, the Negro Savant, at the time the Plenipotentiary of Liberia. His intellectual countenance, his quiet and dignified manner, and his beautiful English made a great impression on all those who met him. My father always considered Dr. Blyden as one of the most remarkable men he knew. Dr. Blyden would often bring Negro missionaries, or merchants, or native princes with him, and he fully convinced his host of the great possibilities of the Negro race.[42]

Blyden also used some of these encounters and forums to challenge the Social Darwinian underpinnings of the Anthropological Society of London, founded in 1863.[43] The society pioneered social anthropology and ethnographic studies, which included descriptions of peoples and races, influenced by evolutionary theorist Charles Darwin and the writings of Count de Gobineau. This method of thinking concluded that African people occupied the lower rungs of the human race. Blyden, like his Sierra Leonean contemporary Horton, challenged these racial theories of African inferiority, which subsequently provided an ideological basis for British imperial and colonial expansion in Africa.[44]

In his opposition to this racist literature, Blyden articulated the idea of a unique African Personality, which he deemed also belonged to Africans in the Americas and West Indies.[45] Blyden believed that Africans personalities are informed by communitarian systems of social organizations, mutual aid communities, polygamy, secret societies, and ritual activity.[46] He contrasted these communitarian systems with individualism, egoism, materialism, and what he called the "cult of science."[47] Proceeding from the idea that all races were equal but distinct, Blyden called for the cultivation of a distinct African Personality—a personality that celebrates Africa's past achievements and that should be nurtured in Africa as well as by Africans in the Americas and West Indies.[48]

Whereas Blyden shared in Amo's public intellectualism, vindicationist scholarship, and Afro-positivist centralization of Africa in public discourse, he, like Protten, maintained an iconoclastic outlook, a distinctive Afro-Christian theology, an emphasis on education, and sophistication in the use of African languages as a way to analyze African cultures and societies. Like Protten, Blyden was a subject of Danish crown and grew up in a similar multicultural environment in Charlotte Amalie, whose residents in the 1830s include Dutch settlers, American missionaries, Sephardic Jews, and free and enslaved blacks, and were influenced by the Danish in official language, architecture, place and city names. Both Protten and Blyden were skillful in cultivating a host of benefactors and sympathizers in supporting their causes, whether ecclesiastical or intellectual, while enabling other blacks or Africans within their orbit and itinerant circuits.

Eighteenth-Century Afropublican Forerunners: Christian Jacob Protten, Africanus (1715–1769)

Christian Jacob Protten, was not quite as successful as Amo or Blyden in eradicating cynical ideas about Africa in his sphere of European influence. This failure was partly because of Protten's iconoclasm, an attribute he shares with Blyden. As is true of many iconoclastic scholars, the iconic intellectual and political activities of Amo, and Blyden after him, defy easy categorization. They both questioned the popular ideas of their age and were, at the same time, innovative in their production of knowledge concerning Africa. Protten's disappointments came despite his publicizing, as Amo did, his birth in Africa, and his making Africa the fulcrum of his intellectual work and reveling in his African cultural identity. He embraced the title of Christian Jacobus Protten, Africanus, even though he was of a dual racial parentage, and contemporaneous European records referenced him as *mulatto*, which historically was a derogatory term for the crossbred progeny of a horse and a mule. This is in contrast to Blyden who is described in the *Washington Post* as "a full blood African, with expressive eyes and diplomatic bearing."[49]

Unlike Blyden, Protten and Amo were born on the Gold Coast. Protten and Blyden, however, share the heritage of growing up within the Danish colonial sphere of influence. Blyden was born in the Danish West Indies, and Protten was born in the Afro-Danish enclave at Osu (Danish Accra), where the sprawling Christiansborg Castle hugs the Atlantic coastline of the Gold Coast. A substantial portion of the close to 60 percent of the Danish slave trade from West Africa would have passed through Protten's Christiansborg to Blyden's Danish West Indies. Protten was descended from Ga royalty on his maternal side. Protten's mother was a granddaughter of the erstwhile king of the Ga, Okai Koi, which makes Protten the grandson of Ofoli, king of Popo and cousin to Ofoli's successor at Popo as well as the great-great-grandson of Dode Akabi, the only female king in Ga history.[50] Protten was fathered by a Danish sailor-soldier, Jacob Protten, of whom very little is known.[51]

Protten thus was a biological byproduct of the cultural and economic encounter between Europeans and Africans in Osu, which began with a seventeenth-century land grant by his maternal great-grandfather, King Okai Koi of Ga, Accra, to the Danes. Danish beginnings in West Africa can be traced to 1624, when Danes first arrived on the Gold Coast and established a stable presence through numerous forts and castles between 1652 and 1661. They later expanded east as far as the Bight of Benin.[52] Osu, which was their primary base, eventually became a cosmopolitan trading city on the Atlantic seaboard and was home to diverse African and European traders, Ga political refugees, Akan migrants, and ex-slaves from the Bight of Benin.[53] The predominantly male Danish population of this coastal mélange married or engaged in various liaisons with Ga women, which gave them a decided competitive advantage over other European traders on the Ga coastline.[54] Thus, by the close of the eighteenth century, there was already a group of Africans and Afro-Europeans who through intermarriage and trade partnerships came to be known as "Mulattofoi" or mulatto people on the Gold Coast.[55] At Osu, Protten was socialized into his African heritage through the religious and cultural perspectives of his maternal relatives. But within and about the Danish fort, he was influenced by Europeans, especially Danish traders and sailors, and a mixed-race group of friends and relatives who were intimately connected to their fathers' European culture on the Gold Coast as well as to their Ga/African families and polities.[56] Afro-Danes, like Protten, were often employed by their Danish relatives to serve in a variety of capacities as brokers, messengers, and interpreters. In addition, they often performed as trading assistants and diplomatic envoys to West African chiefs.[57]

As part of their expanding activities on the Gold Coast in 1722, the Danes established the Christiansborg Fort School for the mixed-race offspring of their Danish officers. After they were baptized, these children were often enrolled in the military.[58] Protten was one of the first students at this school, enrolling between 1722 and 1726, under the guidance of a Danish Lutheran minister, Elias Svane. It was Svane, who like his Dutch counterpart in Amo's case, recommended Protten and Frederik Pedersen Svane for religious training in Denmark. Thus in 1727, together with Pedersen Svane, Protten left for Denmark to be trained as a preacher of the Christian gospel.[59]

Protten left Africa at the much older age of eleven compared to Amo. He arrived in Copenhagen on August 14, 1727, just before his twelfth birthday, on September 1. Protten was baptized after arriving in Copenhagen, with King Frederik IV serving as his godparent. Compared to Amo, though, Protten did not benefit from the royal largesse. That is, royal patronage or godparenthood did not assure him free tuition. In fact, Svane initially enrolled Protten and Pedersen Svane as apprentices to learn blacksmithing as a trade with the idea that it would be lucrative as a profession on the Gold Coast. In spite of this, the young Protten and Pederson Svane reportedly objected and were eventually enrolled at the University of Copenhagen, where Protten studied for three years, 1732–1735.[60]

It is apparent from here that Protten, like Amo, and Blyden later, had benefactors who supported his intellectual and theological ambitions. Amo had the missionary Johannes van der Star and the royals of Brunswick-Wolfenbuttel to help him. Blyden also had Rev. John Knox, his parents, and John B. Pinney and Walter Lowrie, who were both Presbyterians and members of the American Colonization Society. They urged Blyden to go on to Liberia to pursue his ministerial and academic ambitions. Protten, on the other hand, had Svane and Frederick IV of Denmark as his benefactors. Protten differed from Amo and was similar to Blyden in the sense that, in addition to these supporters he began to nurture relationships with a host of patrons who would support his ambitions. This nurturing began during his time in Copenhagen, when he became enamored with the emotional and demonstrative forms of Christianity, which had been encouraged by the pietistic Lutheran and Moravian denominations. Under these circumstances, Protten experienced an epiphany of sorts and refused to return to the Gold Coast under the direction of the Danish West India and Guinea Company. He met Zinzendorf and decided to travel to the Moravian base in Herrnhut, Saxony (now eastern Germany). Protten learned to speak and write German, in addition to Danish, Ga, and Fante. In Herrnhut, Protten encountered the racism of the European Christian church, eventually falling out with Zinzendorf.

From this point on, Protten's Afropublican life encompassed navigation of the cultural worlds of the Moravian church in what is now eastern Germany and in the Netherlands, the Danish colonial establishment in Copenhagen, the Danish West Indies islands, and the Gold Coast. Protten therefore presaged Blyden as a true Atlantic denizen, even though Blyden had a much larger scope of influence in the Atlantic World as well as in West Africa and the Mediterranean. Protten's central contributions to the *Weltanschauung* circulating in the Atlantic world were his polemics, scholarship, and institutional challenge of the Christian church, through which he sought to legitimate his African origins and place his African-ness at the forefront of conversations surrounding what it means to be human. Protten did so in a variety of ways very similar to Amo and Blyden. Blyden later described this position as the "African standpoint"—celebrating an

African identity, valorizing the African past, centering Africa in intellectual debates, and understanding African languages and cultures.[61]

First, as stated earlier, Protten professed his African birth and proclaimed his African identity by signing all of his written communications as Christian Jacob Protten, Africanus. For example, when he published his *Ga-Danish/Akan-Danish dictionary*, Protten signed off as "Christian Protten, . . . born on said [Gold] Coast."[62] This signature reveals that he was not just a Western-educated person studying the languages and cultures of a society he was vaguely familiar with, but was actually born and raised in "said" society. However, his insistence on his African background was one of the reasons Protten was not as successful as Amo in convincing Europeans of Africa's prominence. In the dictionary publication, Protten expressed his reservations about Europeans' capability of understanding and writing about African societies. He deemed that one "must have the correct pronunciation with one's mother's milk, or from childhood and up through adolescence" to understand African societies and languages.[63]

Second, Protten's *Ga-Danish/Akan-Danish dictionary* is itself an embodiment of his groundbreaking work as a linguist. Thus, while Johannes A. Zimmerman (who published in 1858 *A Grammatical Sketch and Vocabulary of the Akra- or Ga-Language*) and J. G. Christaller (whose numerous publications about the Akan language included *A Grammar of the Asante and Fante Language called Tsi [Chwee, Twi]*) earned reputations as pioneers in transliterating Ghanaian languages, Protten, in his attempt to influence Danish society's understanding of Gold Coast cultures, initiated the translation of Ga and Fante into Danish and vice versa for the benefit of his mixed-race students at the Christiansborg school.[64]

In this intellectual practice of understanding African languages as a means of properly interpreting African societies, Protten serves as a trailblazer to Blyden. Blyden made a conscious effort to learn African languages. Thus, like Protten, Blyden became a student of African languages, learning to speak Fula and other Senegambian languages. He writes about this in a letter to his sympathizer on the ACS board, William Coppinger, "I am here

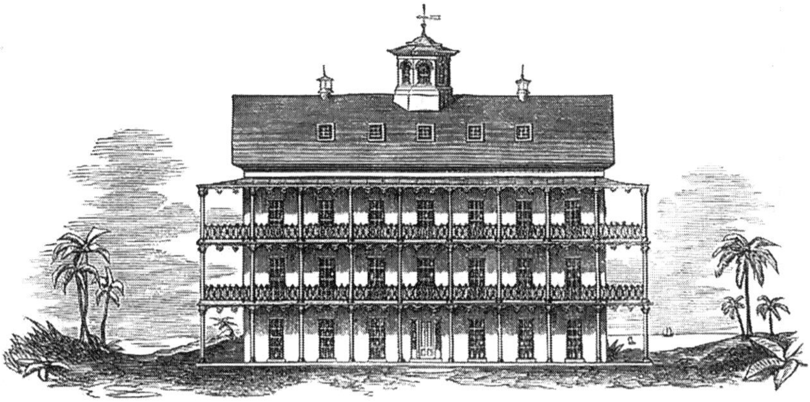

FIGURE 7. Liberia College.

FIGURE 8. Christiansborg castle.

at work among the Mohammedans. I am trying to establish among them to be supported by themselves, a school of teaching the English language and literature, as well as the great vernaculars-Foulah, Mandigo, Aku, and also Arabic."[65]

Records show that, between 1757 and 1762, when Protten served at Christiansborg Castle as the teacher at his alma mater, the "mulatto" school, he reestablished and aligned himself with his Ga/African kin network in Osu, Accra, Akwamu, and Little Popo rather than with Danish officials at Osu, Christiansborg. This alliance provided him a strategic advantage over Danish officials who detested Protten's sundry critiques of their actions and inactions at the Danish fort. However, they had to restrain their displeasure with him because they were wary of his strong connections to African royalty on the Gold Coast.[66] This reaction demonstrates that Protten did not simply assert his African birth and identity but actually lived it.

The publication of the dictionary and its African content additionally exhibits that, although trained in the West, Protten chose to make Africa the central focus of his only known major intellectual exposition. Protten viewed his mission as an African public mediator as illuminating Africa and African culture to interlocutors in the European public sphere, including Zinzendorf, who thought the worst of Africans. This undertaking is even clearer in Protten's systematic demolishing of false accounts of a purported African proclivity for incest and the stereotyping of African women as adulterous and licentious. Two examples should suffice here. The first illustration is that of Protten's masterful defense of his family relation, Helena Platfues, née Svendsdatter, who had been accused by a Danish administrator, C. J. Bertram, of being promiscuous. The allegation was the latter's vile attempt to avoid a debt he owed Svendsdatter by blackmail. Protten subsequently utilized his knowledge of Danish law to successfully defend his "sister," resulting in a ruling that caused Bertram's salary to be shaved to pay Svendsdatter.

Protten's actions were not confined to the courtroom; he was, in fact, disdained for using his understanding of Western modes of thinking to defend African culture and Africans. A second illustration of Protten's quest to portray African culture in a positive light is his consulting of African informants, including his own relatives, about the sexual mores of African families. After Governor Jessen of Christiansborg began circulating stories of widespread incest among Africans to his influential European guests, Protten challenged the governor with his findings, noting that adultery was reviled not only by the Ga on the Gold Coast but also by Africans in the Danish West

Indies, where Protten lived between 1742 and 1745 as a missionary. Protten again earned the ire of Governor Jessen, who criticized him for "siding with the heathen."[67] In this instance, Protten independently began investigating an assortment of accusations by Danish officials and, as a consequence, defended the composition of the African family, thereby anticipating Blyden's study of the African family structure among the inhabitants of Sierra Leone.

It is evident that Protten's European education did not negate his African birth and identity. Thus, his erudition was not necessarily because of his Danish background; yet neither had he lost his African heritage because he was Western educated. Protten transferred this Afro-positivism into his activities with the Moravian church. While at Herrnhut, Protten was known in the Moravian community to offer prayers in the Ga language during choir meetings and devotions.[68] Here again, Protten predates Blyden's advocacy of the use of West African languages in church missiology and doxology. This self-identification with Africa and African languages conversely made Protten a target of the overt racism of the Moravian brethren and their leader, Nikolaus von Zinzendorf, and ultimately resulted in Protten's banishment from the community.

The final provocation appears to be Protten's iconoclasm, revealed in his anger and remonstration that Guinea or West Africa had been omitted from a publication offering thanks for Moravian congregations and missions all over the world.[69] In their records, the Moravian brethren describe Protten as an African savage and Moorish. Other diarists refer to him as a lost but found-again sheep. The greatest condemnation came from Zinzendorf, who believed that Protten, much like the enslaved Africans in the Danish West Indies, had a "high opinion of himself. Presumptiveness and a high opinion of oneself only prostitutes a person and carry no weight with the Saviour, who has his ways of bending such people." Zinzendorf believed that such bending came through enslavement because the "Lord wishes to make slaves of the Moors first before they are blessed, because they are so proud."[70]

Consequently, in contrast to Amo, who had been, to a considerable extent, successful in convincing Europeans of Africa's dignity, Protten's iconoclastic approach as well as the racial and cultural feeling of superiority within his sphere of influence seemed to have impeded his mediatory role for Africa. But all was not in vain; despite Protten's calamitous departure from Osu following his accidental shooting of a child, he was offered a reprieve by King Frederick V of Denmark, who believed "Christian Protten is a very useful person, in that he understands the language of the country and has already been active in instructing the mulatto children."[71]

When advising the Moravians, Gold Coast–based Danish merchant Ludewig Roemer deemed that Protten could be of "great service" and that "[his] kinship with noble Accra's especially Ashangmo can still be very useful for your purpose."[72] An acknowledgment similarly came from C. G. A. Oldendorp, who in his *History of the Mission* first published in 1770, wrote: "I have taken this idea of the relationship between the minor gods and the supreme deity from the diary of Christian Protten, a native of Africa who spent time with the Brethren," in Herrnhut and the Danish West Indies. This was a compliment to Protten's doggedness about his African birth and his scholarship on Africa; it was, however, posthumous. In the nineteenth century, another Afro-Danish intellectual, Edward Wilmot Blyden, along with his cohort of Africa-born intellectuals, would nevertheless continue the tradition Protten and Amo helped establish in the prior century.

Edward Blyden as the Nineteenth-Century Successor

Blyden and his peers became heirs to these eighteenth-century Africa-born intellectuals who understood the need to refute the wrong assertions about African life and history disseminated by European Enlightenment thinkers of their era. Unfortunately, Blyden's views have been treated and portrayed by others as emerging solely from the wellsprings of European thought. On the contrary, Blyden and his cohort of nineteenth-century West African scholars like James Africanus Horton (1835–1883) ably procured the mantle from the previous century. Blyden's Afropublican engagement with various thought communities in West Africa, the Middle East, the Caribbean, Europe, and the United States challenges this curious exclusion of African involvement in the cultural and intellectual exchanges of the Atlantic.

Blyden Afro-positivist discursive practice is organically similar to the plantation intellectuals in the Americas who insisted on African ways of life. This similarity is evident in Blyden's desire for autonomous African nations, his pride in an African past, his valorization of African social and cultural practices as well as his return to Africa. Afro-positivism as a philosophical tradition is also evident in the discourse of eighteenth-century Africa-born intellectuals in Europe and the Americas who not only rendered Africa the center of their writings but also insisted on being called African. In fact, Blyden directly references this collection of scholars as his predecessors in his first pamphlet, titled *A Voice from Bleeding Africa*, which includes a list of accomplished black intellectuals: Olaudah Equiano, Ignatius Sancho, Francis Williams, Job Ben Solomon, among others. In this list, Blyden directly mentions "A. W. Amo," describing his heritage, education, and intellectual accomplishments in Latin and Greek, philosophy, and mathematics.[73]

Although Blyden was not born in Africa, he claimed an ethnic-African heritage as an Igbo; and like Protten, he insisted on a lived African experience to articulate African historical and contemporaneous realities. Blyden, the Afropublican, therefore eulogized Africa not only by writing from his experiences with various African communities in Liberia, Sierra Leone, and the Greater Senegambia region, but also by formulating through these experiences his concept of the African Personality, which regaled Africa and African cultural and sociopolitical practices, much as his eighteenth-century Afro-positivist predecessors had done. But not being born in Africa did not preclude Blyden from the challenges of racism faced by black folk worldwide. Much like the overt racism Protten faced in the Moravian community, Blyden was refused entry into U.S. colleges on account of his race. Faced with the systemic racism advanced by the Fugitive Slave Law and the risk of being blackbirded by slave catchers, Blyden chose to go to Africa just as Amo did when he seemed to be no longer welcome in Europe.

Eurocentric writers tended to describe Africans in uncharitable terms. In response, the Gold Coast's theologian Protten and philosopher Amo and other members of their cohort produced an alternative canon of eighteenth-century literature.[74] However, these have yet to be recognized in contemporary academic conversations about the fashioning of the Atlantic world and the Black Atlantic.[75] As a scholar, Blyden inherited from these African polemicists of the eighteenth century the necessity to correct the narratives of African life and history written by Europeans. Blyden used this vindicationist narrative as part of his Afro-positivist strategy and eventually influenced his peers like Alexander Crummel and a black organization like the ANA to adopt such an approach.

Thus, building on the unique contributions of the eighteenth-century Africa-born thinkers, Edward Blyden emerges as the successor and exemplar of this West African class of intellectuals in the nineteenth century. This legacy is exemplified in Blyden's Afropositivism, iconoclasm, theological disposition, transcendent scholarship as well as ideas on education.

Like both Amo and Protten, Blyden used his understanding of Western modes of thinking to articulate the African viewpoint. Blyden's contemporary E. D. Morel explains his recognition of this strategy when he writes that:

> More fully versed in the literature of Europe than any other Negro, Blyden's studies only made him more of an African soul, an African culture, an Africa of clearly demarcated and peculiar racial needs . . . He labored to show that Africa had a soul and a civilization-the latter worth preserving in itself, the former if destroyed, leading to the destruction of the race.[76]

Blyden, therefore, not only used his training in European discourse to explain peculiar African social and cultural practice, but, as Protten did with the Moravians, when Blyden wrote about religion, missiology, or biblical interpretation, he followed the Afro-positivist practice of centering Africa. This practice is evident in theological essays such as "Phillip and the Eunuch or The Instrument and Methods of Africa's Evangelization, Christianity and the Negro Races, the Return of the Exiles and the West African Church," in which Blyden advocates for African-centered ways of evangelizing African peoples and instituting churches among them. Similar to Protten's insistence with the Moravians on the use of African languages, Blyden insisted on the use of African languages in the West African Church as part of his West African Ethiopianism. In many ways, Blyden's insistence on the Africanization of the West African church was transcendent in that, in the years following his demise, it became the staple strategy for many missionary groups in West Africa.

Blyden was closer to Protten than Amo in iconoclasm and education. In iconoclasm, while Protten was banished from the Moravian community—in large part due to his pro-African stance—Blyden resigned from the Presbyterian church to become a *Minister of Truth*. Owing to theological, racial, and regional tensions between the conservative and liberal elements within the worldwide Presbyterian denomination and magnified in Liberia and the United States, on December 8, 1886, Blyden, "after much thought and earnest prayer," asked the Presbytery "to release [him] from the sacred office."[77] Blyden explained in later correspondence that he gave up the collar because of his "deep love for Africa and for the truth and for freedom," insisting that he had not converted to Islam but that he "prefer[s] what is good for [his] people in the method of its propagators to what is evil in the methods of Christian teachers."[78] Blyden, therefore, stood for his principles on African missiology and disdained the "bigotry of ignorance" he believed prevailed in the Presbyterian Church.[79]

In education, just as Protten returned to the Gold Coast to teach at his alma mater, the Christiansborg School, Blyden taught at his Alexander High School in Liberia. Much more importantly, like Protten's interest in the children at the Christiansborg School, Blyden was interested in enabling other African students to aspire to great heights. The *Sierra Leone Weekly News*, for example, reports that, as Director of Mohammedan Education, Blyden helped organize two schools at Fourah Bay, and one each at Foulah Town, Aberdeen village, and Magazine Cut for Muslim Children.[80] Much like Protten took the side of his African kin against the Danish colonial establishment, Blyden took the side of the Kru, Grebo, and other indigenous inhabitants of Liberia against the Americo-Liberian elite.

Blyden disagreed with his contemporaries whenever he deemed fit. He disagreed with acquaintances and foes alike, including Herbert Spencer, black Nationalist Martin Delany, and Bishop Henry McNeal Turner on the issue of emigration. This intellectual independence can also be gleaned from an inaugural address he gave on January 5, 1881. As President of Liberia College, Blyden eruditely engaged with "The aims and methods of a liberal education for Africans," and took a position analogous to Du Bois's stance in his famous debate with Booker T. Washington. In his disagreement with Washington, Du Bois asserted the primacy of liberal over industrial training for blacks.[81] Blyden on the other hand, in an open letter to B. T. Washington published in the *New York Age* on January 24, 1895, commended Washington for his industrial schemes, wishing him God's speed in his work "on God's line for the race."[82] However, in 1911, Blyden in a confidential letter to the editor of the Charleston, South Carolina *News* and *Courier* characterized Washington as not possessing a "gleam of real racial knowledge—anything that showed appreciation of racial conditions and adaptations."[83] Blyden questioned Washington's purpose to "train the Negro to believe that the difference between him and the white man is that between tweedledee and tweedledum—that black man only needs money, a balance at his bankers, to make him the social equal of the white."[84] Blyden, the consummate iconoclast, defies easy classification. However, unlike other black iconoclasts, Blyden's ideas stretched beyond the contours of a specific black geographic community.

Edward W. Blyden's Intellectual Transformations investigates his views of Africa as they circulated through the lecture circuits of the United States, Europe, and Africa as well as in newspapers and journals of the Black Atlantic world.[85] West Africa had a central place in the formation of Atlantic bodies of knowledge and provided important knowledge responsible for black intellectual life in the nineteenth century. Demonstrating West Africa's centrality is significant because Blyden and other critical nineteenth-century writers, having acquired Amo's and Protten's intellectual baton, produced important articulations of Pan-Africanism for their own era. Additional expressions of Pan-African reasoning in West Africa include Horton's *West African Countries and Peoples* and Joseph Casely Hayford's *Ethiopia Unbound*.[86] Most scholars of Pan-Africanism, nonetheless, agree that Blyden was the first academic to offer an extensive scholarly exposition of the idea of Pan-Africanism.[87]

Blyden, building on Armistead's previous work, is also arguably the scholarly progenitor of the vindicationist canon used by the American Negro Academy cofounder Alexander Crummell (1819–1898). Because of him, Blyden was elected to be a corresponding member of the academy in 1897.[88] Blyden and Crummell were already personal friends and had collaborated in Liberia before Crummel established the ANA in 1897. One of the aims of the academy was the vindication of the "Negro Race."[89] Four decades before the formation of the ANA, Blyden penned an essay, published by G. Killian of Monrovia, that included an introduction by Crummell. In the original essay, titled "A Brief Examination of the Arguments of African Inferiority: A Vindication of the African Race," Blyden sought to negate pseudoscientific claims about Africans as substandard humans because of their physiological makeup.[90]

It is abundantly clear that Blyden's vindicationist ideas had an enormous influence on the ANA. John Gibbs St. Clair Drake describes the vindicationists as encompassing the "most educated black men and women" who, two centuries prior, spoke and wrote against the institution of slavery and the characterization of people of African descent in inhuman terms.[91] The ANA asserted its conceptual task as "the Defense of the Negro against Vicious Attacks."[92] This school of thought consequently encompassed the primary goal of the deconstruction of the pseudoscientific claims on which ideas of black inhumanity and cultural inferiority were based—a pseudoscience that, in turn, encouraged the justification of a racist U.S. society and its accompanying social institutions.[93] W. E. B. Du Bois and Carter G. Woodson were the last vanguards of black intellectuals who belonged to this school of thought. This perspective encompassed what Manning Marable characterizes as the "corrective" dimension of the black intellectual tradition.[94] Like most of the members of the ANA, Blyden was a vindicationist; like most pioneers in African history and African American studies, he saw the task as correcting the misrepresentations of Africa and Africans.

Whether one calls it vindicationist or corrective, these terms clearly denote the Afro-positivist discourse initiated by the plantation intellectuals and Africa-born scholars of the eighteenth century. Thus, it is obvious that Blyden refined and rearticulated the Afro-positivist tradition originated by enslaved Africans born in Africa. The first systematic articulation of Pan-Africanism was propounded by Blyden, a West African of diasporan origin, and the U.S. vindicationist tradition was launched by this West Indian returnee to Africa. That Blyden began to articulate Pan-African ideas following his stay in West Africa speaks volumes about West Africa's status in the origination and evolution of Pan-Africanism.

Africans or Africa-born individuals conceived and initiated the formulation of ideas of Africa as homeland: as a place of origin and a place of belonging, including as a destination of physical or spiritual return that would become a central element of early Pan-African ideas. In maroonage, rebellion, ontological beliefs, aesthetics, polity, or revelry, Africans laid the foundation for the emergent "polycultural African-American communit[ies]" throughout the Americas.[95] Compared to their (American-born) descendants in the Americas, the Africa-born enslaved did not have to imagine but could remember a lived Africa. And it was this lived Africa that they passed on either in languages, customs, traditions, or religious practices and beliefs. These plantation intellectuals also passed on reflective traditions about colonial societies in the Americas, questioning Afro-pessimism or "invented traditions" and negative ideas about Africa that had allowed for their capture, enslavement, and dehumanization on the colonial plantations.

Thus, since the early Atlantic age, Pan-African sentiment or ideas have continued to exist in several black communities around the world. Contemporarily, assorted interpretive schools in academe have turned to new models of conceptualizing Africa and the African diaspora. A plethora of terms has since emerged seeking to replace or illuminate Pan-Africanism, including African diaspora, Global Africa, diasporic Africa, Black Atlantic, and more recently Afropolitanism. While these new terms signal capacious analytic approaches to the study of Africa and the African diaspora, they are not original in their discursive underpinnings. Their foundations can be traced directly to enslaved Africans who first arrived in the Americas in the sixteenth and seventeenth centuries and insisted on African modalities of living in the Americas.

The concepts can similarly be traced to Africa-born Atlantic intellectuals who transmitted the tradition of questioning Western civilization, its education, and its claims as the sole arbiter of modernity. Equiano, Cugoano, Amo, and Protten were all instrumental in Pan-Africanism's early conceptual stage. It is, therefore, erroneous for Peter Esedebe to argue that "Pan-African thinking originally began in the so-called New World becoming articulate during the century starting from the declaration of American independence (1776)."[96] The scholarship of these eighteenth-century Africa-born intellectuals is especially poignant because, in addition to their training in Christianity and at Western educational institutions, Cugoano, Protten, Amo, and Equiano based their arguments against Western modernity on their lived African experience. Although they spent a considerable portion of their adult lives traveling and studying in Europe, the topics that drew abundant attention to them in the intellectual world of the eighteenth century were their writings on Africa.

Equiano was abducted in Africa but spent much of his life in the West Indies, the United States, and Europe. Amo earned a doctorate of philosophy in Germany, becoming a celebrated public figure in Europe before returning to the Gold Coast, where he died. All of these Africa-born litterateurs were consumed with Africa and their African identity, and concerned with the image of Africa and Africans in European public spheres. They therefore used Afro-positivist strategies to confront these negative perceptions head on.

Scholars often argue that African diasporans, particularly African Americans, who experienced the worst forms of slavery, were quick to adopt the idea of Pan-Africanism because slavery had eroded their ethnic-African identities. On the contrary, Sylviane Diouf and others have maintained enslaved Africans employed an ethnic identity in their resistance to slavery and the slave trade. Vincent Harding additionally points out that Pan-African-based resistance began with the "multiformity" of African captives in the castles and forts on the shores of Africa.[97]

These are all legitimate claims; however, while ethnic identity in the United States may have assumed a racial character that encouraged a Pan-African identity, it is evident that in other sections of the Americas, ethnic identity persisted alongside a black racial identity.[98] The Aponte Rebellion of 1812 in Cuba reveals that ethnic identities did not quickly dissipate, nor did they prevent the development of a racial identity for collective Pan-African action.[99] The lesson here is that, in most cases, ethnic and pan-ethnic identities are necessary steps in the development of African nationalist and Pan-Africanist identities. Furthermore, even in the United States, where there is a heightened racial identity, such identities as Salt Water Africans, Gullah, and Creole existed alongside a supra-black identity—at least until the great migration of African Americans from the South into the Midwest and the northern United States.

Conclusion

Despite the diverse definitions of Pan-Africanism, there is a consensus that, as an idea, Pan-Africanism entails considerations of a shared homeland, racial equality, advocating unity, and enhancing the social conditions of African-descended communities globally. Contemporary writings such as "Critical Departures in the Practice of Pan-Africanism in the New Millennium," *Pan Africanism and African Liberation in the 21st Century*, and *Pan-Africanism and Integration in Africa* reinterpret Pan-Africanism in light of current developments in communities of African heritage.[100] Also imperative to this study is understanding why twenty-first-century African academics continue to reimagine Pan-Africanism as an interpretive tool for today's

African people. In visualizing Pan-Africanism for the twenty-first century, Paul Zeleza writes:

> Recalling and reclaiming our histories is a pre-requisite to any serious project of emancipation and liberation whether today or tomorrow in the 21st century. This is especially so in our era of willful historical erasure and amnesia, of easy despair and the arrogant pessimisms of post-humanist scholarship.[101]

As Zeleza suggests, historical knowledge is key to Pan-Africanist thought. Zeleza is remarkably similar to West Africans like Amo, Protten, and later Blyden, who were all keenly aware of the importance of historical reclamation, as their actions and writings indicate the magnitude with which they regarded the task of recording Africa's history during a period when African history had been described as nonexistent.

In the nineteenth century, intellectuals of African heritage rode on steamboats to journey from one geographic region to the other; they read serialized versions of foreign newspapers and magazines to learn about the conditions of other peoples of African descent. Travel and literacy were very significant means by which Pan-African leaders or intellectuals came to their notions of Pan-Africanism. Swifter means of transportation, communication, cyberpolitanism, and an increased literacy among people of African descent in the twenty-first century are already reshaping the discourse on Pan-Africanism. In the future, scholars may no longer refer to these ideas as Pan-Africanist. They may instead use terms like *Afropolitanism* because ideas often mutate and adapt to their historical conditions. It is essential that, as these new thoughts or terms are propounded, the philosophical foundations on which they are based are accorded their proper place in Pan-Africanist historiography in particular and the worldwide study of African-descended peoples in general.

This linking of Pan-African scholarship over three centuries, however, should not be read as an Afrocentric exercise that links the exertions of all people of African descent across time and space. It is, rather, an exegesis on the profound scholarly career of an African public intellectual who served not only as a discursive bridge between various black communities of thought but also as a cultural interpreter mediating the encounters between Africa and the global community. It is a mistake to receive all articulations of Pan-African sentiment as an expression or an ascription to all peoples of African descent with a set of immutable characteristics.[102]

Yet, foundational ideas like Blyden's *African Personality* frequently come up for such predictable critique in the works of Gilroy and Appiah. Such misconstruals ignore Blyden's careful, if flawed, articulation of race in contestation and divergence from the European racial theorists of his day. Such analyses disregard or fail to pay attention to Blyden's meticulous distinction of the peculiarities and idiosyncrasies of the polities, religions, and cultures of various ethnic groups and societies he encountered in West Africa as well as Blyden's own claim to a distinctive Igbo identity.

Finally, sworn critics often gloss over Blyden's acknowledgment of some of the precepts and benefits of Africa's encounter with modernity. The argument here is that like enslaved Africans and his Africa-born forerunners, Blyden believed that at the vanguard of these encounters, particularly Africa's encounter with European civilization was violence. In Blyden's own words, "the fringe of European civilization is violence," and African intellectuals intimate with the foundations of Western learning should be at the forefront of confronting a spurious imperialism disguised as a paternalistic modernity.

Thus, while Wilson Jeremiah Moses's brilliance in *Classical Black Nationalism: From the American Revolution to Marcus Garvey* and *Afrotopia: The Roots of African American Popular Culture* reveals Blyden as a black nationalist and precursor to Afrocentric intellectual traditions, this book connects him to an earlier tradition, which is Afro-positivism. The goals of the Afro-positivists, as compared to Moses's black nationalists, were different from "those of upper-class Europeans and white Americans."[103] Afro-positivists were interested in a return to a lived and remembered Africa, and therein lies the importance of the historicization and evolution of Blyden's ideas. The genius of Blyden was not only his ability to evolve his thinking on different subjects concerning Africa such as Ethiopianism, but also to combine, with great sophistication and non-dogmatism, the earlier Afro-positivist tradition with contemporaneous ideas including those espoused by black nationalists. This distinguishes him from other Ethiopianists and providential historians alike: Alexander Crummel, Martin Delany, and Henry McNeal Turner.

Edward Blyden's Ethnoscapes: Igbo, Afro-Danish, and Jewish

"Of ebony hue," he later claimed to be of "pure Negro" parentage from the Ibo tribe in eastern Nigeria.

—Hollis R. Lynch, *Edward Wilmot Blyden, Pan-Negro Patriot 1832–1912*

At the birth of African diaspora studies, the historical experience of the Jewish diaspora was often cited as the classic dispersion on which the study of the African diaspora should be based. This was also, however, a critically contested supposition. Critics argued that the African diaspora was distinct and required studying on its own terms.[1] The life history and Afropublican career of Edward Blyden offers an opportunity for an alternative approach to this early discourse about the study of the African diaspora. Blyden himself wrote, "I have taken and do take, the deepest possible interest in the current history of the Jews—especially in the marvelous movement called Zionism. It has been for many years my privilege to study the question from the African *standpoint*. And the history of the African race—their enslavement, persecution, proscription, and sufferings—closely resembles that of the Jews."[2] Thus, at the confluence of Blyden's claim to an Igbo ancestry and his upbringing while living among Jews on the Danish West Indies island of St. Thomas involve historical events, ordeals, and sentiments that intersect the Jewish and African diasporas—an infrequent consideration in diaspora studies.

These points of imbrication include the transatlantic slave trade, the Inquisition, slave rebellions in the Danish West Indies and the Caribbean, the American Revolution, Igbo identity in Africa and the Americas as well as black and Afro-Danish identity in the Caribbean. While this manifold approach to Blyden's biography helps in the social and historical examination of the meanings and layers of his identity, Blyden's life also serves as an indubitable historical source. Together, Blyden's own accounts of his life and his multifaceted identity collapse various temporal constructions of history, be they linear, cyclical, or genealogical continuums of history.

In addition, these accounts about Blyden's racial and cultural heritage challenge the definitiveness of biological, racial, cultural, and religious exceptionality and provides some clarity for ethnogenetic *processes* and *conditions* of cultural contact in the Atlantic world.[3] In other words, in this historical structure, Blyden's Afro-Danish identity and his claim to Igbo ethnicity cannot be separated from his connections to the Jewish communities of St. Thomas and St. Eustatius. For Blyden, the African diaspora and the Jewish diaspora intersect and therefore cannot be treated as separate historical diasporas with people from distinct racial origins who have experienced isolated historical events and therefore occupy separate historical temporalities.

The recent emergence of literature about Black Jews, African Jews, and Igbo Jews makes this exploration of Blyden's Igbo and apparent Jewish cultural heritage even more compelling.[4] In order to fully understand Blyden's journey to Afropublican status, insight into his socialization to ethnicity, racc, and culture is imperative.

Afro-Danish Drama

A significant contribution to Blyden's social identity formation occurred on July 2, 1848. On this day, sixteen-year-old Blyden witnessed a rare drama of slave resistance staged on the Danish West Indies island of St. Croix.[5] This enactment of slave resistance is especially significant to Atlantic history because the actors included both free and enslaved blacks on the one hand, and both Danish West Indies–born and Africa-born slaves on the other. Thus, the Africa-born plantation intellectuals and Danish West Indies–born blacks came together to form a successful nonviolent and popular emancipation movement in what can be described as the *makings* of an Afro-Danish or black identity.

The main protagonist in this tragic play was "General Buddo," also known as Gottlieb Bordeaux, John Gottliff, or Moses Gottlieb. The opening scene presents Buddo living on the Estate La Grange, a large sugar plantation located just outside of Frederiksted, St. Croix, where he was born an enslaved child on March 19, 1820.

This historical drama continues by depicting Buddo as belonging to or owned by the Lutheran Church but being a child of unknown paternity.[6] However, his mother was the well-known Maria Rosina, who was herself born enslaved on the La Grange plantation in 1799 and mother to two girls, Mathilde and Leah Petrus.[7] Buddo grew up to be a skilled artisan in and around Frederiksted, St. Croix, and endeared himself to some of the island's European population, including the governor of the Danish West Indies, Peter Von Scholten.

In 1792 Denmark had promulgated a law that would abolish Danish participation in the slave trade by 1803. This law did not, however, emancipate enslaved blacks in the Danish West Indies. Between July 2 and 3, 1848, General Buddo led a number of free and enslaved blacks in revolt against the Danish colonial government.[8] What makes this historical event a rarity in

Atlantic history is that General Buddo strived to make sure no "white" blood was shed during the course of the uprising for emancipation.

Further, the demonstration, unlike African revolts that preceded it, was not organized along ethnic lines but on racial grounds. For example, unlike the St. John rebellion of 1733, the Antigua slave rebellion of 1736, and the St Croix revolt in 1759, whose protagonists identified by ethnic and class designations, the enslaved plantation laborers and their free black counterparts who participated in this nonviolent and popular revolt were identified and self-identified by their race.[9] The events of the revolt by the enslaved blacks, as earlier noted, led to the proclamation of freedom for the islands' enslaved population on July 3, 1848. This declaration was later confirmed by a Danish royal proclamation on September 22, 1848.[10]

The rebellion ended in tragedy when the Danish colonial government exiled Buddo to Trinidad, from whence he later, according to some sources, relocated to the United States and subsequently vanished from the historical record.[11] Buddo's place in this drama shows how freedom in the Atlantic world was often fleeting. The irony is that Buddo himself is documented as having arrived in the United States as a destitute man after being deported from St. Croix following the rebellion.[12] His exile and subsequent disappearance into historical oblivion, just like Toussaint Louverture, imparted lessons about how freedom was never free or without cost; this circumscription of freedom had a definite impact on Blyden. The Buddo-led movement also was influential in the development of an Afro-Danish identity for the Danish West Indies' black population.[13]

Thus, while there is no direct commentary to show a connection between Blyden and Buddo, as a literate sixteen-year-old living in the Danish West Indies, the rebellion must have been didactic for Blyden. What makes this link more certain is indirect written evidence from the *Tidende* of May 6, 1848, that features an announcement by Blyden's childhood mentor, John P. Knox, proclaiming the second anniversary of the St. Thomas Bible Society, which was to be celebrated at the Reformed Dutch Church on May 8, 1848.[14] However, Blyden had more than the example of Buddo from which to learn.

In Cuba and other parts of the Caribbean, African recaptives and enslaved Africans emancipated by the British Naval Squadron still had to work to pay for their freedom or have their status determined by the multinational mixed commission courts.[15] In the United States, Blyden would later learn of Solomon Northup's twelve-year travail in enslavement after having been born free.[16]

Ultimately, these considerations influenced a young Blyden, especially in 1850 when he acknowledged that it was his "great fear of being seized for a slave under the operations of the Fugitive Slave law which was at the time causing great excitement in the country," driving him eventually to leave America for Liberia to pursue his education.[17] The Buddo rebellion also served as a historical benchmark in Blyden's life for a different but equally remarkable period of Danish West Indies history—the era of both the enslaved or "country-born" and the "freeborn" black. In other words, the 1848 emancipation permanently split time into before slavery and after (freedom). Edward Blyden personifies this temporal rupture. At the time that Buddo and others were fighting for their freedom, Blyden was a freeborn black living in the predominantly Jewish English-speaking community of Charlotte Amalie. However, even though he was born free, Blyden almost certainly had an inkling of what the enslaved population experienced in the wake of the upheavals following the revolt led by General Buddo.

As a free black person living in a Jewish community and a larger society *conditioned* or built on the institution of slavery, Blyden was inevitably affected by the actions of Buddo and his compatriots. Reflecting on racial identity and the lessons of Buddo's "freedom" following the upheavals in St. Croix, Blyden decided to go to the United States first and later at age eighteen to settle in Liberia. Blyden's own claim to freedom did not come, however, from the gains of the drama that showcased Buddo. Unlike Buddo, Blyden was born to skilled and free parents who had earlier immigrated to St. Thomas.[18] The Blyden family, on the evidence of their St. Eustatius background, appears to have been following Jewish benefactors possibly connected with the Senegambian Jewish diaspora and the Dutch Jewish diaspora that birthed the Caribbean Jewish community of St. Eustatius. The St. Eustatius Jewish community migrated to St. Thomas Curacao and other destinations in the Caribbean following the British capture of the island in 1781. This was the same time that Blyden's parents arrived in St. Thomas.[19]

Another possible reason why the parents chose St. Thomas over other locations in the Caribbean could be that the lingua franca of the island was Dutch, and blacks in St. Thomas and St. John spoke Dutch Creole even though the official language was Danish.[20] What is noteworthy here is that we see the Blyden family paralleling the Jewish migration in the Caribbean again when Blyden was ten. Blyden and his family—his parents and six siblings, Robert, William, Romeo, John, Jane, and Lavina—moved to Puerto Cabello, Venezuela, where Blyden acquired Spanish as a language.[21] The family later returned to St. Thomas in 1844.[22] Thus, despite the Buddo-led uprising, Blyden enjoyed a relatively peaceful upbringing.

As explained earlier, during his schooling years, he had three major influences: his mother, father, and mentor J. P. Knox. For Blyden, they represented school in the morning, tailoring apprenticeship in the afternoon, and Protestant Christianity on Sunday, respectively.[23] Blyden continued this itinerary for four years, during which he also studied privately with his mother, Judith, of whom he wrote: "the influence of my excellent and devoted mother . . . more than to any other earthly cause, can I trace whatever literary tastes and religious aspirations I possessed."[24] Later in life, Blyden dedicated his book *From West Africa to Palestine* to his mother "whose careful and prayerful teachings, in [his] early years, produced impressions and awakened aspirations which, God's blessing, have determined thus far, the course of [his] life."[25] Thus, here we see Blyden attribute his intellectual life to the Christian notion of Providence by way of his mother.

Blyden also imbibed providential ideas from Rev. Knox, who was secretary of the St. Thomas Bible Society and would influence Blyden to travel to the United States.[26] However, when Blyden arrived in America aboard Captain Davis's ship, the *Oxholm*, he was confronted by the U.S. system of social inequality and oppression based on race, which subsequently blocked his goal of higher education. Blyden spent a short period working as a servant in a New York home while attending night school.[27] This was the period in which the "Back-to-Africa" movement was at its height. Blyden, influenced by the prevailing sentiments of the time, immigrated to Liberia for an education that was unavailable to him in the United States on account of his race. Like General Buddo, who advocated for the Afro-Danish population of St. Croix, Blyden became a voice of consciousness and a defender of Africa and people of African descent worldwide. It is entirely plausible that Blyden's cognizance of an African race was first influenced by Buddo's rebellion, as the slave rebellion was the first in the history of the Danish West Indies to be based on race, rather than ethnicity (Akwamu, Ga, Igbo etc.), such as was witnessed in the 1759 St. Croix rebellion. Buddo's rebellion involved the combined participation of Africa-born blacks, free blacks like Buddo himself, and the enslaved black population. Subsequently, Blyden's ideas about race likely began to crystallize in this period.

Blyden's journey to Afropublican status that began in the Danish West Indies continued in Liberia.[28] He left the comforts of his parents, siblings, and home—his natal St. Thomas. He also left a host of benefactors and well-wishers in St. Thomas and in the United States.[29] There were, however, memories, people, and places in St. Thomas that would never leave Blyden's mind. One of these was the Jewish community of St. Thomas; another was his claim to an Igbo ethnicity and, ultimately, to a racial identity shaped by General Buddo and his contemporaries. These were the building blocks on which Blyden would formulate a theory on racial identity he called the African Personality.

Igbo/African Ethnicity

With very few exceptions, scholars and Blyden biographers generally agree that Blyden was of Igbo ancestry. One source of this claim is found in the work of pioneering historian of Pan-Africanism P. Olisanwuche Esedebe.[30]

Although Esedebe claims that Blyden's paternal grandfather was from Igboland, it is still unclear as to how Blyden went from a claim of coming from "the purest Negro parentage" to a conclusion that he was of Igbo heritage.[31]

Nonetheless, the fact that Blyden claimed an African ethnicity in the Danish West Indies is not surprising given the Afro-positivist traditions established by Africa-born plantation intellectuals on the Danish West Indian Islands. Besides, claims to African provenance or a connection to Africa was a well-established tradition among both Africa-born and diaspora-born leaders of African-descended communities in the Americas, which is in itself evidence of the integral role Afro-positivism and old-world African identities, cultures, and forms of knowledge played in the making of Atlantic commerce, culture, ideas, and religion.

One possible reason for diasporic black leaders' insistent claims to African heritage, even centuries removed, is that, throughout the late eighteenth and early nineteenth century, black "conspirators" sought to "make full use of the peculiar gifts of those native-born Africans [plantation intellectuals] who had remained close to the cultic practices of the homeland."[32] Thus, Denmark Vesey (1773–1822), who led the 1822 Charlestown, South Carolina, conspiracy, was, by some accounts, born on Blyden's birth island of St. Thomas, and is not only believed to have spent some time in Africa but also had Gullah Jack as his co-conspirator or fellow plantation intellectual in plans to change the public culture of the plantation. With Gullah Jack in the fold, the collaborators "already had Africa and its spirits with them," because Gullah Jack was considered "a conjurer from among the Gullah people who lived on the coasts of the homeland, and his comrades in the conspiracy believed that he would call on the fathers in their behalf and would develop potions and powders to protect them."[33]

Nat Turner (1800–1831) led a revolt in Southampton County, Virginia; it was believed that his family was "not too far removed from Africa" and that he dabbled in the "ancient crafts of Africa and Asia."[34] From Jamaica, Blyden may have heard or read about other plantation intellectuals like Gold Coast leaders Nanny (ca. 1686–1733), her lieutenants Cudjoe and Quao, and others who successfully established maroon communities following protracted warfare with British troops. Nanny, an Akan Gold Coast–born woman and leader of the Windward Maroons of Jamaica, was instrumental to the successful establishment of a community of escaped African men and women in the 1740s.[35] Some accounts reference Nanny as outmaneuvering British soldiers through her mystical and spiritual, Africa-derived powers.[36]

Still in the Caribbean, Blyden would have learned of the enslaved plantation intellectuals of Akan and Ga royalty, born on the Gold Coast, who led the St. John rebellion of 1733, the Antigua slave rebellion of 1736, and the St Croix revolt in 1759.[37] In Haiti, Dutty Boukman was the leader of the 1791 slave revolt that set off the Haitian Revolution. It is believed that Boukman, before the start of the uprising, led the rebels in a religious ceremony alongside an Africa-born woman—Cecile Fatiman and/or Mambo Marinette.[38] The Haitian Revolution inspired African-derived ethnic associations, known in Cuba as *Cabildos de naciones*, to enact insurrections throughout the island nation. Enslaved Africans rose up against their enslavement in Cuba with the belief that help would come from the kings of either Kongo/Angola in Africa, or from Haiti.[39]

Martin Robison Delany (1812–1885), socialized by "his parents and maternal grandmother" to be "deeply conscious of their noble African heritage," claimed an "unadulterated African" heritage such that "when honors fell upon him" and "when he entered the council of Kings, the black race entered with him."[40] Bishop Henry McNeal Turner (1834–1915) of the AME Church believed he was freeborn because his grandfather, an enslaved African prince, was freed "owing to some British Statute or law which forbade the enslavement of royal blood."[41] Not even twentieth-century scholar W. E. B. Du Bois failed to embrace this Afro-positivist tradition of associating with Africa. Du Bois wrote about his great-great-grandmother passing on an African lullaby through his family for two hundred years.[42] It is safe to extrapolate that Blyden and his nineteenth-century contemporaries utilized this black leadership tradition of connecting to Africa and sought to use it to establish their leadership credentials in the African Atlantic world.

In this way, Afro-positivism and African ethnicity continued to shape and influence Atlantic societies even though most African diaspora communities in the Atlantic world were by this time no longer in their formative stages.[43] However, these polycultural societies, which were centuries removed from Africa, continued to imagine, re-create, reinvent, and invest their related place of origin—Africa—with myth, ancestral pride, and respect. Because of this, Afro-positivism rooted in an African episteme was still the starting point for black leaders and political organizations in the nineteenth century. It is therefore not startling that Blyden would claim an Igbo ethnicity, a primary foundation for his ascent to Afropublican status in the black world of the nineteenth and early twentieth centuries.

Nonetheless, who were the Igbo and why would Blyden claim a Danish West Indian or diasporic Igbo ethnicity among the plethora of African ethnicities? While there are still debates as to exactly when an Igbo identity emerged during the Atlantic period, most scholars of Igbo history agree that the Igbo people are autochthonous to the Bight of Biafra. There, they first emerged in the Niger-Benue confluence and then populated and migrated to their present location in the Niger Delta and Cross River valley.[44] The Igbo living in this location before and during the Atlantic period may be said to have been localized or living in segmented or several hundred independent towns and villages. In these village republics, power was shared along gender (dual-sex), age, and occupational lines. Igbo people spoke one language that included an assemblage of major and minor dialects.[45]

Igboness in the Atlantic period came to constitute a belief in Chukwu or Chineke (God) with veneration for a pantheon of male and female deities and special reverence for two major deities, Ala/Ani/Ana (earth deity) and Chi (personal deity), indicating a belief in a form of reincarnation; an emphasis on individuality and personal achievement (Ikenga) epitomized by title taking; and exaltation of two major crops, yam and kolanut—products of the Igbo people's early history of success in iron working and a sustained agrarian economy.[46]

The questions then are: from what Umunna (extended family), Obi (family compound), and Ogbe (village) did Blyden's Igbo ancestors originate; what personal deity (Chi) or group of deities did his ancestors revere; were these ancestors peasant or nobility, free or servile? Unfortunately, for many people who crossed the Atlantic, such personal details are unavailable, just as they are not available for Blyden's ancestors.

Myron Jackson, a native of St. Thomas and a Blyden family acquaintance, avers that Blyden likely learned of such information through oral traditions and stories passed down in his family.[47] While Jackson's response about Blyden's knowledge of his Igbo heritage is reasonable, some may question the authenticity of the oral claim since it is not verifiable through any definitive historical evidence.[48] This has very much been the case in the current debate about another member of the African diaspora, Olaudah Equiano, who not only claimed an Igbo ethnicity but also birth in an "Igboland" village, Essaka, in his much-acclaimed slave narrative, *The Interesting Narrative of the Life of Olaudah Equiano*. Vincent Carretta has questioned Equiano's claims on the basis of two written documents: a baptismal record of Equiano from 1759 and a Royal Navy ship muster list from 1773. Both of these documents suggest that Equiano was born in South Carolina, not Africa. Other scholars have raised an issue with Carretta's potential over-reliance on written documents to the neglect of linguistic and collected oral histories.[49]

Some written and statistical evidence that establish Igbo/Bight of Biafra presence in the Danish West Indies can support Jackson's supposition. The records of the Trans-Atlantic Slave Voyages Database indicate that about one in seven enslaved Africans shipped from Africa to the Americas came from the Bight of Biafra; that is, about a million and a half Biafrans. Of this number, close to 20,000 disembarked in the Danish West Indies (DWI). This might seem like a small percentage, but the total of all forced exports of enslaved Africans from Africa to the DWI (from 1680 to 1838) was 129,867, and 16,641 of those who arrived in the DWI were from the Bight of Biafra, compared to 48,016 from the Gold Coast, the largest exporting region to the DWI, and a combined 5,172 from the Windward Coast and Sierra Leone, the lowest exporting region excluding Southeast Africa and the Indian Ocean seaboard, with a mere 25. The remaining souls came from the Senegambia, West Central Africa, and the Bight of Benin.[50]

Further historical evidence can be gleaned from contemporaneous Danish West Indian newspapers like the *Royal Danish American Gazette* (1770–1775), the *St. Thomas Gazette*, the *Sanct. Thomae Tidende*, and the *St. Croix Avis*, all of which suggest that Jackson's claims are well founded. These newspapers show advertisements of slave ships arriving in the DWI with enslaved "cargo" from various slaving ports in Africa, including the ports of the Bight of Biafra. The newspapers also feature announcements of runaway slaves of Bight of Biafra origin: Igbo and Moko, among others.

The following selections from the *Royal Danish American Gazette* (*RDAG*) demonstrate the Igbo/Biafran presence in the DWI. The *RDAG*, for example, advertised on October 11, 1775, that one George Walker had "just imported 35 Choice New Negroes" into Christiansted, and they were to be sold that day on Kings Street. On Company Street, George Vance and Edmund Burke were looking to sell "a Few Fine Young Slaves of the Ebbo [Igbo] nation."[51] On July 28, 1770, the *RDAG* reports the running away of "An Ebbo Negro Fellow. By profession a distiller, named George was purchased at Mr. Woodfruf Haynes venue."[52] On August 1, 1770, the running away of two blacks, "Rose an Ebbo, about 5ft high with her child a suckling boy, [and] Christina, a girl about 4ft high" was reported. "A wench of the Ebbo country named Sue, yellow, 30 years. Speaks bad English. [Who also] took [her] child with her" was also reported to have runaway on October 6, 1770.[53] Other mentions of Igbo runaways were very descriptive, indicating that, by the close of the first half of the eighteenth century, certain characteristics had come to be associated or discerned about Igbo peoples on the Danish West Indian islands. For example, one runaway woman by "name Hazard of the Ebbo country, [is described as being] marked on both arms as the Ebbo Negroes" whilcs Pierre who runaway about "2 months ago, [is described as] middle aged, midsized, [with] Ebbo country marks on his forehead."[54] Another Igbo woman who had been reported in the Gazette as being on the run since August 22, 1770 is finally identified as an Igbo woman after it was noticed

TABLE 1. Total Exports from Cultural Regions in Africa to the Danish West Indies, 1500–1838

CULTURAL REGION	NUMBER OF ENSLAVED AFRICANS
Sierra Leone and Windward Coast	5,172
Senegambia	5,867
Bight of Benin	17,070
West Central Africa	16,208
Gold Coast	48,016
Bight of Biafra	16,641
Southeast Africa and Indian Ocean	25

Source: Trans-Atlantic Slave Trade Database, www.slavevoyages.org.

TABLE 2. Country Total Exports of Enslaved Africans to the Danish West Indies, 1501–1866

YEAR	SPAIN/ URUGUAY	PORTUGAL/ BRAZIL	GREAT BRITAIN	NETHERLANDS	UNITED STATES	FRANCE	DENMARK/ BALTIC	TOTALS
1680–1700	0	0	411	0	0	0	22,199	22,610
1701–1725	0	0	129	5,756	0	0	5,027	10,912
1726–1750	0	0	334	505	0	0	4,793	5,632
1751–1775	0	0	3,004	0	1,244	0	17,508	21,756
1776–1800	0	0	14,279	0	1,195	0	28,027	43,501
1801–1825	0	0	10,309	0	926	3,527	4,835	19,597
1826–1838	307	0	0	0	0	5,551	0	5,858
Totals	*307*	*0*	*28,466*	*6,261*	*3,365*	*9,078*	*82,389*	*129,866*

Source: Trans-Atlantic Slave Trade Database, www.slavevoyages.org.

that she was passing as a "Mullata." The *RDAG* noted that a "yellow negro woman, of the Ebbo nation formerly the property of Alex Davis. She is well known in town and country by the name of mulatta Nancy. She is a stout thick well limbed wench, speaks good English and Dutch and reports in every place she is detected as a runaway that she is working for her owner. Has been seen by several negroes selling or trafficking goods in West End and Plantations."[55] The April 17, 1773, edition of the *RDAG* also announced "runaway from subscriber, a negroe wench, called Mary, of the Ebbo country: She is about ten years old, with her country marks on her forehead; had on when she went away a piece of old sail cloth and a long chain about her body."[56] On September 30, 1772, the *RDAG* reported "absented from the estate of Andrew Irwin, Esq. commonly called the Fountain, slim yellowish fellow, named Mocco Sam, active and shoots well."[57] On November 4, 1775, one John Harrison also advertised that a "runaway from the subscriber a New Negro Man, named January of the Mocco country. He was bought last Sunday from Mr. Richard Forster at West End. He has thick lips, a scar upon his right shoulder."[58]

The well-established presence of enslaved Africans from the Bight of Biafra in the DWI is evident. Blyden could very well have been acquainted, encountered, or related to DWI blacks of Igbo/Bight of Biafra origin. What is curious, though, is that Blyden failed to mention such an acquaintance in the DWI in any of his available memoirs and writings, other than the claim that he was of Igbo origin. What is certain is that Blyden also described his fellow black intellectual Henry McNeal Turner as an Igbo person, who "when in company with him he has furnished a most puzzling object of study." Blyden proceeded to imbue Turner with Igbo personality traits, which if closely scrutinized, bear a close similarity to descriptions of Igbo cultural idiosyncrasies offered by current scholars of Igbo history and culture.

This is particularly evident in the writings of Chinua Achebe, arguably the most popular and influential Igbo person since the second half of the twentieth century. For example, Blyden writes that Turner's "intellectual versatility and resourcefulness . . . when contrasted with his restlessness, if anything is said which he cannot just fit in with his preconceived notions; his fits of irritation growing, probably out of an uncomfortable and *nervous organization*, characteristic of the *impetuous and intractable Eboe* tribe from which he sprang."[59] Here, Blyden, like Achebe after him, references an Igbo civic culture that stems from, in Achebe's words, "the threat of anarchy, always attendant on the Igbo choice of political organization" and that made them vulnerable to the Atlantic slave trade. In using "nervous organization," Blyden seems to have anticipated Achebe's description of the Igbo village republics, describing, "The Eboes, currently spelt "Ibos" are the dominants ethnic group of Eastern Nigeria."[60]

Achebe alludes to Blyden's "nervous organization" when he writes, "those hundreds of autonomous Igbo villages and towns, so deeply suspicious of political amalgamation[,]would be stretched to the limit should they ever face an enemy able to wield the resources of a centralized state."[61] Blyden infused Turner with another Igbo characterization: "impetuous and intractable." He then goes on to explain this characteristic as "a pedigree, which goes far to explain, if it does not excuse, [Turner's] ferocity of utterance. But, as with the Eboes, whose anger is very short madness, the clouds of wrath readily disperse and sunshine appears as if there had been no storm. There is in this character much that is generous, much that is hearty and spontaneous."[62]

In this instance, Blyden presaged Achebe. Achebe, explaining the cosmological and philosophical reasons behind Igbo social organization as well as the "threat of anarchy" that undergirds the Igbo's segmentary political organization aver that Igbo individuality and competition have been the features of Igbo life "from antiquity through precolonial times to the present." Achebe, therefore, concludes:

> The Igbo have always lived in a world of continual struggle, motion and change—a feature conspicuous in the tautness, overreach and torsion of their art; it is like a tightrope walk, a hairbreadth brush with the boundaries of anarchy. This world does not produce easygoing people. Those who visit the Igbo in their home, or run into them abroad or in literature are not

> always prepared for their tense and cocky temperament. The British called them argumentative.[63]

Achebe appears to agree with Blyden's description of Igbo "impetuousness and intractability." Blyden, in some of his other depictions of Turner's temperament, also seems to have anticipated Achebe's descriptions of the Igbo. Blyden writes:

> In spite of his contemptuous and often abusive attitude toward adversaries; in spite of his too frequent indulgence in terms of scorn and vituperation; in spite also of the fact that clever people have always a little malice against the stupid; no man has a warmer heart or more expansive and unrestricted sympathies; none is more abundant in generosity toward the unfortunate and helpless.[64]

Thus, by Blyden's estimation, Bishop Turner exhibits the same Igbo cultural traits that Achebe and others later described as individuality, competition, and spirituality, as well as a high sense of achievement, oral dexterity, and a penchant for speaking truth to power. Incidentally, some of the same traits are identified in recent studies of the Igbo in the Americas.[65] What is evident in reading Blyden through Achebe is that Blyden appears to have had a deep, if not a firsthand, understanding of Igbo society and culture. Blyden's father was a tailor, a profession often associated with enslaved Igbo in Atlantic history literature. Blyden therefore likely acquired this knowledge from the Igbo community in the DWI, whose eighteenth-century ancestors were interviewed by Moravian missionary C. G. A. Oldendorp.[66]

Reading Blyden's statements authored in 1900 about Turner through the lens of Achebe's twenty-first-century writings may seem anachronistic to those wedded to linear history; but, as stated earlier, a nonlinear historical materialist approach to Blyden's work is imperative to understanding and providing increased clarity to the ethnogenetic processes and conditions that shaped his Afropublican status.[67] Thus, Blyden's imagined or real

FIGURE 9. Dr. E. W. Blyden in 1894.

connection to Igboland, the apparent land of his ancestors, was his cue for adopting the Afro-positivist conceptualization of Africa begun by the Africa-born plantation intellectuals.

Blyden's understanding of the Igbo more than likely came from experiential encounters with the Igbo in both the diaspora and Africa. It is therefore safe to say that if Blyden imbued Turner with what he perceived to be Igbo characteristics, then he believed the same about himself, which is why he claimed an Igbo ethnicity. Ultimately, what can be gleaned from the oral accounts, slave trade statistics, newspaper accounts, and Blyden's statements on Turner is that there are many possible etymologies from both oral and written documents that one can deduce to explain Blyden's Igbo claim. What is more important here, however, is what such a claim would have done for Blyden. Claiming Igbo allowed him to be like the many Igbo plantation intellectuals in the Americas who valorized their lived African experience and longed to return physically or spiritually to Ala/Ani/Ana (the earth, earth deity) in order to relive the experience of the Umunna (extended family), the Obi (family compound), and Ogbe (village). In addition, as it did for many Diasporic African leaders and black intellectuals throughout the eighteenth and nineteenth century, Blyden's claim to be of pure Igbo heritage established his authenticity as a spokesman for Africa and black folk worldwide. It accentuated his place as a black leader and gave him a platform from which he could launch his Pan-African agenda.

Recent scholarship on the African diaspora has shown both the salience and mutability of ethnicity as an important category in the analysis of diasporic communities. These works have been useful in the effort to understand processes and conditions of cultural creativity, identity formation, religious practices and beliefs, and forms of social grouping in African diaspora communities of the Atlantic world.[68] The significance of ethnicity in Blyden's life is critical to understanding the development of his identity and eventually his intellectual career.

AFRO-JEWISH OR JEWISH ACQUAINTANCE

Another realm of current research that informs the intellectual career of Edward Blyden is the intersection of the Jewish and African diasporas. In Blyden's own words, he lived in the same neighborhood with Jewish families such as the "Benjamins, Azvedos, Da Costas, Bensilas, Wolf, and other—names well known throughout the West Indies." Blyden recalls playing with Jewish boys, with whom he looked forward "to the annual festivals and feasts" of the St. Thomas synagogue. Yet, Blyden writes that he "always went to the synagogue on the solemn day of Atonement—not inside."[69] The Sabbath remained important to Blyden throughout his career. His ability to visit Egypt on his way to Jerusalem was, therefore, a dream fulfilled. He explains that it was "the land which every Sabbath-school boy desires to see, as he reads the simple narratives of Joseph and his brethren . . . and exodus of the Jews–of the haughty and tyrannical Pharaoh."[70] When he eventually arrived in Jerusalem, he grieved that the Sabbath was no longer sacred in Jerusalem. He decried how economic activities were carried on by both "Jews and Muslims who form a great bulk of the population" on the Sabbath. He observes seeing "camels go to and fro with their loads, and every other form of activity engaged in, showing that the people no longer 'Remember the Sabbath-day to keep it holy.'"[71]

In fact, when Blyden returned to the island in 1862 to visit his mother he recalls "how cordially [he] was received by his Jewish acquaintances . . . [including] the thoughtful hospitality of a Jewish neighbor living opposite, [who sent] tea and other refreshments to give [him] a practical and . . . a most grateful welcome."[72] Nonetheless, it was in the Reformed Dutch Church of St. Thomas that Blyden was received and not his much coveted and hallowed confines of the St. Thomas synagogue.[73] Although he was unable to enter the St. Thomas Synagogue, he made time to visit several synagogues during his visit to Jerusalem, including the Spanish and Polish Synagogues.[74]

Over a century later, on July 30, 1976, Edward Wilmot Blyden III, the Sierra Leonean ambassador to the United Nations, arrived in Charlotte Amalie, St. Thomas, where his grandfather Edward Blyden was born. Blyden III was embarking on a "ten-day comprehensive return visit to the Virgin Islands" that would include visits to "St. Croix, St. John and Tortola."[75] Ambassador Blyden was a citizen of Sierra Leone, but his great-grandparents were born on the Island of St. Eustatius and migrated to St. Thomas. His grandfather, and our subject, Edward Blyden, eventually settled in Sierra Leone, where he died and where his remains are interred.

Blyden III's visit seemed to capture the multiple departures, homes, and belongings of African diaspora people, but even more poignant is that on the evening of his arrival he entered and addressed the St. Thomas synagogue, a place that his grandfather was unable to enter as a young boy. According to Rabbi Shimon Moch, the Hebrew Congregation of St. Thomas was first built on Synagogue Hill in the late eighteenth century with a congregation comprised of nine Jewish families, who were later joined by thirteen migrant families from England, France, St. Eustatius, and Curacao. After being twice destroyed by fire, the synagogue that Blyden would come to revere was built in 1831 with a congregation now numbering sixty-four families.[76]

Unlike his grandfather, who "took up an outside position from which [he] could witness the proceedings of the worshippers, hear the prayers and the reading, the singing and the sermon," Blyden III addressed the Jewish community from within the synagogue. Blyden, about a century earlier, viewed the grounds of the synagogue as a "mysterious assembly" and had watched through "breathless silence" and "with an awe and reverence which followed [him] all the days of his life."[77]

It was a reverential curiosity that led Blyden to desire to "understand the Hebrew language—to read with facility the poets and prophets of the Old Testament, and the Talmud in the original."[78] Blyden's curiosity about the rituals of Judaism would ultimately send him down the path of Oriental scholarship and even a "visit to the original home of the Jews—to see Jerusalem and Mount Zion, the joy of the whole world . . . the land of the patriarchs and prophets."[79] As Blyden learned to read a number of Mediterranean and Romance languages, including Hebrew, he continued with a study of the "literature and history of the Jews . . . philological, historical, and even theological information."[80]

I describe Blyden as a Black Orientalist who employed an *Africa-centered Orientalist discourse* to illuminate African histories and cultures as he engaged with other intellectuals throughout the world. First, as part of his Orientalist academic training, Blyden became quite familiar with Latin, Greek, Hebrew, and, as I will show later, Arabic. I use "Black Orientalist" and "Africa-centered Orientalist discourse" in contradistinction to James Dorman, who describes Blyden as a "western-trained Christian Orientalist," when Blyden was in fact self-taught.[81] That is, as an autodidact, Blyden was not socialized or pressed to be in a specific school of thought or analytical persuasion, and in fact came to Orientalism from an African perspective. Blyden's critique of the Orientalist approach to translating the Bible into Arabic demonstrates his occupation of a different conceptual space as compared to his other Orientalist colleagues.[82]

Further, Blyden's Orientalist discourse and position on Africa differs from that of his Orientalist colleagues—Christian, European, or African diasporan. Blyden's 1898 essay "The Jewish Question" is a great testament to Blyden's Africa-centered Orientalist discourse. In this essay, Blyden makes it clear that he was examining the history of the Jews and the current thinking about Zionism—that is, the future of persecuted Jews in Europe as well as Judaism "from an African standpoint."[83] Blyden's intervention in this global public discourse is significant not only because he was the single African public intellectual engaging the debate on Zionism, but also because he himself was "born in the midst of Jews."[84]

Blyden's Afropublican stance toward making factual representations of African peoples and cultures is revealed in how he pairs the African condition with the Jewish Question and thus again makes Africa the center of his public intellection. As Benjamin Neubergher points out, Blyden deployed "Homer, Herodotus, and the Bible" to paint a richer history of Africa compared to "books written by foreigners and for a foreign race."[85]

Nonetheless, it is curious that all we learn about Blyden's relationship with the Jewish community in St. Thomas is his childhood memories of playing with Jewish boys and him standing on the outside of the St. Thomas synagogue. Blyden uncharacteristically fails to inform readers about how his parents came to live in the Jewish neighborhood or how his family's travel to Venezuela was connected to the Jewish Caribbean diaspora, which leads me to ask whether Blyden's interest in Jews and Judaism was because of a peculiar Jewish heritage—a heritage he perhaps did not wish to triumph over his Igbo, black, and Pan-African identities. Is this curious Jewish legacy why Blyden chose to emphasize an African perspective in addressing the "Jewish Question," or Zionism, "the great question now uppermost in the minds of thousands of Jews, if not millions of Jews"? And did he notice the resemblance of "the history of the African race . . . to that of the Jews" because he had heritage in both societies?[86]

In order to understand the intersections of the African and Jewish diasporas in Blyden's life, we must begin with Blyden's earliest known ancestor. As intimated earlier, past scholars on Blyden generally held that it was Blyden's paternal grandfather who was initially displaced by the transatlantic trade in enslaved Africans. Grandfather Blyden presumably survived the Middle Passage and disembarked from either a European slave ship or perhaps a Jewish merchant ship on what was the Dutch island of St. Eustatius.[87] The name and ethnic origins of Grandpa Blyden, as well as when he arrived in St. Eustatius, where Blyden's father, Romeo, was born, remain murky. Holden, however, speculates that the name Blyden, Romeo's received name, is an anglicized form of the Dutch name Blieden.[88] This is entirely plausible, given that the Blydens of St. Thomas originally came from St. Eustatius, the Dutch island where Edward Blyden's grandfather likely came into contact with the ancestors of the Jewish community of St. Thomas, who had also migrated from St. Eustatius.

Besides this, it appears that the names Blieden, Bliden, and Blidstein are actually Jewish names derived from the Hebrew word *Blîde*, meaning joy.[89] We may never know for certain whether Blyden's grandfather had been enslaved, manumitted, or affiliated with a Dutch Jew named Blieden when he first arrived on the Island of St. Eustatius or how his son Romeo came to possess an anglicized version of this supposed Jewish name. Some answers may be found with the "Honen Daliem," the Jewish community of St. Eustatius founded between 1722 and 1737 by Dutch Jews and other Jews deriving from the Portuguese-Spanish Jewish diaspora. By 1750, they comprised more than half of the 802 free citizens of St. Eustatius.[90] The identities of Blyden's paternal grandmother and maternal grandparents, and whether they were among these 802 free citizens of St. Eustatius, is, however, unknown.

Meanwhile, Romeo Blyden married Judith (née Nicholson) Blyden, and as a couple, they moved from St. Eustatius to St. Thomas.[91] Superseding language considerations pointed out earlier, it is more likely that the Blydens' migration to St. Thomas was because they accompanied the last group of Jewish people leaving St. Eustatius or were following the Jewish people who had earlier migrated to St. Thomas after the British invasion and capture of the Dutch island in 1781, during the American Revolutionary War.[92]

In fact, when the Blydens departed for Venezuela in 1842, they were following the migratory patterns of the Curaçao Jews, who were strongly

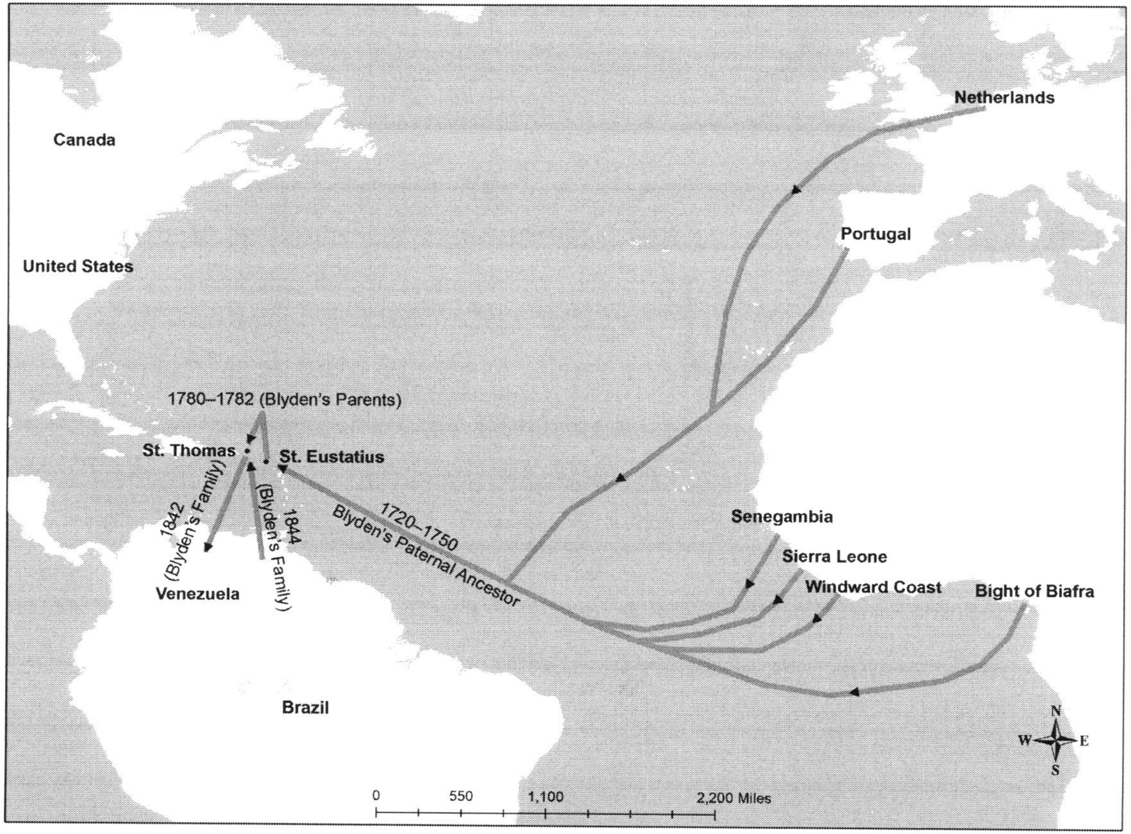

MAP BY CHARLES YORKE

MAP 2. Blyden's family travels. This map shows the Atlantic travels of Blyden's family beginning with his grandfather's journey from Africa to St. Eustatius and subsequent travels by Blyden's parents and family.

affiliated with St. Eustatius Jews and who had begun to settle on the island from the 1830s following Simón Bolívar's liberation of the island from Spain. Also, when the Blydens quickly returned to St. Thomas from Venezuela in 1844, it was likely because of anti-Jewish and anti-black sentiment in Venezuela, which would lead to anti-Jewish riots in 1848 and 1854.[93] The Blydens' departure from St. Eustatius, St. Thomas, and Venezuela were therefore conditioned or at least influenced by activities that directly affected the Jewish Caribbean Diaspora. These facts are more than passing commentary; they present strong evidence that the Blydens were more than just acquaintances to Jewish families in the Caribbean.

At this point, an excursus is necessary to show why the Blydens could have originated in any region of Atlantic Africa and Europe and also to explain why Blyden thought that the history of the African race—their enslavement, persecution, proscription, and sufferings—closely resembles that of the Jews."[94] It may seem that these events are completely unrelated; nonetheless, the intersections of the Jewish and African diasporas in the Caribbean have a long history reaching as far back as the beginnings of Atlantic commercial, cultural, and intellectual exchange. This history shows that while scholars like Esedebe accept an Igbo heritage for Blyden's paternal forebears, both Blyden's paternal grandfather, and the Nicholsons, his maternal ancestors, could have come from anywhere in Atlantic Africa (Senegambia, Bight of Biafra, Gold Coast, West African Islands), Portugal, or the Netherlands.

Besides this, the European Jewish diaspora is not unrelated to the Danish West Indies' African and Jewish diasporas. For example, as early as May 7, 1684, Jews played significant roles in the Danish West Indies Islands, when Gabriel Milan, a Danish Jew, with relatives and family connections in Portugal, Flanders, and Hamburg was appointed Governor of the Islands by the Danish Crown. He began his commission on October 13, 1684, and served until 1686. From 1686 to 1695, "A Spanish Portuguese Jew, Moses Joshua Henriques [was] appointed factor in Gluckstadt for ships sailing in the slave trade from Gluckstadt to Guinea and St. Thomas," and in 1695 he sought to involve other powerful Jewish financiers by transferring the rights of trade granted him by the West Indies company directors.[95]

Tudor Parfitt argues that perhaps "at some deep level in western consciousness, Jews are actually assumed to *be* black," and *Edward W. Blyden's Intellectual Transformations* highlights the possibility that this assumption comes from early intersections of African and Jewish diasporas in the Mediterranean that led to the construction of European race narratives that often portrayed Jews as being black and blacks as being Jewish.[96] An investigation of these intersections may very well seem to have no direct connection with Blyden; nonetheless, it is as important an exercise as the preceding analysis of Blyden's claim to be Igboness. Blyden may very well have known of these junctures, and they likely formed the basis for how he conceived of and theorized the Black Atlantic Diaspora. In fact Blyden explains that his interest in Jewish history was from firsthand experience and not just because of the "fascinating stories of the Patriarchs, of the Judges, of the Kings of Judah and of Israel." Blyden refers to a "special teaching outside of books, which comes from contact with living illustrations."[97] This special teaching, from "living illustrations" more than likely included the circuitous journeys Jews took through the Iberian Peninsula, Atlantic Africa, and Europe on their way to the Caribbean. This knowledge was what led Blyden to compare the African and Jewish Diaspora. We begin with the connections of the Jewish and African in the Mediterranean.

Given that black Africans have been present in the Mediterranean world since ancient times and that a Jewish presence in Africa parallels the same historical timeline, it is not surprising that the African and Jewish diasporas should intersect and lead to an exchange of culture and traditions. For example, a black African presence is recorded in Naples and Sicily in the thirteenth century before the Atlantic slave trade took off.[98] As Parfitt's work shows, "the last Jews were forced to leave Naples in 1541," and by the late sixteenth century, Africans comprised 83 percent of the enslaved population in Naples.[99]

Beyond an encounter in the Mediterranean, as late as the eighth and ninth centuries, a Jewish presence is recorded in Senegambia's Walata and

Tenderima regions.[100] Centuries before the Atlantic era, Africans were also known throughout the Iberian Peninsula, due in part to their participation in the Almoravid, or "Moorish," conquest during the early expansion of Islam and also later through the trans-Saharan trade, which brought enslaved Africans through North Africa into the peninsula.[101] However, for the purposes of this study, we are more concerned with the junctures of the Jewish and African diasporas in the Atlantic period. As it relates to Blyden, however, one may particularly identify in the Atlantic era, a linking of the two diasporas in Portugal, Senegambia, the Netherlands, and the West Indies.

In his pioneering work on the early Atlantic world, Philip Curtin suggests that the eastern Mediterranean plantation complex was the basis of early Atlantic African plantations in the Azores, Canaries, Cape Verde, and Madeiras islands. These early Atlantic plantation societies established off the West African coast, in turn, became the foundation for plantation complexes in the Americas and Caribbean.[102] It is instructive that some of the settlers of these early Atlantic African plantation societies that Curtin describes were free and enslaved Africans as well as Jewish-Portuguese *degrados* (convicts) and *Novos Christaos* (New Christians). Early Atlantic meetings of the African peoples with the Jewish diasporas, therefore, began in Africa. Besides this early intersection of African and Jewish diasporas, the link between the Jewish and African diasporas in Portugal can be directly traced to the advent of Atlantic trade between the Portuguese Empire and West Africans following the former's circumnavigation of the western and central African coasts by the close of the fifteenth century. Diplomatic ties between Portugal and West Africa date to this period. It is entirely possible that Blyden's ancestor emerged from these Atlantic convergences of Jewish and African peoples.

Portuguese ties with the Senegambia region, for example, go as far back as the 1470s, to the extent that the nephew of the ruler of Jelof and the ruler himself, King Jeleen, successively visited Portugal. A delegation from the Oba, of the kingdom of Benin, also arrived in Lisbon in 1486 and later in 1516. A steady stream of Kongolese also arrived in Lisbon beginning in 1484, including Henrique, son of the Mani Kongo, Afonso. Prince Henrique, who was sent to Portugal for studies in 1508, later led a Kongolese embassy to Rome in 1514, was ordained a priest in 1518, and was consecrated as a bishop by Pope Leo X in 1520.[103]

With the Atlantic slave trade now firmly in place, Portuguese ships increased the number of enslaved Africans they were bringing from Atlantic Africa into Spain and Portugal, so much so that by the second half of the sixteenth century, Africans made up 10 percent of the population of Lisbon and about 8 percent of the population of Seville.[104] During this period, throughout southern Portugal (in the Algarve, Castro Marim, Evora, and particularly Lisbon), black Africans and their descendants encountered and lived with Jews.

By the eighteenth century, Lisbon was not only a vibrant Atlantic cosmopole, but also "about one fifth of the inhabitants of Lisbon consist[ed] of blacks, mulattoes, or of some intermediate tint of black and white." As James Sweet notes, Lisbon was a "racially mixed amalgam of poor whites, Africans, and Jews," to such an extent that one traveler wondered whether Lisbon was still in Europe and fearing that "in a few centuries not a drop of pure Portuguese blood will be left here, but all will be corrupted between Jews and Negroes."[105]

With the amalgamation or encounter of Jews and Africans established in Portugal, both groups of people became victims of the Inquisition in grand public spectacles. Sephardic Jews were forced to flee Spain in 1492 and to depart Portugal in 1496–1497. As Peter Mark and Jose da Silva Horta explain, Jews in Iberia faced either forced conversion to Christianity or expulsion. About 50,000 Jews chose expulsion, subsequently migrating to locations in the Ottoman Empire, West Africa, Asia, the Netherlands, and the Americas. Those who remained were forced to become so-called New Christians—as distinct from Old Christians, that is, European Christians of non-Sephardic descent. Some Portuguese New Christians, however, practiced their faith in secret, earning them the sobriquet crypto-Jews or Marranos.[106] For some Jews escaping the general antagonism toward Jews in the Portuguese Atlantic world, their destination was the Senegambia region of West Africa, specifically Senegal.

Some Portuguese Jews, specifically Sephardic merchants who sought to escape the Inquisition and state-sponsored harassment emanating from Portugal, settled in two communities on Senegal's Petite Côte, Porto D'Ale, and Joal, in the seventeenth century. Under the protection of local Muslim rulers, these two communities were able to once again freely practice their faith not as New Christians, but as public Jews, away from the agents of the Inquisition.[107]

Two significant factors about these Petite Côte Jewish communities relate to Blyden's heritage. First, they included Jews of mixed heritage: Afro-Portuguese Jews as well as Sephardic Jews, who married African wives and bore multiracial offspring. Senegambian Jews raised their offspring, as well as taught their wives and servants, to adhere to Jewish religious practices such as circumcision, mainly because Jewish law, halakhah, required "Jews to convert their slaves, black or white, to Judaism."[108] In fulfillment of this dictate, some of them sent their mixed-race Jewish children and wives to Amsterdam for education and conversion but primarily to affirm and reestablish their Jewish identities.

Secondly, these early-seventeenth-century Portuguese Sephardic merchants established commercial relationships throughout the Atlantic world that encompassed Ceuta, Lisbon, Amsterdam, and ports in northern Europe. The principal commodities in this trade were blades or swords, which became instrumental in warfare in the Senegambia region. The Senegambia Jewish diaspora benefited greatly from the commercial ties, particularly with the Portuguese Jewish diaspora community in Amsterdam. They established commercial as well as spiritual links to the Amsterdam community, which provided the Senegambia diaspora with rabbis for spiritual guidance. Eventually, most of the Jews of Senegambia and their descendants left for Amsterdam.[109]

Having established the connections between the Iberian-Senegambia-Amsterdam Afro-Jewish communities, I now turn to the connection between the Amsterdam community and the Jewish Caribbean Diaspora. The Amsterdam community and other post-expulsion Jewish communities in Antwerp, Hamburg, London, and Valencia as well as returnee Jews from the failed Dutch colonization of Brazil became the basis for the establishment of Jewish settlements in the Dutch Americas: St. Eustatius, Curaçao, Suriname.[110] According to early historiographers of the Jewish presence in St. Eustatius, the formative stage of the Jewish community can be traced to the period between 1660 and 1720 with the arrival of Sephardic Jews from Brazil, Curaçao, and Amsterdam. By 1722, there were four Jewish families totaling twenty-one people—six adult men, four women, six girls, and five boys. This community had among them sixteen slaves.[111]

If Blyden's ancestors were among these sixteen enslaved persons, and if he arrived directly from Atlantic Africa, or from Portugal, Amsterdam, or Curaçao, verification is absent in the limited records of St. Eustatius. Another noteworthy fact that suggests a connection between the Blyden family and St. Eustatius is that the Honen Daliem Synagogue was built within sight of the large Dutch Reformed Church. This was the same Christian denomination that Blyden worshipped with in St. Thomas and through which he came under the influence of J. P. Knox.

Was Blyden part Jewish either in cultural heritage or in genealogy? It is plausible that Blyden's forebears earned their freedom under Jewish law, which enjoins Jews to convert and free their slaves. Grandpa Blyden or the Nicholsons may have been freed after the seventh year of their enslavement according to Judaic law, in which case they would have converted to Judaism. There is however no evidence of this conversion to Judaism even if nominally. What we can say definitively is that the foregoing seems to suggest that Blyden may have been partly Jewish or at the very least was influenced in diverse ways by the culture, religion, language, and history of the Jewish peoples of the Caribbean.

What is even more important here is that, just as Blyden may have learned about an Igbo heritage through oral accounts, he also learned through firsthand accounts about the multiple migrations and merging of the Jewish and African Diasporas including his family's unique relationship to the Jewish Diaspora in the Caribbean. Blyden points out in "The Jewish Question" that he had been engaged in such a comparative analysis of both diasporas since 1895, when he "delivered in the city of Washington [D.C.], in America a lecture on 'The Work and Destiny of the Races.'"[112] Thus, long before Robin Cohen's *Global Diaspora* which describes both African and Jewish Diasporas as victim diasporas, Blyden was already theorizing and explaining from research and experiential encounters the connections between both the African and Jewish Diaspora.[113]

Conclusion

The foregoing discussion of Blyden's family genealogy and wandering through the Caribbean proves two things. First, it shows that the discourse on totally separating the Jewish and African diasporas does not hold much merit—particularly so for the Atlantic period during which they intersect and merge at different historical events and moments like the Portuguese Inquisition and the American Revolution. Second, the preceding historical analysis serves to emphasize why Blyden would become the foremost black or Afropublican intellectual of the nineteenth century given his connection, or early exposure, to different cultural communities. Overall, Blyden's family genealogy and movement across the Caribbean show that while the historical *conditions* that occasioned the Jewish and African diasporas were not always the same, the *processes* of dispersion for each largely mirrors the other.

The evidence, written and statistical, presented here strongly demonstrates that it is most likely that Blyden's ancestors came from Igboland, in the Bight of Biafra. He likely claimed an Igbo heritage because he lived with people of Igbo descent in St. Thomas and also heard oral traditions and stories passed down in his family. In addition, Blyden admired and eulogized Igbo traits, and so laid claim to Igbo identity, a necessary building block to his racial identity. Igboness served Blyden the same way that an African origin functioned for other black intellectuals and leaders like Vesey and Nanny who preceded him. It also functioned for him in the same ways that it did for his contemporaries such as Delany, Turner, or Du Bois, who is described as the most influential black intellectual of the twentieth century. Igbo identity signified a belonging to a real or imagined African homeland: land of the ancestors, a place of dispersal as well as departure and, most importantly for Blyden, a place of return. In claiming an Igbo identity, Blyden made the symbolic voyage of an African return, which will be followed by a physical return and domicile in Africa.

Thus, even if Blyden's ancestors hailed from Senegambia, Portugal, or Amsterdam, Blyden was able to return to the original place of departure—Africa. Further, the juxtaposition of Blyden's Jewish heritage with his Igbo identity and return to Africa helps in making the larger point about the complex and dynamic ethnogenetic *processes* and *conditions* of cultural contact in the Atlantic world. More poignantly, these locations and communities associated with Blyden not only signify sites of intersection for both the African and Jewish diasporas; they also mark the Blyden family's geosocial movements throughout the Caribbean that were necessitated by historical conditions affecting both diasporas. In fact, in Blyden's scholarly opinion, "the history of the African race—their enslavement, persecution, proscription, and suffering—closely resembles that of the Jews."[114]

Finally, Blyden, a seasoned Black Orientalist and, according to Michael Echerou's early work, an avid reader of the newspaper *Nineteenth Century*, was well situated to engage in the intense scholarly debates of the nineteenth century touching Judaism and Zionism. What is most significant is that Blyden chose to tackle the so-called Jewish Question from an African standpoint, applying an African-centered discourse to engage the global and/or Jewish public sphere. This ethnohistorical examination of Blyden's life reveals that, like the Jewish and African diasporas, the layers of his cultural and racial identity do not fit a neat linear continuum of history. Clearly, neither the Jewish nor the African diaspora can be definitively confined regarding culture, race, or religion, as the ethnogenetic processes and cultural contacts of the Atlantic world were not only varied but intertwined. Blyden's family is itself a microcosm of the cultural histories of the Atlantic world, in particular the encounter of the African Jewish diasporas.

The Blyden family's movement from the African Atlantic world through the Dutch and Danish West Indies and Venezuela shaped his Pan-African outlook through early socialization to diasporic Igbo and Afro-Danish identities. Although the *processes* of dispersion that they lived through mirrored the peripatetic sojourns of many Jews in the Atlantic period, similarity is not sameness. Thus, the *conditions* of diaspora, including racism, enslavement, or religious persecution, were not always the same. In addition, Blyden's grandson, Blyden III's visit to his grandfather's birthplace is significant in showing the distinctiveness of the African Diaspora and its unique relationship to Africa. This is because it helps illustrate the essence of what Tiffany Patterson and Robin Kelley describe as the ongoing process of diaspora; Ruth Simms Hamilton's *continuous* physical and social processes of geosocial mobility of African peoples; and more recently, Kwame Essien's *Z Paths*, which explain the situation of Afro-Brazilian returnees to Ghana and other parts of West Africa, their initial journeys to Brazil and reverse migrations to West Africa, and their present remembrances of Brazil as home.[115]

Edward Wilmot Blyden and the "Africanization of Islam" in West Africa

> Tonight's proceedings are unique. Here you have a body of British Muslims assembled in the second city of the British Empire congratulating an African Negro on being decorated by the Sultan of Turkey. This event will live in history.
>
> —Edward Blyden, Lagos, May 1905, Award Ceremony, Decoration of the Imperial Order of the Medjidieh

On September 6, 1871, Edward Wilmot Blyden, a new resident at Freetown, Sierra Leone, reports that an embassy of nine leading Muslim old men from Fulahtown gave him a formal welcome. These Muslims blessed him in Arabic, ending with the *bibarakat al-nabi* (blessings of the Prophet). Blyden, in turn, informed them of his reason for coming to Sierra Leone: that "the word of God—His truth—should spread over all Africa . . . that [he] might teach the Arabic language to young men who are to be the future teachers and [Christian] missionaries, that they may be able to understand the Moslem Ulema's [priests] and carry the word of God to Futah, Jenne, and Timbuktu." This meeting marked a watershed moment in the reciprocal relationship that continued to develop between Blyden and the Muslim communities of the Upper Guinea region, which spans modern-day Liberia, Sierra Leone, parts of eastern Guinea, and northwestern Ivory Coast. According to Blyden, the group of nine who called on him saw him as "chosen of God" and began to call him *Mukhtar*—"the chosen one"—in contrast to Abd-al-Kerim, which name had been given to him for his work among Muslims in the interior of Liberia.[1]

A great deal has been written about Blyden's foundational contributions to the notion of Pan-Africanism as well as to African and African diasporan intellectual history.[2] Very little of the existing scholarship, however, deals directly with his encounter with the Muslim peoples of Upper Guinea and his academic engagement with their histories, philosophies, and distinctive practice of Islam. Therefore, I examine Blyden's study of Islam in West Africa during the nineteenth century and argues that he is the intellectual progenitor of the notion of Africans making Islam their own—an idea now popularized by the phrase "Africanization of Islam."[3]

As a Presbyterian-trained minister, his stance on Islam and its redeeming qualities for African people earned him many enemies in the Christian and British colonial establishment who accused him of having converted to Islam. I provide a historical context for Blyden's presence in West Africa, which led to his encounter with Islam and Muslims in Upper Guinea and throughout the region. I show Blyden's revered place in both African studies in general and Pan-African intellectual history and the historiography on the "Africanization of Islam." I will also systematically detail his specific contributions to the study of Islam in the areas of Islamic scholarship, Arabic and African languages, the institutionalization of Arabic/English schools, and cultural immersion in Muslim African societies. I show Blyden's systematic study of the spread, localization, and practice of Islam among Muslim Africans.

Historical Background, Context, and Atlantic Encounters

Since the thirteenth century, non-Muslims, nominal Muslims, Muslim clerics, traders, merchants, landlords, and craftsmen along with religious and educational specialists of the Greater Senegambia region had, through intermarriage, conquest, and political alliance, been seeking commercial relationships, political space, and spreading Islam to the region's Atlantic seaboard communities.[4] The cross-cultural encounter that ensued between the inland and coastal communities further accelerated with the formation of the colonies of Freetown, Sierra Leone (1787), and Cape Mesurado, in what would become Liberia (1821). Blyden, for instance, observes that formerly enslaved or "recaptive" Yoruba (Aku) domiciled in Freetown indebted their Muslim faith to the "intelligence, zeal, and energy" of Fula clerics from the interior. Furthermore, "many of the Aku Mohammedans, who have acquired some means by traffic, send their sons to Futa Jallon to be educated in the language and religion of Arabia."[5] Within this intellectual, political, and social milieu he commenced a dynamic relationship with Upper Guinea's Muslim communities, specifically those in modern-day Liberia and Sierra Leone.

Blyden, a lifelong autodidact, increasingly sought to understand African communities and institutions following his repatriation to Liberia from the West Indies in 1851. Before then, various groups pursuing emigration arrangements to the African continent influenced Blyden. These were the white abolitionists and missionaries associated with the American Colonization Society and the Board of Foreign Missions of the Presbyterian Church, USA, and the Church Missionary Society in London and the African diasporan intellectuals and missionaries, such as Martin Delany and Henry Highland Garnett.[6] While these emigrationist traditions occasionally worked together, they were quite discrete.[7] In spite of their racial phenotypic and philosophical differences, these emigrationist groups collectively led Blyden to believe that God had providentially prepared folk of the African diaspora to civilize and evangelize their heathen brethren in Africa.[8] His encounter with Islam would gradually dissipate such beliefs.

Blyden's continued quest for knowledge and his subsequent arrival in Sierra Leone coincided with Upper Guinea's Muslim clerics' search for an intellectual connection with the Atlantic world. As a result of his aim "to establish Christian schools in the great Mohammedan centers" in the interior, a dialectical relationship ensued between him and the region's Muslim communities and its leading intellectuals.[9] For instance, one of the Muslim scholars, Alfa Suleiman, who was also imam of Fourah Bay College, advised Blyden that it was best to translate the Bible into Fula by using Arabic letters (Ajami) because of West Africans' familiarity with it through trade, the mosque, and school.[10] This burgeoning relationship between Blyden and the Muslim communities of the Senegambia not only impacted his intellectual views of Islam but correspondingly influenced the growth of Muslim intellectual communities throughout West Africa, notably in Sierra Leone, Liberia, and Nigeria.[11] The relationship stimulated exchanges between the Muslim communities in West Africa and the *Umma* (community of Muslim believers) in Great Britain as well as Syria and Turkey in the Mediterranean.

From these interactions, I argue that, ultimately, Blyden's study of Islam brought him to a better understanding of the history of human movement in Africa including Africans' engagement with cultures other than their own. Specifically, he attained an understanding of the dynamic engagement of varying cultures within and outside the African continent. Blyden came to understand that African autonomy and agency mediated the inflow of Arabic and Mediterranean cultures into Africa that transformed their indigenous social, political, cultural, religious, and economic institutions. It was on this basis that Blyden engaged African, African diasporan, and European intellectuals alike on the status of Africans in global modernity.

In an August 24, 1871, letter, Blyden informs Henry Venn, honorary secretary of the Church Missionary Society, of his arrival in Sierra Leone following thirteen days of travel from Liverpool, England. Additionally, he lays out his plan of action after being appointed as a linguist at Fourah Bay College, which was later established by the CMS in 1872. This letter marks the first of many Blyden would write to Venn, as well as to William Coppinger, secretary of both the Pennsylvania Colonization Society and the American Colonization Society. Coppinger also managed the publication of the ACS mouthpiece, the *African Repository*, in which some of Blyden's literary contributions to the nineteenth-century Back to Africa movement are recorded.[12]

Blyden's letters to Venn detail how he planned to use Arabic in the propagation of the Christian gospel among West African Muslims. These letters preceded Blyden's travels to the interior of Sierra Leone. He later embarked on various expeditions and missions to the interior, including one to Boporo. Blyden's goals for undertaking these missions, in his own words, were that "the Christian Negro confronting and working with the Mohammedan Negro will do more than any other human instrumentality in this country to supersede the Crescent by the Cross."[13] This statement and the first epigraph demonstrate Blyden's Christianizing goals through the use of Arabic. Ironically, it was during this period that he published several essays on Islam ("Islam and Race Distinctions," "Mohammedanism and the Negro Race," and "The Mohammedans of Nigritia"[14]), which drew accusations of sacrilege from contemporaneous Christian advocates. Blyden was therefore in many ways deserving of his nineteenth-century European colleague Mary Kingsley's description of him as a Black Arabic scholar par excellence and a "perfectly typical True Negro [African]."[15] Kingsley was, however, not the only one who recognized his contribution to Arabic and Islamic studies.

In May 1905, the sultan of Turkey rewarded Blyden with the Decoration of the Imperial Order of the Medjidieh. This award recognized his contribution to Muslim education (that is, modern Islamic schools or English/Arabic schools) in West Africa.[16] This recognition was significant because it was the highest class of award that a civilian could receive from Sultan Abdul Hamid Khan, the ruler of the Ottoman Empire, who laid claim at the time to be Caliph and Commander of the Faithful, the political and spiritual leader of the *Umma*. Sultan Abdulmecid I originally instituted the order in 1851 to reward British and French army personnel who had helped the Ottoman Empire during the Crimean War against Russia.

Blyden's letters, his knowledge of Arabic, the award by the Sultan of Turkey, and commendations by his peers all testify to Blyden's contribution to the systematic study of West African Muslim societies. In addition, they show the painstaking travels, training, and translations Blyden undertook in pursuit of an understanding of West African societies. Plus, it is evident that Blyden pioneered the establishment of what became known as Arabic/English schools in West Africa, which combined Western education with Islamic/Arabic instruction.[17]

Edward Blyden, African Studies, and Pan-Africanism

In his presidential address in 2010, Charles Ambler, then African Studies Association president, framed his speech around the exemplary scholarship and ideal of Blyden's archetypical Africanist work. He described Blyden as someone whose combined vision of research, social justice, cultural immersion, and cultural particularism in the study of Africa needed to be duplicated by contemporary African studies practitioners.[18] Indeed, the Caribbean-born Liberian intellectual is fondly remembered by many people in academia for his Pan-African activism and his authorship of several acclaimed essays. Above all, he is best known for his magnum opus, *Christianity, Islam, and the Negro Race* (1889), considered one of the seminal intellectual texts on Pan-Africanism. While Kwame Nkrumah's *Philosophical Consciencism* is more deeply rooted in the discipline of philosophy than Blyden's early work, in many ways Blyden's was a theoretical antecedent to Nkrumah's work.

Nkrumah, like Blyden, argues that Africa's external Islamic and Euro-Christian influences need to be brought in tune with "the original humanist principles" of traditional Africa.[19] Blyden also viewed Islam as less racial and discriminatory compared to Christianity as practiced by Europeans. He consequently saw Islam as a more successful medium for the regeneration of the African Personality he envisioned.[20] For him, the prior introduction of Islam to Africa is an important stage to a true Christianity. He believed that Islam, as practiced in much of West Africa before the introduction of Christianity, helped preserve African traits that constituted the African Personality—being in tune with nature, spiritual, industrious, communal, or socialist.[21] Plus, in making a distinction between the Christianity of contemporaneous European Christian missions and an indigenous African Christianity that was more aligned with extant African practices, he clearly preferred the latter.[22]

According to Blyden, the "Oriental aspect of Islam . . . [was] largely modified in [Africa]." Through this understanding of the localization of Islam, Blyden advocated the localization of Christianity in West Africa. After Blyden's intimate study of Islam as practiced in Africa, he began to compare his observations of Africanized Islam with Christianity as taught to Africans by European missionaries. In Blyden's comparative analyses, he came to the conclusion that African Christians were docile, servile, and blind imitators of European Christianity—"All tendencies to independent individuality were repressed and destroyed. Their ideas and aspirations could be expressed only in conformity with the views and tastes of those who held rule over them. All avenues to intellectual improvement were closed against them, and they were doomed to perpetual ignorance."[23]

In other words, African Muslims when compared to their Christian counterparts were independent of Arab Muslims, and their ideas and motivations were distinct from the Arabic peoples who introduced Africans to Islam. It was on this basis that Blyden advocated and influenced the emergence of the indigenous African church movement in West Africa. This movement was led by the likes of James Holy Johnson and Mojola Agbebi with the formation of the Native Baptist Church in 1888.[24] As a result of this line of thinking, Blyden advocated a "spiritual decolonization" of the African mind, a task that was taken on by the leaders of the indigenous African Christian church movement such as Johnson and Agbebi.[25]

Blyden, through his call for European education and Christianity to be adapted to local African conditions, had prefigured Nkrumah's attempted synthesis of the best aspects of Euro-Christian ideas, Islamic civilization, and "African humanism." Ali Mazrui further expounds on Blyden's and Nkrumah's ideas on Islam, Christianity, and Africa in his famous *Triple Heritage* documentary series and in subsequent lectures on Pan-Africanism in the era of globalization.[26] These subsequent engagements with Blyden's scholarship is one of the reasons he is considered to have authored the first sophisticated explanation of Pan-Africanism, which was later embraced by Nkrumah and more recently by Mazrui. However, fewer academics and Pan-African enthusiasts are aware of Blyden's specific contributions to the systematic study of Islam in West Africa.

In fact, some of the early historical studies of Islam in Africa, its localization and contact with traditional African religions, by the likes of E. G. Parrinder and later Lamin Sanneh rarely mention Blyden's pioneering contributions.[27] Blyden rather finds indirect acknowledgment in Black nationalist historiography in the United States, which examines how Afro-American Islam drew on the discursive space provided by his writings on Africanized Islam to create rhetorical strategies and to form religious social movements. Noble Drew Ali's *Moorish Science Temple* and later Elijah Muhammad's *Nation of Islam* each drew on Blyden's writing to claim Islam as an African/Black religion as opposed to Christianity as a European/white religious tradition.[28]

Glocalization and Africanizing Islam

To explain the two stages of African agency that Blyden identifies in the Africanization of Islam, I employ the conceptual term *glocalization*. Glocalization is seen as a less marginal way of thinking about or conceptualizing globalization. It recognizes globalization as a simultaneous process of universalizing and particularizing rather than a system where one party is globalizing and the other is simply on the receiving end of an exchange of goods or ideas.[29] In this way, globalization is not Europeanization, Americanization, Arabization, or the *ization* of anything for that matter. Glocalization is, therefore, the reciprocal process of the *externalization* and *localization* of an idea, product, or phenomenon, and in this particular instance: religion. So one can talk about Glocalized Islam–the simultaneous spread (externalization) of Islam from the Arabian Peninsula to other parts of the world beginning in the seventh century, which was accompanied by a *localization* of Islam wherever it gained a foothold.

Thus, in the areas of the world where Islam found traction, Islam took on an indigenous character reflecting more of the cultural sensibilities of the local population and less of Islam as practiced in the Arabian Peninsula. Blyden describes this African agency or process of glocalization beginning with its externalization to West Africa as follows:

> There are numerous Negro Mohammedan communities and states in Africa which are self-reliant, productive, independent, and dominant, supporting, without the countenance or patronage of the parent country, Arabia, whence they derived them, their political, literary, and ecclesiastical institutions. In Sierra Leone, the Mohammedans, without any aid from Government—Imperial or local—or any contributions from Mecca or Constantinople, erect their mosques, keep up their religious services, conduct their schools, and contribute to the support of missionaries from Arabia, Morocco or Futah when they visit them.[30]

Blyden goes on to summarize the glocalization process: "the Arab superstructure has been superimposed on a permanent indigenous substructure, so that what really took place when the Arab met the Negro in his own home was a healthy amalgamation, and not an absorption or an undue repression."[31]

The phrase "Africanization of Islam" appears to have first been used by Nehemiah Levtzion in writing about ancient Ghana and Mali when he opined, "the Islamization of Africa was accompanied by the Africanization of

Islam."[32] Levtzion was describing the parallel process of indigenization that went along with the spread of Islam in sub-Saharan Africa. David Robinson subsequently used this phrase as the title of a chapter in his *Muslim Societies in African History*. In this book, Robinson explains Muslim African use of architecture, calligraphy, amulets, and visual culture in different parts of the African continent.[33]

John Hunwick, a longtime specialist on the history of Islam in Africa, commenting on Afro-Arab relations in the twentieth century, credits Blyden as one of the pioneers in the fostering of relationships between Africans south of the Sahara and Arab Africans to the north.[34] This acknowledgment makes sense because Blyden was one of the early scholars to begin the systematic study of the origins, nature, and practice of Islam among Muslim Africans. Long before current African historians studied the Africanization of Islam in West Africa, Blyden had begun an examination of the African cultural underpinnings of Islam in the region. Thus, while Blyden did not coin the term *Africanization*, he certainly was the first scholar to begin a systemized study of Islam as practiced in Africa. He provides fresh insights into the religion even as he used it for his Pan-African "propaganda machine." Blyden's contribution to the systematic study of Islam includes his analyses of Arabic and African languages and literature, Muslim African historiography, Islam and Islamic scholarship in Africa, and English/Arab education, as well as his cultural immersion in African Muslim communities.

Mukhtar Abd-al-Kerim Blyden and the Systematic Study of Islam in Africa

In his zeal to study Islamic African societies, Blyden began with Arabic and then turned to Fula/Pulaar. However, prior to his study of Arabic, he was familiar with languages in Oriental scholarship: Latin, Greek, and Hebrew. With his acquisition of Arabic, Blyden became a full-fledged Black Orientalist who could employ an Africa-centered Orientalist discourse to illuminate

African histories and cultures. Because Blyden received his early education while living in Liberia, in West Africa, he balanced his Orientalist training with his day-to-day experiences within Muslim African societies. His Orientalist discourse and orientation to Africa was therefore fundamentally different from that of his Orientalist colleagues—Christian, European, and African diasporan. Blyden's Africa-centered Orientalism was shaped by his travels and stays in Islamic centers of learning in Egypt, Syria, and Kankan, the famous Islamic city of West Africa. Moreover, he was influenced during his tenure at Liberia College, where he institutionalized the study of Arabic and correspondingly invited African clerics to study and translate Islamic documents. It was as a result of these actions that African Muslims gave Blyden the sobriquet *Mukhtar*—the chosen one.

Ever the consummate scholar and linguist, Blyden began his Islamic journey by taking a linguistic pilgrimage to the Syrian Protestant College in Beirut, Syria, in 1866. The same year, he traveled through Egypt and Jerusalem.[35] Blyden, already minimally familiar with Arabic, explained his purpose in going to Syria:

> The other day, while on a visit to a native town, I met a couple of itinerant Mohammedan priests, with their books and papers. They could not speak a word of English. I wrote an Arabic passage from the Koran from memory. They read it and raised their hands in astonishment that I should know anything of the language. They then showed me their papers, but I was not sufficiently acquainted with the language to read them. But I hope by perseverance to be able to learn that and several other native languages.[36]

Evidently, this encounter with Muslim clerics in the interior of Liberia was a critical moment in his quest for Arabic fluency and knowledge of Islam. The meeting is also evidence of Muslim clerics' desire to spread Islam in the Atlantic belt of the Greater Senegambia region of West Africa. At this time, Blyden already spoke Spanish and Dutch, but likewise was interested in teaching Arabic at Liberia College. He, therefore, set aboard Captain Thomas

Milbourne's screw steamer the *Pioneer* on May 11, 1866, en route to Syria to study Arabic.[37] On July 16, Blyden arrived in the port of Beirut and traveled twelve miles inland to the Syrian Protestant College, in Abieh, on July 19.[38]

In 1867, Blyden returned from his studies to teach Arabic at Liberia College. Later on in 1872, while serving variously as a linguist at Fourah Bay College and as agent for the colonial government of Sierra Leone, Blyden helped champion the creation of an Arabic Translation Bureau.[39] He even proposed sending two young translators to the Syrian Protestant College where he himself had studied.[40] He hired two translators, Momodou Wakka and Mohammed Sanusi, who would later be hired into the service of the British colonial government on Blyden's recommendation.[41]

Sanusi first met Blyden on one of his visits to Fulahtown, Sierra Leone. According to Blyden, Sanusi, who was an Aku (Yoruba) man, had been educated at Futah Jallon by a Fula teacher. Sanusi made a great impression on Blyden when he expressed interest in Arabic translations of the New Testament.[42] When Blyden met Sanusi, the latter was already literate in Arabic and English. To Blyden, he was an example of how the Christian clergy were ignorant of the intellectual abilities of African Muslims. It was Sanusi and one Suleiman, an *Imani Ratib*, who actually set up a study plan for him to learn Fula. In addition, Sanusi helped with his translation of African-language texts on Islam.[43] In addition to his government appointment as a linguist, Sanusi, now Blyden's mentee, taught Arabic at Fourah Bay College and, because of his translation skills, became an important medium of exchange between West African Muslims and the British Muslim community of Liverpool, who published the *Crescent* and *Islamic World*.[44]

Drawing from both his Orientalist training in the Middle East and the African oral traditions, Blyden additionally took his time to describe the literary character of the Qur'an and how Africans put its prosaic qualities to oral use. As a result, Blyden not only contextualized the literacy of African Muslims for his readers but correspondingly documented their historical writing traditions and their production of oral and textual communities embedded in African society. For example, he offers the following remarks on Islamic education under the leadership of learned West African ulemas, whom he describes as capable of reproducing from memory any chapter of the Qur'an:

> First they [students] are taught the letters and vowel marks, then they are taught to read the text, without receiving any insight into its meaning. When they can read fluently they are taught the meaning of the words which they commit to memory; after which they are instructed in what they call the "Jaleleyn," a running commentary on the Koran. While learning the Jaleleyn they have side studies assigned them in Arabic manuscripts, containing the mystical traditions, the acts of Mohamed, the duties of fasting, prayer, alms, corporal purification, etc. Young men who intend to be enrolled among the Ulemas take up history and chronology.[45]

Blyden had clearly taken important steps in his study of Islam. First, through travel and formal studies, he became literate in Arabic, adding it to his existing repertoire of Oriental and European languages. Second, he began to study some of the African languages, such as Fula, spoken in the Upper Guinea region. The latter not only set him apart from other Oriental scholars, but also showed his sustained ethnographic study and interaction among African Muslim individuals, communities, and centers of learning, which prepared him for the Africa-centered Orientalist discourse that he would profess in his various writings on African Islam.

In addition, Blyden spearheaded the institutionalization of the study of Islam not only by consistently engaging or befriending Muslim clerics, but by making them scholars-in-residence at Fourah Bay College and adding Arabic to the curriculum of the college. Blyden's institutionalization efforts included the establishment of an Arabic Translation Bureau for the colonial government of Sierra Leone. He began to collect, archive, and translate indigenous African texts, while providing extensive commentary on the Africanized nature of the texts. He described how they were written through the use of African languages, African orality, and the Arabic written tradition.

These texts later became known as Ajami texts. Lastly, he made it a point to offer a description of the existing processes of instruction and education set up by the region's Muslim intellectuals. This systematic engagement was the bedrock on which he developed a canon of scholarly work on African Islam while engaging with other scholars of Islam.

Scholarship on Islam and Islamic Africa

Blyden debated most of his contemporaries' writings on classical studies, Islam as religion, and Islam as practiced in Africa as well as Oriental culture. Notably, these scholars included R. Bosworth Smith, Trinity College, Oxford; Syed Ameer Ali Moulivi, Inner Temple, London; J. Addison Alexander, Princeton University; Professor Draper, New York University; Monier Williams, the Boden Professor of Sanskrit at Oxford; and Bishop Crowther of Nigeria.[46] Blyden was without a doubt conversant with the existing body of scholarship on Islam, as he was on Christianity. He used his knowledge of West African Muslim communities to contest Herbert Spencer's views on African intellectual and organizational abilities. He was quick to point out in his review of Smith's work on Islam that many Muslim West African communities were self-reliant, arguing that Islam had transformed rather than totally changed indigenous African practices.[47] Blyden's paramount involvement, as far as Islam was concerned, was less with Oriental Islam and more with Islamic Africa. In his contribution to the scholarly discourse on West African Islam between 1871 and 1905, Blyden wrote at least five articles. These include "Mohammedanism in Western Africa," "Mohammedanism and the Negro Race," "Islam and Race Distinctions," and "The Mohammedans of Nigritia."[48] He also wrote "Islam in the Western Soudan" and "The Koran in Africa."[49]

The central theme of Blyden's writings is the indigenous character of Islam in Africa or Africanized Islam. He argues that, unlike Christianity, Islam did not have a harmful effect on Africans. Rather, in many cases, Islam helped maintain some African practices, particularly kinship and marriage systems such as polygamy. Each article reveals various aspects of his understanding of the African nature of Islam in West Africa. In 1869, after Blyden went on a learning expedition to Boporo, he produced "Mohammedanism in Western Africa," in which he explains Muslim African literacy. He describes Muslim Africans at "Boporo, Misadu, Medina, and Kankan" as showing great appreciation for the poetic qualities of the Koran. In addition, he explains the practice of Islam in various Muslim African cities he visited.[50] Emphasizing his theme on the Africanization of Islam, Blyden explains the collective or communal nature of the African societies he visited. He argues that Islam had not been forced on Africans. Rather, it had fostered sobriety or alcoholic abstinence and a sense of unity among various ethnic groups, whether they were "Jalof, Foulah or Mandingo."[51]

In "Mohammedanism and the Negro Race," Blyden reckons that Islam arrived in Africa in three different historical periods and routes: "from Egypt through Nubia, to Bornu and Hausa; another, from Abyssinia [Sudanic Africa] to Yoruba and Ashante; the third, from the Barbary States across the desert to Timbuktu."[52] He subsequently details how West Africa had historically been connected to the Mediterranean and European worlds through trade across the Sahara and along the various routes he had identified.[53] In the same article, he elaborates on how Islam arrived in North Africa and spread into West Africa.[54] In addition, he describes the "Hausas, Foulahs, Mandigoes, Soosoos, Akus" as having a somewhat Pan-Islamic cultural federation because they not only mingled and worshipped together but similarly were "united by a common religious sentiment, [and] by a common antagonism to paganism."[55] In addition, he describes for the first time the ways in which Africans produced amulets and charms based on their African approach to Islamic "art of healing, and as a wonderful storehouse of charms and divining power protecting them from danger and foretelling events." Blyden describes these amulets as "passages from the Koran, written on slips of paper and enclosed in leather cases about two-three inches square—after the manner of the Jewish phylactery—and worn around the neck or wrist. The passages usually written are the last two passages of the

Koran, known as the 'Chapters of Refuge.'" Blyden goes on to describe how African Muslims "wear constantly about their person's certain texts from the Koran called Ayat-el-hifz, verse of protection or preservation, which are supposed to keep away every species of misfortune."[56] As noted earlier, these early descriptions of Africans' use of Islamic amulets and calligraphy have been recently expanded on in the work of David Robinson and others.[57]

In addition to these descriptions, Blyden wrote about Islamic manuscripts composed by Africans. Here, the purpose was not only to focus on West African jihadist figures of the nineteenth century such as Al Hajj Omaru of Futah Toro but also to counter the negative prevailing view of Africans as intellectually deficient.[58] Blyden provides a brief biography on Al Hajj Umar plus other Black pioneers of Islam, such as Bilal, the famous muezzin. In describing the latter, he writes that "the eloquent Azan or 'Call to Prayer', which to this day summons at the same hours millions of the human race to their devotions, was first uttered by a Negro, Bilal by name, whom Mohammed, in obedience to a dream, appointed the first Muezzin or Crier."[59]

Blyden capped these publications with a contribution to an 1871 book, *The People of Africa: A Series of Papers on Their Character, Conditions and Future*.[60] It is reputed that of the ten chapters of the book, seven were written by Blyden, and another was his English translation of an Arabic letter written by the king of Musardu to the president of Liberia.[61] Blyden's scholarship was more than that of a roaming ethnographer; he contributed original insights into the nature and practice of Islam in West Africa that countered previous descriptions or conceptions. This pioneering scholarship is evidenced in his careful description of Muslim African historiography.

Muslim African Historiography

Ajami texts are the corpus of writing produced by African Muslim clerics and intellectuals in African languages but utilizing an altered (Africanized) Arabic script. This body of Ajami literature covers translations of Arabic documents, religious tracts, Islamic jurisprudence, trade and administrative records, documentation of hitherto oral/cultural histories, and personal and diplomatic correspondence as well as pharmacopeia formulas.[62] *The Meanings of Timbuktu* is a contemporary book that includes contributions from recognized and long-standing researchers of Islam in Africa. These include Souleymane Bachir Diagne, John Hunwick, Paulo F. de Moraes Farias, Mohammed Ould Yobba, Murray Last, and Beverly Mack. It is, therefore, astonishing that in his contribution to the volume, Moulaye Hassane writes that "although the script of the Holy Qur'an has played such an important role in the transcription of languages of certain Islamized African peoples, this field has aroused little interest among researchers—because of a lack of sources."[63]

This stance is curious because Blyden had, over a century and a half earlier, set the stage for researchers through his seminal contribution to the study of Islam in Africa. He anticipated various commentaries on the textual, poetic, phonetic, syntactic, and other linguistic qualities of Ajami historiography. Blyden writes of an instance when he is advised by his Muslim acquaintances to use the Arabic script in his translation of the Gospel of Matthew into Fula and acknowledges that "the Roman letters will never prevail or be read in Mohammedan Africa."[64] Blyden subsequently recognized the distinctive way in which West Africans spoke Arabic and utilized it for written purposes. He writes:

> Among the Moslems of West Africa, there are some peculiarities in the sounds of the letters. The fourth letter of the alphabet is generally pronounced like *s*; the seventh like the simple *k*; the ninth like *j* in jug; *seen* and *sheen* have both the sound of *s*. The fifteenth letter is sounded like *l*; the nineteenth, whose guttural sound is so difficult for western organs, is sounded like *k*; the twenty-first like *g* hard.[65]

In "Mohammedanism in Western Africa," Blyden informs us of the various manuscripts and *tarikhs* (books/histories) that were being produced in

Boporo, Misadu, and Kankan, one of which was the *Makamat of Hariri*. Blyden, in a comparative examination, describes the texts produced in Kankan and the other named sites as:

> better written, and . . . of a much more edifying character, than those we have seen from the Gambia and that region of the country. Some of the latter consisting of childish legends and superstitious details are often curious philologically, being mixtures of Arabic and the vernacular dialect.[66]

Some of his descriptions of the texts, admittedly, are condescending. Nonetheless, it shows that Blyden had a bias for the Muslim societies he was familiar with over those he was minimally conversant with, even as he expertly described the nature of the Ajami texts.

Additionally, Blyden provides some details on the literary careers of some of the Ajami writers. He describes Sheikh Al-Hajj Omaru of Futah Toro as an extraordinary personality who "influenced the history of the country between Timbuktu and the West coast" through his complex warrior, prophetic, and literary career. Blyden opines that Sheik Omaru wrote works of prose and poetry and that these "poems are recited and sung in Mohammedan town and village, from Foulah-town in Sierra Leone, to Kano . . . for his many extraordinary deeds, and see his successful enterprises, literary and military proofs of divine guidance."[67] In sum, Blyden describes the literary nature of these *kitabs* (writings) and, in the process, foresaw contemporary discussion on the existence of a written tradition in West Africa. This tradition is the intellectual heritage of Muslim African civilizations in West Africa. He understood that a history of Africa without an account of the history of Islamic knowledge (philosophy, history, language) is insufficient history.

Institutionalization

In addition to establishing the language bureau in Sierra Leone and creating various translation and language-study networks, when Blyden returned to Liberia from his travels to the Middle East, he began to champion female education and an Arabic curriculum at Liberia College. He did this by befriending and involving several Muslim traders and priests from the interior of Liberia. He is believed to have received several visitors from Futa Jallon and Kankan and made several trips to the interior, going to places like Vonsua, Boporo, and Musardu.[68] Blyden wrote in the spring of 1868 that "Mandigoes, who visit me from time to time, express strong desire to have schools established among them, that they might learn the English language." In October of the same year, another group of people from the Vey ethnic group called on Blyden to assist them in acquiring copies of the Bible that had been translated into their language by Mr. Koelle, a German missionary.[69]

By 1869, Arabic was being offered at Liberia College, and students were examined in Arabic and called on to read an "elegant manuscript Koran, written at Boporo, seventy-five miles interior from Monrovia, by learned Mandigoes."[70] External examiners from Kankan were furthermore employed to offer senior examinations on the "Seventh Makamat, and portions of the Koran."[71] Blyden's ability to bring scholars from Kankan, an important African Islamic learning city, perhaps second only to Timbuktu, shows his important contribution to the pedagogy and study of Arabic and Islam.[72]

Later in 1891, he was influential in convincing the colonial government of Sierra Leone under the leadership of Governor Hay to establish an Anglo-Muslim school named Madrasa Harunia, where Islam and Arabic were combined with English and science lessons. Eventually Blyden, for all his hard work, was appointed the director of Mohammedan education in Sierra Leone as part of efforts to combine Islamic education with English curricula. It was on this basis that William Henry Abdullah Quilliam, the British Muslim solicitor and confidant of the sultan of Turkey, recommended

Blyden to the sultan, who decided to award him the Imperial Order of the Medjidieh.[73] The award is an affirmation of Blyden's efforts to institutionalize the academic study of Arabic and Islam into existing West African educational systems.

Blyden pioneered "modern" Islamic, or English/Arabic, schools in West Africa through his conscious cultivation of Arabic study networks and translation agencies. The fact that these schools not only were replicated and expanded but still exist in West Africa is a testament to his visionary leadership as not just a theoretician but a practical man of affairs with adequate, if not great, organizing ability.[74]

Cultural Immersion

Blyden's study of Islam in West Africa was not limited to examining texts and collecting data or documents. In other words, Blyden wrote from experience; he visited and lived with Muslims. His studies and writing built on the social capital that he earned with the Muslim communities he encountered and studied. Blyden is reported to have often received Muslim traders at home, some of whom spent several days in his company. One Muslim priest, who arrived in Monrovia after about an eighteen-day walk from Futa with a dozen pupils, spent three days reading Arabic works at Liberia College and enjoying his hospitality. The warm welcome he received from Blyden created a "favorable impression on him and his followers," and he responded in the affirmative for establishing Muslim/English schools in Futa. Another Muslim priest who arrived from Kankan likewise spent a few days in Blyden's house holding conversations with him in Arabic.[75]

With this reputation among Muslim clerics, Blyden was welcomed in many Muslim African communities. The people of Fulah town were known

MAP 3 (*opposite*). Blyden's Senegambian travels. This map shows Blyden's travel route into the interior communities of the Senegambian region, 1872.

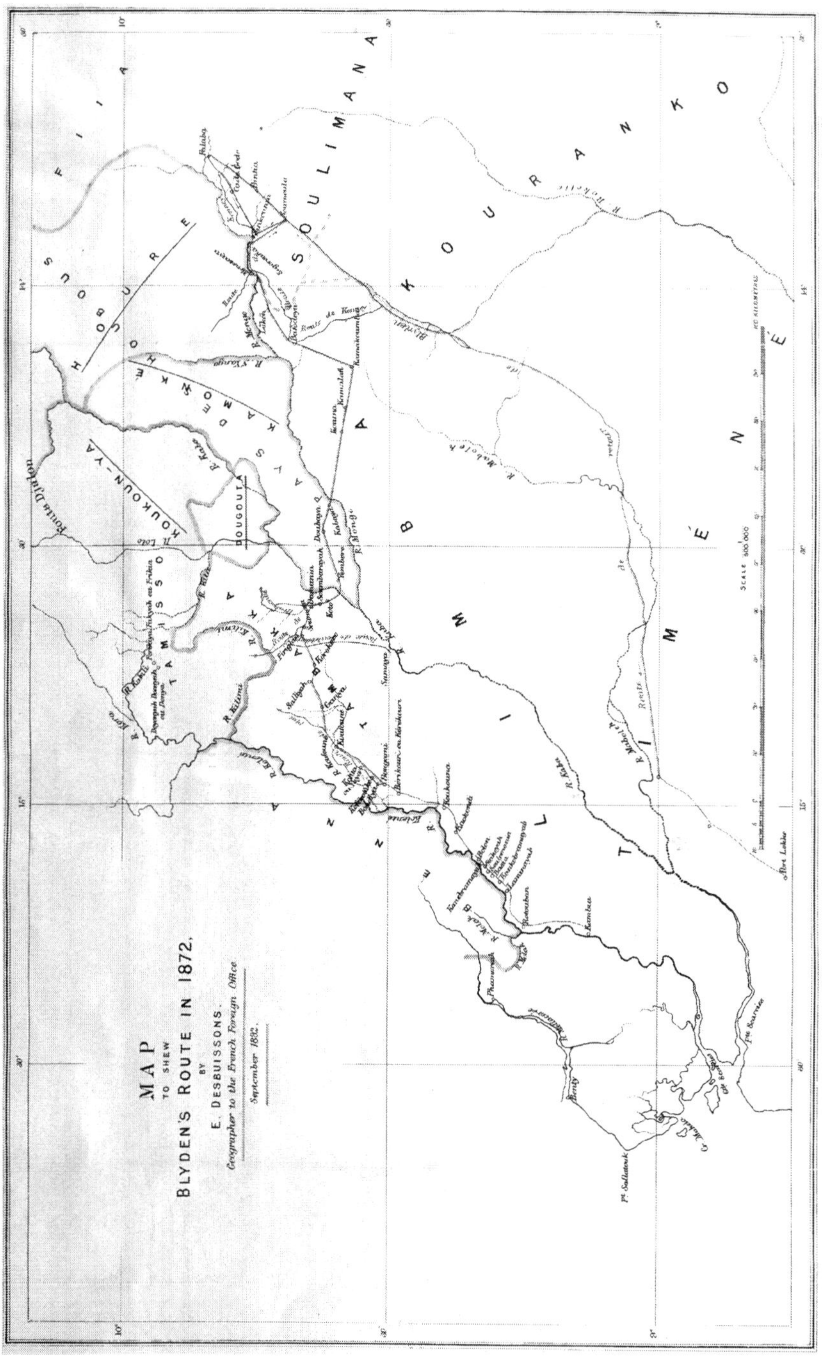

NATIONAL ARCHIVES, KEW GARDEN, UNITED KINGDOM

to provide for his upkeep. On one occasion, he received a "large basket of yams, and a dozen fowls" from Fulah town's "principal men."[76] But it was not just food; the Muslim communities truly believed that "one of their race [African] had been permitted by the Almighty to visit the Holy Land and to return and tell them all about it in the Arabic language."[77] For this reason, they presented Blyden with some of the best primary documents for his scholarly work. During his second visit to Vonsua, five miles north of St. Paul's River near Monrovia, Blyden wrote of receiving a drawing of the "plan of the temple of Mecca with a description in Arabic" from a Mandingo priest, which Blyden subsequently sent for publication.[78]

Blyden was furthermore an important diplomat, the central conduit of communication between both the governments of Liberia and Sierra Leone and the inland Muslim communities. He helped the Liberian government settle boundary disputes and was called upon by the governor in chief of the British West African Settlements, Sir Arthur Kennedy, to welcome "Fulah Mohammedans from the country about Futah and Sego" and to translate their communication with the governor in Arabic.[79] With diplomatic support from the governments of Liberia and Sierra Leone, as well as the goodwill of the Muslim communities, Blyden traveled to West African Islamic centers of learning and held conferences with leading scholars. He collected manuscripts on their societies, their distinctive practice of Islam, and reflective writings for translation.

Blyden also embarked on several exploratory expeditions on behalf of the governments of Liberia and Sierra Leone—traveling to places like Timbo, Falaba, and Boporo.[80] On his visit to Boporo, for example, Blyden reported being received kindly by the king of this region, who feted the visiting delegation and presented his children and those of his brother as a nucleus of students for any future schools.[81] Some of Blyden's travel accounts are contained in his article titled "The Country East of Liberia; Monrovia to Boporo."[82]

It is evident from Blyden's numerous reports to various colonial administrators in Sierra Leone that he was seeking to intervene in the imposition of formal colonial systems in the societies he visited. Blyden saw what was inevitable and wanted to influence which European overlord was going to succeed—and, indeed, there were certainly differences between the British, French, German, and Belgians. It seems from his letters that Blyden had made his bed with the British. For example, in his letter to Governor Kendall, dated February 1, 1872, he writes about the political institutions and affluence of Garyah, one of the towns he visited on his way to the city of Yembereh.[83] Blyden notes that Garyah is a moderate town of a thousand people presided over by a Muslim chief, Seyyu Surri. He describes Garyah's rich prairie, patches of forest, and good soil, as well as local iron smelting and the great abundance of agricultural products like groundnuts, guinea corn, rice, potatoes, guavas papaws, and more. Blyden recommended the construction of a railroad from Kambia to Falaba that passed through Garyah.[84]

Blyden goes on to describe Falaba as the "emporium" of trade from the interior to Freetown, and "Billeh, a sort of University town—the Oxford of this region" and Kambia as a great commercial center of about three thousand persons, where one meets Foulahs, Mandigoes, Susus, Seraculis, and Temnes.[85] Thus, although Blyden curiously advocated European colonization of certain territories in Africa, he had a different understanding of how such colonization should take place—through trade, infrastructural development, and intellectual engagement. Blyden's symbiotic relationship with Muslim communities in West Africa was such that in 1883, when a new stone mosque named Jami Us-Salam was opened in Fulah town, Sierra Leone, the clerics made sure to offer special prayers for Blyden.[86]

Perhaps one of the most important things to come out of Blyden's cultural immersion, besides the systematic study of the history of Islam and the general history of the Greater Senegambia region, is his documentation of resistance to domestic slavery in the region. His proficiency is evinced in his personal accounts of Islamic slave rebellions—that of the Hubbu, led by the Muslim cleric Mamadu Juhe, and his son Abal, against the Futa Jallon state in the 1850s as well as the Bilali rebellion (ca. 1838–1872), led by Bilali, the son of Alimami Namina Sheka Dumbuya (a deceased king) and his slave concubine wife.[87]

Blyden initially described the Hubbu uprising as "renegade Foulahs in rebellion against the King of Timbo."[88] He however later explained in more detail how Islamic ideas of freedom and social equality were used by the so-called renegade Fulas to establish independent Islamic communities that were separated from those ruled by the Futa Jallon's aristocracy. Blyden avers that the "Hooboos or Hubus" were so called because in separating themselves and forming new communities, "they chanted a word from the Koran in which the word *Hubu* appears twice. The verse says: '*Nuhibu* Rusul Allahi *huban* Wahidan,' meaning 'Those possessed of the love of God's messenger.'"[89]

In the case of the Bilali revolt, Blyden shows how the transatlantic slave trade transformed both domestic and Islamic conventions on servitude. According to David Skinner, Bilali's father, Alimami Dumbuya, raised Bilali and his maternal siblings as free children and, by domestic and Islamic convention, promised freedom on the death of their father. On the death of Alimami Dumbuya, however, his would-be successor, Alimami Mummineh, chose to treat Bilali and his family as property—to be shared as part of his royal inheritance. Bilali, his family, and other servile followers fled in 1838 and settled in Laminyah, an independent community at Tonko Limba. Laminyah, led by Bilali with support from his Limba hosts, became a safe haven for fugitive slaves. Alimami Mummineh and other slaveholding elite sought unsuccessfully to curb the expansion of Bilali's fiefdom, resulting in widespread war and truncation of Atlantic trade.[90]

Again, it was Blyden's personal intervention in the colonial scheme that gradually brought the war to an end. On the one hand, during his Falaba expedition, Blyden impressed upon Alimami Mummineh that, in order to be treated fairly by the colonial government of Sierra Leone, he must abandon the proslavery policy he had pursued for thirty years. The alimami subsequently agreed to meet with Bilali and government officials at Kambia to bring an end to the war.[91] On the other hand, Blyden managed to convince the colonial government that the war between Bilali and Alimami

Mummineh was injurious to its trade and abolitionist ideology, consequently forcing it to intervene militarily and through negotiation.[92]

Conclusion

From these experiences of cultural immersion in African Muslim communities, Blyden concluded that Islam, more than Christianity, was suitable to African dignity—his African restoration project that was to cultivate the African Personality. He disliked the fact that European Christian missionaries tried to sow discord between African Christians and Muslims.[93] It is important to note that Blyden remained a Christian to the end. As late as 1872 Blyden was committed to obtaining victory "in the cause of the Master [Jesus]."[94] His missionary intentions in the *Arabic Bible in the Soudan* make this very clear for those who assume he was a crypto-Muslim. More importantly, however, is that, Blyden's study of Islam and subsequent elevation of it above European Christianity, reflects an often glossed over evolutionary stage in his Afropublican intellectual career. Early in his career (in the 1860s), Blyden wrote essays like "Liberia—the Foundation of an Empire" and "The Call of Providence to the Descendants of Africa in America," which reflect a belief that an African renaissance was to come from the Americas, particularly from Black folk in the African Atlantic diaspora.[95] Following Blyden's study of the Africanization of Islam (1870s–1880s), however, he began to strike a different tone. In a series of essays published after 1885, Blyden notes how "the nation now being reared in Africa by returning exiles from this country (United States) will not be a reproduction of the American. The restoration of the Negro to the land of his fathers will be the restoration of a race to its original integrity." Other statements read, "Time Not Ripe for Negro Exodus."[96] This latter period of Blyden's career, which follows his practical engagement with Africanized Islam, was a prelude to his immersion in African culture, which in turn, culminated in publication of his final work, *African Life and Customs*, in 1908.

This book, written a few years before his death in 1912, was an amalgamation of Blyden's writings about African social systems, cultures, family traditions, and economic structure. These essays had been earlier serialized in the *Sierra Leone Weekly News*. The significance of his journey through various intellectual transformations to this final work has been lost on various treatments of Blyden's intellectual career. Indeed, Blyden's final foray and scholarly transformation in his understanding of African society are derived from his penultimate rational transformation as a result of his encounter with Islam—Africanized Islam. His studious encounter with Africanized Islam allowed him to appreciate how Africans domesticated foreign influence, and included seeing traditional African societies from a different perspective. Africanized Islam was, therefore, the analytic lens through which he valorized traditional African societies. Blyden's engagement with Africanized Islam was also the basis for his advocating the establishment of Africanized Christian churches, which inspired the new Ethiopianist movement throughout West Africa, but specifically in Sierra Leone, Ghana, Nigeria, and Liberia.

In other words, Blyden's study of Africanized Islam afforded him the opportunity to truly understand African social institutions, cultures, and traditions. In "The Return of the Exiles and the West African Church" (1891),[97] for example, he defends the incorporation of African traditions in West African Christian practice by writing a scathing critique of the "godfather" of European Christianity:

> Consider the conditions under which Europe received the Gospel. Had the hard conditions now imposed on African Chiefs been required of European sovereigns and chiefs, Christianity might never have been permanently established on the west of the Bosporus. The Christian Emperor, Constantine, was half a pagan to the end. He erected in the new capital, Constantinople, a statue of himself. At the base of this statue, it is said he placed a fragment of what he believed to be the true Cross. In the same place, he deposited the palladium, the cherished relic of Pagan Rome, which Aeneas was said

> to have rescued from the flames of Troy, and which Constantine himself stealthily removed to his new capital. This was his fetish, brought over from heathenism. . . . Constantine was at one and the same moment the summoner of the Nicene Council, and the chief priest of heathenism. At one moment he was preaching sermons to his courtiers, and discussing dogmas with his bishops; at the next, he was issuing orders for the regulation of some Pagan ritual.[98]

It was the sort of critique that Blyden had earlier advanced against African customs. At this moment of his intellectual journey, however, he was more accommodating and perhaps accepting of the integrity of African religion, tradition, and culture. Africanized Islam provided him the gateway to understanding African life and customs. Blyden recognized that there was a distinct particularity with which traditional African societies experienced the world, and this needed to be cultivated and nurtured for the benefit of the world.

Blyden's specific and general contributions to the study of Islam demonstrate that through Islam he arrived at a more sophisticated understanding of African humanity and culture. His learned appreciation of the process by which Africans blended Arabic written culture, Islamic religion, and Oriental culture with African languages, African orality, and extant African practices showed him how long and dynamic African history had been. Blyden saw something different from what he had learned about Africa as a young boy living in the Caribbean and in the United States. Residual influences of the Back-to-Africa movement in the United States were gradually dispelled through his encounter with African Muslims.

Blyden's Africa-centered Orientalist discourse, while still Pan-African, had a different tone from the one he previously engaged in with Atlantic interlocutors. He previously thought African salvation should or would come from their African brethren in the diaspora. His new knowledge about African transformation through Africans' agency and autonomy to mix and blend incoming Arabic and Mediterranean cultures with their own social, political, cultural, and economic institutions, however, steered him to look within Africa for its regeneration. On this basis, Blyden engaged Atlantic, Oriental, and European intellectuals alike on the status of Africans in global modernity. His works were not only received and debated in black cosmopolitan circuits in Africa and the Americas; they were read in Victorian England and Oriental cities such as Damascus, Beirut, and Constantinople.

This transformation reveals two things about his intellectual career. First, at the time of his passing, Blyden had a heightened appreciation of African societies than when he first arrived in Liberia, where as a teenager he joined the Americo-Liberian militia in not only bearing arms against the indigenous groups of Liberia, but also denigrating their ways of life. Second, by the end of his career, Blyden—influenced by various adaptations to African life—had become an advocate for indigenous groups in both Sierra Leone and Liberia. He correspondingly inspired an alternate form of the Ethiopianism. No longer part of the Back-to-Africa movement, with its emphasis on the African diaspora providentially helping civilize and Christianize their "native" brethren, Blyden, through his immersion in Africanized Islam, believed that civilizing and Christianizing should come from within Africa and not from without. By the time of his passing, accordingly, while Blyden was not a Muslim convert, Africanized Islam had become central, if not essential, to his thinking on diverse fields of study about Africa.

Finally, while it is a worthwhile intellectual pursuit to treat all of Blyden's writings collectively in order to establish the main tenets of his ideas, their consistency, and contributions to African history and philosophy, it is more revealing to trace the epic transformations, the exact moments of change, and the causes for modifications in Blyden's assessments on various subjects. Rather than simply attribute all of his reasoning to "race," the idea of Providence, or Victorian ideas, it is important to trace how Blyden abandoned, adapted, and transformed his thinking on these subjects as they relate to Africa and African-descended peoples.

Future academic investigation of Blyden's life and intellectual work will be more fruitful if his various publications are contextualized in the historical periods in which they were written and if the purposes for which they were written are made clearer. Thus, Blyden's evolving study of Islam would lead him to advocate for the Africanization of the Christian church in West Africa. Blyden's views on Islam and Race had flaws and contradictions. Some flaws, such as his understanding of race and miscegenation as well as a nonthreatening Islamic proselytization, are not resolved, but other contradictions are resolved in his book *African Life and Customs*. He subsequently used his intellectual sway in West Africa to inspire African-centered missiology and the emergence of indigenous West African churches, as well as to inspire succeeding generations of West African elite in Nigeria, Gambia, Ghana, Sierra Leone, and Liberia.

Dr. Edward Blyden, They Know Your Name: Blyden and West African Ethiopianism

Let us do away with the sentiment of Race. Let us do away with our African Personality and be lost, if possible, in another Race.

—Edward Blyden, quoted in the *Sierra Leone Times*, May 27, 1893

Edward Blyden was undoubtedly popular within several spheres of black intellectual life across the Atlantic world. His reputation was, however, not restricted to urban and cosmopolitan or elitist black publics. In fact, Blyden was so popular a figure in the rural American South that he received letters through the ACS from black southerners seeking relocation to Liberia, West Africa. Blyden's reputation and integrity suffered a huge dent, however, when he was arrested while traveling through central and eastern Arkansas promoting emigration to Africa. Why was Blyden popular in the rural South? Why were blacks in the South writing to him with desires of emigrating to Africa? Answers to these questions are extremely helpful for our understanding of the historical circumstance and reasons why Blyden was detained for organizing emigration clubs in the United States but also help us appreciate why Blyden was the most influential black intellectual of the nineteenth and early twentieth centuries. He was such a prominent figure that during a visit to Lagos, an Afro-Brazilian repatriate who was a mechanic, produced a lantern in honor of Blyden as a testament to black ingenuity. This lantern was marked with the inscription, "Africa's destiny lay hid in night, God said 'let Blyden be' and all was light."[1]

In the aftermath of the early to mid-nineteenth-century disagreements between black and white colonization societies, Blyden, along with Henry McNeal Turner and Alexander Crummel were the only blacks to have any institutional affiliation with the white-led ACS.[2] He was also self-evidently a successful migrant, having emigrated to Liberia in 1851, and emerged as an Afropublican intellectual. From Liberia, Blyden championed emigration to West Africa among the black populations of the Caribbean and the United States. By 1891, when Blyden arrived in the United States, he and Alexander Crummell had been appointed commissioner for colonization by the Liberian government. The commissioners were given the mandate to travel to the United States "to present to the Colored people there, and elsewhere [Caribbean], the claims and advantages of Liberia, and to invite them to come over and help build up a Negro nationality."[3]

Thus, between May 14 and November 22, 1862, Blyden traveled through several global black circuits beginning in North America. He began in the United States, making stops in New York, Philadelphia, Harrisburg, Boston, and Baltimore. From New York, he reportedly traveled "as far south as Washington [DC], and as far north as Portland, Maine, where he addressed the Maine Colonization Society.[4] Blyden subsequently traveled to Halifax and Windsor, Nova Scotia, and St. John's, New Brunswick, all in Canada.

From New York, Blyden also took the time to visit his roots in St. Thomas as well as Barbados in the Caribbean. Throughout his journey, Blyden was given the opportunity to preach in historic black churches like the Shiloh Presbyterian Church in Raleigh, North Carolina, and the African Methodist Episcopal Church in New York, and also to speak at meetings of various colonization societies. His activities were published in the *New York Colonization Society Journal*, the *New York Observer*, the *Foreign Missionary of the Presbyterian Church*, and the *Liberia Herald*. Later, in 1874, Blyden again returned to the United States, this time mainly for academic and missionization purposes.

It was during an 1889 U.S. visit when events began to go awry. Blyden arrived at a time when white Southerners were continuing to "redeem" their losses from the American Civil War. Southern "Redemption," which followed the collapse of Reconstruction, marks the historical period that accompanied the U.S. government's official abandonment of its postwar commitment to improving the lives of black folk. The government had reneged on its protection of black citizens by removing federal troops from the South. The period was also characterized by the reemergence of white supremacy through the removal of blacks' civil and political rights. The black people in the South were economically dependent on whites. Promises of redistribution of land were never fulfilled. State legislators and federal courts conspired to institutionalize racism through disenfranchisement laws, vagrancy codes, and other discriminatory measures, as lynch mobs and Ku Klux Klan violence terrorized blacks and enforced segregation in the South.

In this atmosphere Blyden and the ACS began to receive letters from blacks in the rural South, enquiring about emigration to Liberia. The letters poured in to the secretary of the ACS, William Coppinger, and to Blyden from all over the United States, but especially from some parts of the Midwest as well as the South, including from Alabama, Arkansas, Florida, Georgia, Mississippi, and Oklahoma. The tone of the letters ranged from informational inquiries to pleas of desperation. A sampling of the letters should suffice.

From Oberlin, Ohio, the ACS received a letter thanking it "for the annual reports and pamphlets recently given by you to the library." From Dartmouth College, a Cornelius McKare wrote to Coppinger on August 22, 1891, wondering if "Psychology, Chemistry, and Physics could be taught at Liberia College as it is in . . . [U.S.] High Schools and Colleges . . . and recommended [himself] for the position."[5] D. G. Hendricks, writing from Milan, Texas, mentioned that he "noticed an article in the Houston Weekly concerning the deportation of the Negroes of the Southern States to Liberia."[6] Another Houstonian, Horace George, asked to be "furnished with the necessary information as to the present situation of Liberia, I should like to go there if I can, will be of any service, as I am only a common Blacksmith."[7] From Live Oak, Florida, William Gale assured Coppinger that a "great many of us colored people of this . . . County desire going to Liberia. Therefore apply to you for more information in regards to the matter."[8] A desperate plea came from Samantha, Alabama, where Rev. L. Davies reported, "Negroes of Alabama are faring bad." This was because whites were discouraging them with "pistols and whips . . . [not] allowing them to go to African lands." They, therefore, wanted to leave the "land of destruction and go to [a] land of pleasure and happiness where they can teach their sons and daughters to be ladies and gentlemen."[9]

Other letters came from Oklahoma and Louisiana, but few sounded as desperate as those received from about three hundred Arkansans between 1889 and 1893. From Pinnacle Springs, an anxious Arkansan wrote, "why did the executive committee not answer my application? Wants to go to Liberia." John Allington, another would-be applicant, was ready to go as soon as he could sell his place. A despondent J. J. Gary asked Coppinger, "when will I go, when can I go. Would you please answer me? Please let me go this October 1891, please Mr. Coppinger. Please let me go this time without fail." Simply signing as "Moore and Wife," one correspondent wrote that "times is hard here." J. W. Williams expressed his desire to "remove to that country and [wished] to know if the ACS will assist [him] in getting there."[10]

Meanwhile, in October 1889, Blyden had arrived to tour the American South. He spent time with various black intellectuals on the Eastern Seaboard—in the Washington, DC, area, Philadelphia, and West Virginia—including old acquaintances like Dr. James A. Handy, the Rev. Francis J. Grimké, and Frederick Douglass. He spoke in crowded churches and at various educational institutions, where he emphasized Liberia's need "for surveyors, books, and instruments" as well as at McCormick Theological Seminary in Chicago, where he spoke on "the Koran in Africa."[11]

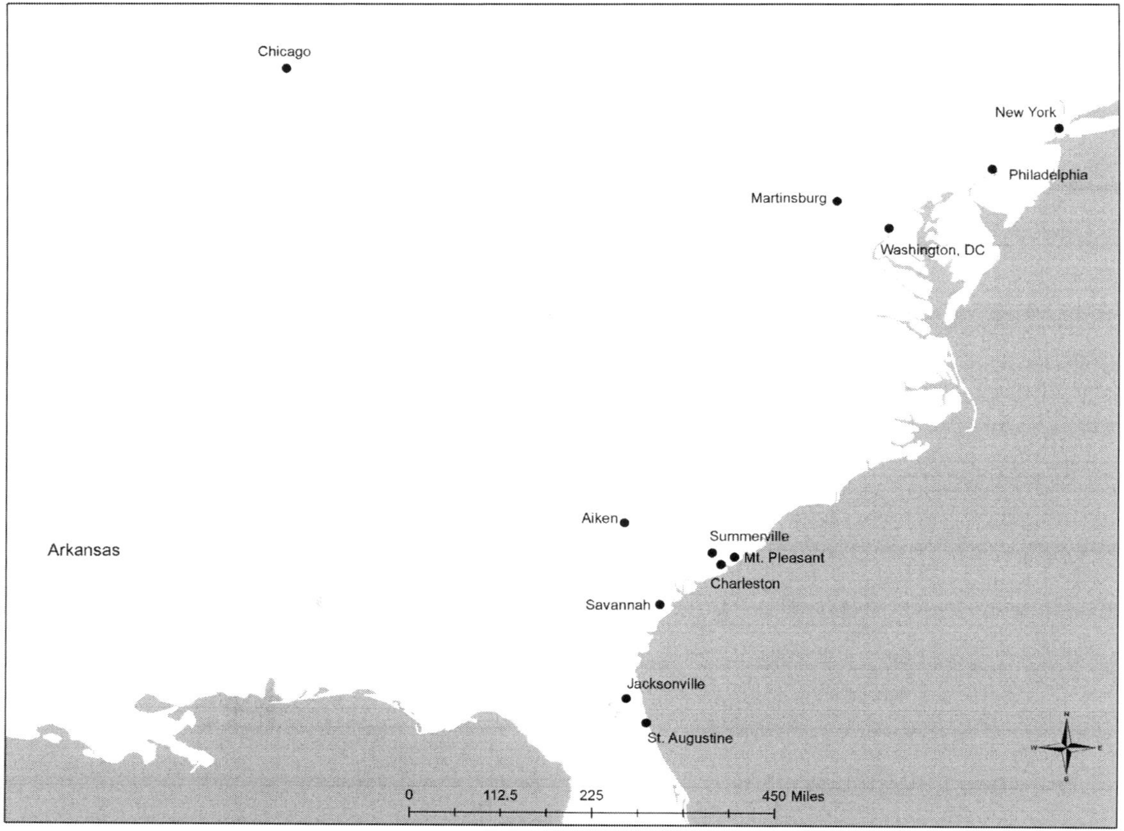

MAP BY CHARLES YORKE

MAP 4. Blyden's southern travels within the United States. This map shows the major cities Blyden travelled, stayed, or lectured at during travels from August 2, 1889, to March 5, 1890, in the United States.

Blyden began his tour of the South in late November by going to Charleston, South Carolina, where he received confirmation that "thousands of Negroes would be ready at short notice to embark for Africa." In Charleston, Blyden preached three sermons in one day to "crowded audiences" at the Morris and Zion AME churches, and "addressed Professors and students of Avery Institute." But his stay in Charleston was not without incident. Charles H. Taylor, former minister to Liberia, attacked him in the press. This allegedly caused Blyden disaffection from the mixed-race section of the population. Blyden, however, continued to enjoy widespread support among blacks in Charleston, who threw banquets and receptions in his honor, and received rave reviews in various newspapers like the *Charleston Recorder* and the *News and Courier*.

He was invited to attend and address the South Carolina Conference of the AME in Aiken, where Dr. W. B. Derrick expressed his thanks to God for meeting "this eminent scholar from our fatherland." Derrick concurred with Blyden that the AME Church and "our people in this country have a mission in Africa." Derrick's plaudits did not end here; he went on to describe Blyden as the "greatest living Negro that the world has produced today and can truly be called John the Baptist, the forerunner of a great movement."[12]

From South Carolina, Blyden traveled to Jacksonville and St. Augustine, Florida, where he did much the same things he had done in Charleston, and received a similarly warm reception from various concerned individuals and associates. Blyden subsequently returned to Washington and Philadelphia. Between July and August 1891, "Blyden" trekked through Pulaski, Lonoke, Prairie, Monroe, and Phillips counties in eastern Arkansas. When he arrived in Monroe County, however, the justice of the peace arrested him for fraud.[13]

While Blyden was touring Arkansas, letters reached Coppinger that Blyden was organizing emigration societies in the state and charging a fee of $1.50 to join the society, and $57.00 to get to Liberia. He also promised emigrants that when they arrived in Liberia, they would receive 150 acres of land plus horses.[14] This must have been perplexing to Coppinger because the Blyden he knew that arrived in the United States to tour the Southern states had written to both him and Reverend Grimké in March 1890 from aboard the RMS *Teutonic* on its way back to West Africa. Coppinger's confusion was resolved when G. W. Lowe wrote from Holy Grove, Arkansas, on August 26, 1891, that "the creature calling himself Blyden is named Meingault. He is now in Phillips County, I think carrying on his work of fraud."[15] Meingault's audacious game of impersonating the most prominent black intellectual of the nineteenth century was up. He was arrested for swindling Arkansas blacks who were desperate to leave for Africa.

West African Ethiopianism

A year following the demise of Edward Wilmot Blyden in Sierra Leone, the prophetic mission of William Wade Harris (1860–1929) began in Liberia. In 1913, claiming instructions from the Angel Gabriel and a prophetic anointing and the mantle of the prophets Elijah and John the Baptist, Harris started to walk from eastern Liberia toward the Ivory Coast. He was clad in white robes and a turban, with a bamboo cross in his right hand as his staff. He also carried a Bible and a gourd bowl for baptismal water as well as a gourd rattle for music in his left hand. Harris trudged along and preached the Christian gospel in villages, towns, and cities from Liberia to the western part of the Gold Coast, all the while baptizing and healing thousands of converts. This feat earned him sobriquets like "Premier African Evangelist," the "most extraordinary one man evangelical crusade that Africa has ever known," and "the Black Elijah of West Africa."[16] Because of his activities, attributes, and accomplishments, Harris is cited in missiology as a pioneer in West African Ethiopianism and the growth of independent African churches. The connection between Harris's activities and Edward Blyden, the true founder of West African Ethiopianism, and an advocate of the West African church are little known.

Inspired by Blyden's writing in the *Negro*, *Sierra Leone Weekly News*, and other publications beginning in the 1870s, West African Ethiopianism emerged in the late nineteenth and early twentieth centuries as a religious, cultural, and political movement. Blyden, through his various publications on the topic, advanced West African Ethiopianism as an anticolonialist critique of European Christian paternalism as well as European political and cultural hegemony. Essentially, West African Ethiopianism was a movement by Africans south of the Sahara against colonialism and European forms of Christianity. Some of its most prominent adherents include James Holy Johnson (1836–1917), Mojola Agbebi (1860–1917), and J. E. Casely Hayford (1866–1930), who in various writings and speeches advocated African liturgical practices and languages, including wearing African clothing in services, using African music in worship, and provisioning African missionaries and personnel to lead a new West African church. Inspired by Blyden, these West African intellectuals supported his push for the Africanization of the West African church and the development of what Blyden called an African Personality.

Blyden emerged as the leader of West African Ethiopianism after he witnessed the effects of the Africanization of Islam in the interior communities of Sierra Leone and Liberia. Seeking the same process for Christianity, he advocated the establishment of independent African churches that espoused African social institutions and cultures: fashion, music, dance, spirituality, and more. This Ethiopianist movement eventually led to the creation of African dress reform societies, a change from Euro-Christian names to African names, and ultimately the secession and creation of new African-led churches. These were the Native Baptist Church of Nigeria, founded in 1888, the Anglican United Native African Church, in 1891, and the United African Methodist Church, in 1917, all in Nigeria. In Cameroon, the Native Baptist Church was established in 1887. In the Gold Coast (Ghana), Blyden's mentee Rev. Mark Hayford founded the Native Baptist Church in 1898 while fostering cooperation with different independent African churches across West Africa.

Harris's twentieth-century evangelism, which led to the creation of the largest independent Ethiopianist church in West Africa, was consequently a successor to this early West African Ethiopianist movement of the nineteenth century. Indeed, Harris had more than a passing familiarity with Blyden's Ethiopianist ideas. A former schoolteacher and ex-government interpreter, he came under the direct influence of Samuel W. Seton, a Blyden confrere and indigenous (Glebo) Liberian who broke away from the Episcopal Church and formed an Independent African church he named the African Evangelical Church of Christ in 1887. Besides this, in 1892 Harris named his newly born son Edward, and by 1904 there was a "Dr. Blyden Literary Union" in Cape Palmas where Harris hailed from.[17]

Furthermore, it is suggested that Blyden, in taking the side of indigenous Liberians against the interests of the settler population in a pro-British speech, influenced Harris and others to mutiny against the Liberian government in favor of Liberia becoming a British protectorate. Even though Blyden was never found to be directly culpable, the incident revealed why Blyden curiously supported the idea of Liberia coming under British protection. Blyden believed the Liberian settlers were high-handed in their dealings with indigenous populations like Harris's Glebo, among whom he had taken refuge in 1882 and 1887 after being assailed by colleagues at Liberia College for teaching on "the principles of polygamy and Mohammedanism."[18]

Blyden also considered Liberia a failed state because the Americo-Liberian settlers were pursuing Western models that he believed would not work in Africa. Blyden's naive hope was that the British would transfer sovereignty to indigenous Africans and that both Liberia and Sierra Leone would become a part of a grander West African state.[19] As such, Harris's success and renown should be placed within the context of the West African form of Ethiopianism that Blyden helped pioneer. Also, it helps explain Blyden's own popularity and influence on West African intellectuals in Liberia, Sierra Leone, Nigeria, and the Gold Coast. Finally, both the West African Ethiopianist movement and Blyden's influence reflect the final evolution of Blyden's thinking on Africa at the time of his passing. We can trace and delineate the historical processes involved in this advancement in Blyden's thinking about Africa through the pages of the *Negro* and the *Sierra Leone Weekly News*.

Historical Context

Throughout his sojourn in Liberia, Blyden was mostly unsuccessful in convincing the Liberian government to "understand that there is an African Social and Economic System most carefully and elaborately organized, venerable, impregnable, [and] indispensable." He had more success in the British colony of Sierra Leone for a variety of historical reasons.[20] First, this was due to the liberal policy of Henry Venn, the honorary secretary of the Church Missionary Society (CMS).

The CMS may be described as an embodiment of the second strand of Euro-American Ethiopianism that was birthed through fear of the growing destitute black British population in England. It also exemplified the various conceptions of modernity, in particular the humanitarian and philanthropic ethos that accompanied the activities of British antislavery exponents who urged a more "legitimate" trade with Africa in the aftermath of abolition. Following in this Euro-Christian abolitionist tradition, the CMS instituted a plan for the establishment of "self-governing, self-supporting, self-propagating native churches and . . . to study the national character of the people and show the utmost respect for national peculiarities." Around the same period, the Select Parliamentary Committee of 1865 recommended that British colonial policy in West Africa be geared toward "encouraging in the natives the exercise of those qualities which may render it possible for us more and more to transfer to them the administration of all Government."[21]

Under this policy of transferring the reins of government to Africans, successive governors of Sierra Leone, Sir Arthur Kennedy (1868–1872) and John Pope-Hennessy, both encouraged and appointed qualified Africans to official positions in the colonial administration. Knowing this, Blyden sought and gained the support of the governors. He was also successful in convincing the CMS hierarchy during a visit to London to appoint him as an emissary for the CMS to the interior regions of Sierra Leone. Blyden's appointment by the CMS was intended to help extend the work of the CMS into the interior with the ultimate goal of implementing his strategy of

Africanization. This decision by the CMS leadership did not, however, sit well with European missionaries resident in Sierra Leone. They not only resisted Blyden's appointment but also schemed to have him suspended for his alleged bigamy with Anna Erskine. They also opposed the creation of a Native Church Pastorate, as Venn had advocated and which as was being pursued by African pastors in Sierra Leone's CMS branches.[22]

Under these circumstances Blyden began to publish the *Negro*.[23] Taking full advantage of his connections with the sympathetic governors, Blyden used the pages of the *Negro* as well as other of his writings to engage the West African public sphere. He bashed the implicit racism and cultural domination in the missionization policies of European Christian agencies like the CMS in West Africa from his Afro-positivist perspective. In the pages of the *Negro*, Blyden strongly advocated for the establishment of an independent West African church devoid of the brand of Christianity taught by European missionaries. It also proposed the founding of a secular West African university led by black scholars who would develop indigenous literature and curricula, and finally the creation of a vast West African British protectorate.[24]

Blyden's Pan-African quest and theorization is also evident in his public activism through the *Negro*, as became clear in the first issue of the newspaper. In this preliminary edition, Blyden explains his choice of the name. He writes that "it has been called the Negro (if explanation necessary) because it is intended to represent and defend the interest of that peculiar type of humanity known as the Negro, with all its affiliated and collateral branches whether on this continent or elsewhere."[25]

Blyden's Afro-positivist discourse was aimed at the foreign missionaries in Sierra Leone, particularly Bishop Henry Cheetham, the colony's CMS bishop. Blyden's rhetoric appealed to Sierra Leone's African intellectuals and clergy but yielded little to the British colonial machinery, exposing his gullibility in believing that the British were sincere in their desire to hand the helm of power to Africans. Cheetham, for his part, was successful in scuttling Blyden's appointment as director of public instruction in Sierra Leone and thereby effectively put an end to Blyden's idea for a secular West

African university. Cheetham also contributed to the Colonial Office coming to the belief that Blyden's appointment would "create a disturbance in Sierra Leone."[26]

However, unlike in Liberia, not all of Blyden's public advocacy in Sierra Leone fell on deaf ears. Through his engagement with Sierra Leoneans, Blyden became even more convinced of the need to Africanize the church in West Africa. Blyden's role as an agent to the interior allowed him to embark on various expeditions within Sierra Leone. Between January 6, 1872, and February 1873, he encountered several Muslim communities like Kambia, Kukumah, Falaba, and Timbo, the capital of the revered Muslim state of Futa Jallon. Through these travels, Blyden became more convinced that Africanized Islam had a better effect on the African Muslim states than had European Christianity among coastal Africans who were Christian.[27]

Blyden, after his experience in the interior of Sierra Leone, dedicated the rest of his academic and public activism to articulating new ideas and reiterating some of his old views on how an Africanization of Christianity project was to be achieved. These ideas filled the pages of the *West African Reporter*, which he helped found in 1874 to foster unity among English-speaking West Africans. Later in 1884, when the paper was discontinued, he helped establish the *Sierra Leone Weekly News* to "serve the interest . . . of West Africa and the race."[28] While these endeavors underline Blyden's conscious contributions to the growth of the West African press, his Afro-positivist discourse is also evinced in his active use of newspapers, tea parties, lectures, historical plays, and luncheons to encourage friendly relations between Sierra Leoneans and Liberians as a stepping-stone to his Pan-African goal—that is, the creation of a larger independent West African state. Blyden's ideas about a West African state, the creation of a West African university, and the Africanization of Christianity had been previously expressed in other mediums; nonetheless, it was in the *Sierra Leone Weekly News* that he would begin to systematically outline his concept of an African Personality.

Blyden believed that people of African descent possessed a distinctive personality that was cultivated and expressed practically through African

FIGURE 10. Dr. Edward Wilmot Blyden: a former Secretary of State and Diplomatic Envoy of Liberia; Born in St. Thomas.

social institutions: religion, family, education, philosophy, communalism, and jurisprudence. Blyden's various enunciations of the African Personality led some West Africans to abandon their European names and to form a dress reform society in Sierra Leone whose aim was to replace European attire with African national dress. Blyden's writings in the *Sierra Leone Weekly News* and his delineation of the African Personality also inspired cultural nationalist spheres in Freetown, Sierra Leone; Lagos, Nigeria; as well as in Accra and Cape Coast on the Gold Coast. Blyden himself began to wear Muslim West African caps along with his suits.

From the Gold Coast, one of Blyden's known associates, Casely Hayford, wrote to the editor of the *Weekly News* describing how "he had followed with keen interest the series of "African Life and Customs" in the *Sierra Leone Weekly News*.[29] In his letter, Casely Hayford reiterated some of Blyden's ideas and endorsed the view that Africa could only be developed along the lines of internally established African social institutions. Approximating Blyden's fascination with the interior societies of the Greater Senegambia region, Casely Hayford cites the interior Gold Coast Asante Kingdom as an example of a society untainted by European culture.

Casely Hayford also endorsed Blyden's secular West African university, describing how, given the opportunity, he would found such "a national University for the Gold Coast and Ashanti." In such a university, Casely Hayford claimed he would found a chair for history that would teach "universal history, with particular reference to the part Ethiopia has played in the Affairs of the world . . . [with] professorships for the Hausa, Fante, and Yoruba languages" that would attract black students from the United States, the West Indies, Sierra Leone, Liberia, Lagos, and the Gambia.

Casely Hayford went on to author books like *Gold Coast Native Institutions* (1903) and *Ethiopia Unbound* (1911), which engage similar themes as Blyden's *African Life and Customs*. In *Gold Coast Native Institutions* and *The Truth about the West African Land Question* (1913), Casely Hayford, like Blyden, looks forward to a *Healthy Imperial Policy for the Gold Coast and Ashanti* (1903) that never came. With its copious quotations from Blyden's *Sierra Leone Weekly News*, his *Ethiopia Unbound* is, in actuality, a literary representation and philosophical expatiation of Blyden's African Personality. This appropriation is personified in the lead character of the novel, Kwamankra. Kwamankra is the literary exemplification of Casely Hayford himself, and thus, explains how he and others in the Gold Coast like Methodist minister Samuel R. B. Solomon (1863–1921), who changed his name to Attoh-Ahuma, had come to embody Blyden's African Personality. Attoh-Ahuma also left the Methodist Church to join the African Methodist Episcopal Zion (AMEZ) mission in the Gold Coast. This AME church was incidentally the Black American church that had itself separated from the Methodist Church in America.[30]

In fact, in 1911 when *Ethiopia Unbound* was published, Blyden commented to the author as follows "The more I read Ethiopia Unbound, the more I see it is not your book, but an inspiration. It has given me more joy and encouragement than anything I have seen for many years."[31] Reveling in such an endorsement, Casely Hayford, in the aftermath of Blyden's passing, also attempted to bring Blyden's vision of West African unity into reality when he spearheaded the founding of the National Congress of British West

Africa in 1920 with branches in Nigeria, Sierra Leone, and the Gambia. Thus, just as the eighteenth-century intellectuals passed on the Afro-positivist tradition to Blyden and his peers, Blyden also passed on a Pan-African mantle to the twentieth-century black intellectual.

It is therefore not surprising that Casely Hayford took a keen interest in William Wade Harris and became one of the few if not the only known ethnographer of Harris's movement. This happened when Harris arrived in Axim, on the western shore of the Gold Coast, where Casely Hayford practiced as a lawyer. Harris, the polygamous Christian, with his African music and African dress personified some of Blyden's articulations of the African Personality. For Casely Hayford, Harris may have seemed like the real-life version of Blyden's theorized Africanized Christian and what an African Christian minister should look like. Harris's movement would also have appeared to him as an institutionalized version of the independent African church Blyden describes in his ethnographic survey of African life and customs.

In using Blyden's missionization methodology, Harris enjoyed success in converting thousands of Africans in Liberia, Ivory Coast, the Gold Coast, and later Sierra Leone. Casely Hayford took notice in July 1914 when he interviewed Harris. He subsequently concluded his ethnographic account by stating that Harris was not only a prophet sent from God but also a West African reformer. Some sources even suggest that Harris had baptized Casely Hayford.[32] It is therefore erroneous to view Harris's movement as the genesis of an African religious movement; his movement, barring its celestial claims, like Casely Hayford's *Ethiopia Unbound*, took inspiration from Blyden's extensive articulation of African lives and customs as well as the African Personality.[33]

Blyden was also revered in Nigeria, especially in Lagos, which had a cosmopolitan population that included various professionals, clergy, and intelligentsia, including his mentee Agbebi, who had changed his name from David Brown Vincent and was instrumental in establishing the Native Baptist Church of Lagos in 1888. Also living in Lagos was Blyden's friend "Holy"

Johnson, who had supported Blyden in Sierra Leone and articulated his ideas about African Christianity. E. A. Ayandele described the latter as both a pioneer of African nationalism and an apostle of Blyden's African Personality.[34] Lagos had also attracted liberated Africans from Sierra Leone and Afro-Brazilian returnees who all read Blyden's work in various newspapers, such as the *Lagos Observer* and the *Lagos Weekly Times*.[35]

It is therefore not happenstance that Blyden was invited by a committee of fourteen prominent Africans to Lagos in December 1890 concerning a dispute between the CMS and its first African bishop, Ajayi Crowther. Blyden arrived on December 20 and was given a formal welcome by the committee on December 21. On January 2, 1891, he delivered a lecture in Lagos, titled "The Return of the Exiles and the West African Church," in which he exhorted Bishop Crowther and James Johnson to form a native African church.[36]

Blyden supported "Holy" Johnson, Bishop Crowther, and the African pastors of the CMS who sought ecclesiastical independence from their parent body in the United Kingdom.[37] The indigenous movement in the Lagos Christian community had no doubt been influenced by Blyden's ideas on domesticated Christianity. This turn of events ultimately resulted in the formation of yet another independent church, the United Native African Church, which was founded in August 1891 following Blyden's departure from Lagos.[38]

Blyden's Afro-Positivism: *African Lives and Customs* and the African Personality

Blyden's thinking on the African Personality, as has been argued from the beginning of this book, is captured in his final book publication, *African Life and Customs*, which represents the height of his transformed thinking about Africa. In his preface, Blyden notes that he kept the "form of the chapters as they had appeared in the *Sierra Leone Weekly News*. More poignantly, Blyden writes that "the following pages have been written with the desire, if possible of unfolding the African who has received unmixed European culture, to himself, through a study of the customs of his fathers, and also of assisting the European political overlord, ruling in Africa."[39] The irony of this statement is that Blyden seemed to be bequeathing to his identified public his own final unfolding from the early Euro-American and Black-American Ethiopianist conceptualizations of Africa and African peoples.

Furthermore, Blyden stressed to his readers that his conceptualizations about Africa and the African Personality were Afro-positivist perspectives derived from the African historical experience. As he puts it in his introduction to *African Life and Customs*, it is a "conscientious investigat[ion] from the spot," as contrasted with the

> noisy and blustering anthropologists of forty or fifty years ago—the Notts and Gliddons, Burtons, Winwood Reade, Hunt, et id omme genus—who invented all sorts of arguments based upon estimates of physical phenomena as conceived by phrenology or physiognomy, using signs and symbols taken from every part of the man—from the heel to the skull—to prove the mental and moral inferiority of the Negro.[40]

Blyden distinguishes his ideas from contemporaneous racialist thinkers. However, this has not stopped many writers including his first biographer, Lynch, from characterizing him as racialist or ethnocentric. His biographers and other writers like Appiah may have rightly argued that Blyden sometimes accepted some of the premises of the leading racial theorists of his day, but they have not brought the same quality of critical analysis to bear on the fundamental distinctions between Blyden and the racist writers of the nineteenth century. This point underlines the importance of engaging Blyden's work and thinking in its chronological development and moments of change.

Blyden, Race, and Women

It is imperative to point out that different social manifestations of the idea of race influenced Blyden's racial cogitations about the mixed-race population of Liberia. He had first been exposed to the racial situation in St. Thomas that led to the Budoo rebellion. He had also been rejected at several U.S. colleges on account of his African heritage. In Liberia, he witnessed the creation of a sociopolitical system in Liberia that favored phenotypically lighter-skinned individuals or Liberians of American heritage. Blyden was undoubtedly also influenced by the leading racial theorists of his day. These multiple influences manifested in three ways: cultural nationalism, racial spirituality, and opposition to miscegenation.

Blyden was adept at forming relationships with indigenous African communities, Afro-Islamic communities, white European and American friends, as well as U.S. mixed-race acquaintances. However, he could not quite fit in with, or seem to like, the "mulattoes"—that is, the Americo-Liberians—in Liberia. He had numerous clashes with them, including over his unsuccessful marriage with Sarah Yates, his various political appointments for the state of Liberia, and his time at Liberia College, where he and Alexander Crummell disputed with J. J. Roberts, president of the college, and members of the Liberian Board of Trustees, all of whom he declared were "mulattoes."[41]

In 1856, Blyden got married to a Virginia-born Liberian emigrant, Sarah Yates, who had earlier arrived in Liberia from Toronto at the age of seventeen or eighteen in 1852. She was the niece of a merchant who became vice president of Liberia, Col. Beverly Page Yates.[42] The marriage was unsuccessful, however, and Blyden often struggled to meet the needs of his family.[43] Blyden complained that his wife was

> of the mind and temperament of the people around her [i.e., of mixed race]. . . . My restlessness and fickleness is largely due to this I am persecuted outside, but more inside. Uncongenial, incompatible, unsympathetic, my

> wife makes the burden of my life sore, very sore and heavy. And if anyone outside—(I have no relatives here) shows any kindness or sympathy, she stimulates a scandal which she knows will readily be believed and circulated in this community.[44]

Friends of Blyden record how Sarah Yates by her behavior and constant threat to leave Liberia scuttled Blyden's chance at the Liberian presidency.[45] Blyden also tried to explain Yates's abusive nature, her intransigence, temper, and tongue, in private letters. Blyden attributed this to Yates's not understanding his African work.[46] Unfortunately, Yates's account of the tempestuous marriage has not survived to make for a more balanced account. Nonetheless, the available records show that, without consulting Blyden, she eventually made good her threat and left Liberia for the United States with their two children, and later Canada, where she stayed with a cousin.[47] Yates is reported to have later returned to Liberia with Blyden's invalid child and a granddaughter, but the two eventually separated when Yates return to the United States. Some reports claim that she never did go back to Liberia in the first place.[48]

Blyden and Yates had three children together—one boy, Edward Jr., and two girls, Uria and Fry. In the aftermath of Yates's departure, Blyden began an alleged adulterous affair with the "Black" Anna Erskine. Blyden described Erskine to his American friends in the following way: "The Day School here is being taught by Miss Anna Erskine and numbers about 25 scholars. I am careful to see that she is regular in her attendance, and consider it a very fine school."[49] Blyden further portrayed Erskine as having no peers because of her knowledge of Latin and French and familiarity with Arabic.[50] Blyden was convinced that had Erskine been of mixed race, rather than black, she would have had more opportunities to excel in Liberia. Needless to say, Blyden admired the daughter of Rev. Hopkins Erskine and Mrs. Eliza Payne Erskine, which may have clouded his judgment.[51] The relationship, however, became a scandal of sorts for Blyden, who was accused of being polygamous. This allegation contributed to his resignation from the Presbyterian Church.

Anna Erskine later bore five children for Blyden, of which only one survived, Isa Cleopatra.[52]

This episode in Blyden's life was symptomatic of the color struggle in Liberia, and directly related to Blyden's "anti-mulatto" positions. The highlight of Blyden's antagonism to miscegenation is captured in various letters he wrote about the conflict between blacks and the mixed-race population of Liberia. In a letter to Crummell, Blyden, quoting the Liberian secretary of the treasury, decried the "terrible conflict . . . ahead between the black and *confounded bastards*."[53] It was, however, another private letter to a board member of the New York Colonization Society, which was accidentally published by the Smithsonian Institute, that brought Blyden trouble in Liberia. In this letter, Blyden catalogued his views on the mixed-race population of Liberia. He attributed their high mortality rate to their dual heritage. He described them as having a high death rate in Liberia owing to their fragility and inability to acclimate to Liberia.[54] Placed in positions of power, he argued, they retarded the progress of the country's education because their constant illnesses led to inactivity and untimely death.[55]

The thrust of Blyden's resentment toward the Americo-Liberians became apparent when he questioned the assumption that people with partial European heritage had "greater aptitude for learning." Blyden accepted that his assumptions were a "vexed question" for many, but opined that miscegenation was not a favorable idea for "inter-tropical Africa."[56] The essay he penned, "The Mixed Races of Liberia," resulted in what Blyden described as a "'mullato-incited mob' of 'forty poverty-stricken and ignorant blacks'" hauling Blyden through the streets of Monrovia, tying a rope around his neck, and nearly lynching him.[57] This incident eventually occasioned Blyden's permanent departure from Liberia to Sierra Leone.

Blyden's antagonism to miscegenation was derived from his experience in Liberia and the general perception during his day that one drop of European blood made one more intelligent than "pure"-blooded Africans. His objection to a hierarchy of race among Africans based on European heritage should be placed in its rightful historical context. Blyden's opposition to miscegenation was limited to Liberia; outside Liberia, his opposition was about self-respect for the African race. He observed that "respect for the Negro is becoming more and more, in progress of events in America, the happy distinction of our age. The Negro being taught to respect himself, and soon he will think it no honour to mingle his blood with that of the Caucasian, Indian or Mongolian."[58] Blyden's aim in his resistance to racial mixture seemed to be an argument against the notion that possessing European or any other foreign heritage made one inherently superior in intellect.

Blyden's views about miscegenation appear to be tangentially related to his views on women. He could be described as also being guilty of exhibiting some chauvinism in this writing even as he was supportive of women's upliftment. For example, if Blyden's relationship with his first wife, Sarah Yates, and his affair with Anna Erskine are anything to go by, Blyden seems to have been more amenable to the company of women who enjoyed his love of languages, and "sympathized with [his] work . . . aims desires and methods," and he "understood her position and work—or rather the work of the African [Blyden]."[59] While these remarks point to Blyden's needs, from the age of twenty, and for the rest of his lifetime, he campaigned for the education of African and black girls to match up with that of boys.[60]

Erskine fit Blyden's desired prototype of a black woman, which led him to complain about their general lack of education, citing the strained marital relationships of Frederick Douglass, Crummell, and Henry Highland Garnet as examples of how "the education of the [black] woman has not kept pace with that of the men."[61] In the case of Erskine, Blyden noted that her being dark in complexion prevented her from climbing the social and intellectual ladder in Liberia.[62] In a letter to one of his longtime correspondents, William Coppinger, Blyden also catalogued the various limitations to education for darker black women in Liberia as opposed to their light-skinned counterparts and decried the status of women of African descent under Christianity when compared to their status in Islam. He wrote, "pure Negro women are nowhere educated up to educated Negro men. In Christian communities the black woman is unpopular. She is at the foot of the ladder. Colored women of all classes of a shade lighter are preferred before her. Her mental and moral training are not attended to."[63]

Blyden thought highly of women's abilities. In a lecture addressed to the AME Church in New York City, he opined that "females see instinctively a great deal further than men with all their logic."[64] However, many of these statements on black women were a reflection of Blyden's experiences with Americo-Liberians of a lighter hue, in general, and his wife, Yates, in particular. In these remarks is also a certain sense of male privilege because Blyden was interested in a black woman who was educated to his standards. He felt that this discrepancy was a problem for many educated blacks, and "you will find [no] one Negro [man] of superior culture who is properly and congenially married."[65]

While Blyden gained a reputation for being "anti-mulatto," outside the context of Liberia, he enjoyed the company of known mixed-race women and men. This included the likes of Anna Julia Cooper, whom he fondly remembered as part of a Saturday circle he had joined when he spent time in Washington, DC.[66] In a letter to Francis Grimké, a mixed-race Presbyterian clergyman, member of the Niagara movement, and founding member of the National Association for the Advancement of Colored People (NAACP) and the ANA, Blyden described the women of the circle in respectful and endearing terms:

> I remember Ella Sommervile who was full of energy, mental alertness and information and a charming companion, in spite of her eccentricities. . . . I can never forget Anna J. Cooper, brilliant, thoughtful, entertaining. Ella Barrier, modest, gentle, winning, tantalizing but with all sound judgment; and towering above all, with her brilliant genius, Mrs. Grimke, scholar, teacher, adviser.[67]

Apart from his observation of these African American women, Blyden also wrote about the importance of black women in Africa, in particular about the role they played in African families, explaining that "plural marriage" could only be engaged with the willing consent of women.[68] He described female societies such as the Bundo society and the Suna among the northern Jollof (Wolof).[69] He offered extended descriptions of women's function as mothers, socializing agents, priestesses, and farmers in these African societies.[70] Blyden notably doted on his daughters, spending the last embers of his life with Isa Cleopatra Blyden, his only surviving child with Anna Erskine. His youngest daughter, Amina Judith Anna (Judith Aminatu), born 1889,

> was said to have been Dr. Blyden's favorite child, resembling her father in intellectual ability, and she was his companion on many of his sea voyages along the coast. When she died in 1909, at the age of 19, it was said that he was completely crushed and never quite regained his former spirit.[71]

Except for the slight traces of male sexism, Blyden's thesis on black women in many ways prefigured contemporary articulations on the "metalanguage of race," by scholars like Evelyn Higginbotham. Higginbotham has argued that the all-encompassing nature of racial categorization, combined with class, gender, and sexuality of black women to cast them in socially negative ways.[72]

But the class and color struggles in Liberia were not the only concerns that shaped Blyden's racial ideology. High on his agenda was a conversation with the leading racial and nationalist thinkers in Europe. Kwaku Larbi Korang has argued that Blyden was in tune with the circulation of ideas throughout the Atlantic including "the romantic racism of Herder, the internationalist nationalism and liberal humanism of Giuseppe Mazzini, and the historical imperialism of Georg Hegel."[73] This book concludes that *African Life and Customs* reveal Blyden as not uncritically taking the ideas of these European thinkers but rather assailing the cultural hegemonies latent in European missionary and colonial administrative discourse.

African Life and Customs, in addition to representing Blyden's final views on the African Personality, reveals the final stage of Blyden's thinking on race. The text shows Blyden's evolved thinking on race as he recognizes the existence of a "human race." Blyden unmistakably points out that "there is no question now as to the human unity."[74] He nonetheless follows this assertion with the idea that all races are equal but distinct, which at face value is erroneous.

However, Blyden's distinctions are environmental rather than biological. In his opinion, "each section has developed for itself such a system or code of life as its environment has suggested—to be improved, not changed by larger knowledge. The African has developed and organized a system useful to him for all the needs of life." It is on this basis that Blyden called for the cultivation of a distinct African Personality—a personality that celebrates Africa's past achievements, a personality to be nurtured in Africa, and that also belonged to Africans in the diaspora.[75]

Racial cogitations aside, in *African Life and Customs*, Blyden advocates the benefits of already-existing African forms of human social organization, explaining polygamy as an essential pillar of the African family structure. He also explains the benefits of African communal systems and African industry and argues the spiritual sanctity of certain traditional African practices.[76] These distinctive African spiritual practices—in Blyden's opinion—were to be further cultivated to enhance the African personality, which was "cooperative, not egotistic or individualistic" and would help provide Africa's unique contribution to humanity.[77] Blyden was thus a nativistic cultural nationalist; he advocated a return to indigenous African practices, which were untainted by European modernity, as the source for Africa's regeneration. However, this was not a naive nativity, because Blyden, through his awareness of the growing influence of Western modernity in Africa, sought to bring these external influences under homegrown ideas and ways of living to nurture the African Personality.

Blyden's combination of race and culture as a form of cultural nationalism derived from his desire to see an Africanization of Western-imported facets of West African life, such as the West African church, which he opined "should be an African, not an English production. . . . The great incubus upon our development has been unreasoning imitation. This we must try to avoid."[78] Blyden was therefore worried that Africans would lose their African

Personality in adherence to those who "reveled in the prospect of hearing some fine morning the 'last of the Negroes.'"[79] Blyden also cautioned that Africans should not merely avoid external influences because they were foreign, but strive to bring the "many good things in foreign customs" to the bidding of the African Personality.[80]

In this race-based cultural nationalism, Blyden had not entirely abandoned the providential interpretation of history embedded in the early Euro-American and African American Ethiopianist traditions. He believed that this African Personality was divinely ordained, which is why he considered "racial peculiarities" God-given. Blyden articulated this spiritual notion of his African Personality to mean that Africans had been assigned a special and distinct place in the universe, just as other races had their own God-given special attributes. Blyden's divinely inspired race "individuality" meant that spiritually Africans were in advance of the "white man," and that the "African spirit is the spirit of service."[81] Blyden explained:

> The spirit of service in the black man is born of his spiritual genius. It is his essential characteristic; and to show you that I connect no servile or unworthy idea with this remark, I hasten to add that I believe that the spirit must lead in civilization before it can become distinctively Christian . . . —how sadly the white man needs it.[82]

Blyden elucidated further that in spite of the past atrocities meted out to the African race, other races need not be afraid of the African Personality because the development of such a personality was free from bitterness, as Africans "were made for the highest glory, which is service to humanity."[83]

Blyden wrote: "It has been said that the fringe of European civilization is violence. All the agencies . . . are tending to fashion us after the one pattern Europe holds out. Society is calling upon us to be like the rest of its worshipers. All the books we read—all the pictures we see beguile us." Thus, rather than acquiesce to Europe's philanthropic and political agencies' call for Africans to "efface [them]selves," Blyden in "The African Problem and the

Method for Its Solution" and *African Life and Customs* developed alternative theories of race.[84] Blyden came to the belief that the various races were "distinct but equal" and not "identical but unequal" as others opined.[85] Thus, while Blyden may have initially accepted the unscientific assertion about the existence of distinct races, he objected to the irrational arrangement of the races into a hierarchy of supreme and inferior races.

African Life and Customs also reveals that Blyden's great desire for "African nationality" was an Afro-positivist discourse and not Mazzini's world citizenship, which was an idealistic harmonization of individual, nation, and humanity. Nor was it Hegel's universality, for both Mazzini and Hegel excluded Blyden's Africa and Africans in their human scheme.[86] Nonetheless, Blyden agreed with Mazzini on the moral equality of all nations and races but claimed it for his idea of an African(Pan-African) nation and race. He, however, emphasized race individuality, which can be described as an expression of African particularity conceived in a human universal. Philosophically, Blyden's theory of race was not an exclusivist theory, but a "duplexive" discourse that meant that his African customs and traditions were particularistic instantiations of the human universal.[87]

Conclusion

In effect, *African Life and Customs* shows that while Blyden was the Black Atlantic's consummate intellectual and its most ardent defender, the center of all his work was Africa. While Blyden had intimate knowledge of the intellectual currents within the Atlantic world, he engaged that community of ideas from an Afro-positivist perspective by raising questions about the claims of the humanitarians, European political theorists, anthropologists, and race polemicists.

His scholarship also transcends the English-speaking transnational units to which Gilroy's work restricts him. It encompassed Muslim West Africa, the Arabic and Hebraic Mediterranean, and the multilingual Caribbean.

Blyden's ideas at the time of his passing also reveal that, much like the plantation intellectuals of the Danish West Indies and the Africa-born Atlantic intellectuals of the eighteenth century, his *African Life and Customs* was an exercise in Afro-positivism—that is, the presentation of an African worldview accompanied by African social institutions as he had observed them in West Africa to vindicate African-descended peoples all over the world.

Two key considerations drove this Afro-positivism, race and providence; but it was his cultural and environmental conception of race that led Blyden to a relativistic conception of society. This was the reason why, although Blyden never abandoned Christianity, he urged "the Christian Negro . . . [not] to look upon the Mohammedans with indifference or hostility . . . but to find ways and means of working with them to mutual advantage."[88] After all, it was African Muslim societies that had forced Blyden to reexamine or recognize the value in African social institutions.

For Blyden, that mutual advantage was the creation of an African Personality and Pan-Africanism. So if race was the idea that led him to cultural relativity, providence was the vehicle on which Blyden's Afro-positivism led him to Pan-African ideas. Providence gave African people a special purpose in humanity. Therefore, while it was no longer providence that diasporic Africans would lead the regeneration of Africa, it was still providence that Africa's hidden destiny or unique contribution to the human universal can only be excavated by the divinely given African Personality. Much like the Lagosians had said of Blyden, Blyden believed that Africa's greatness lay hidden in the peripheries of European civilization, God said, "let the African personality be," and all will be light.

Finally, Blyden's *African Life and Customs* can be viewed as his final and full embrace of the Afro-positivist traditions of his Igbo ancestors. While his Igbo ancestors spiritually or symbolically "flew" back to Ani/land of the ancestors, Blyden's flying back to Africa was both physical and philosophical. He returned physically as an eighteen-year-old filled with an Afro-Christian conception of the future of Africa. However, philosophically, Blyden—like many Western-trained African intellectuals—struggled with the confluence of his Western training and professing of an African identity. This tension was resolved gradually in Blyden's mind through the insights he gained from a rootedness in the lived realities of African societies and an engagement of the African historical experience.

The first steps toward resolution emerged following his moment of regret after participating in a war against the indigenous peoples of Liberia. Blyden, unlike his Americo-Liberian counterparts, abandoned the abrasive attitude toward the indigenous peoples. The next moment toward his transformation came through Blyden's encounter with Muslim African civilization and its intellectuals in the interior of Liberia and Sierra Leone. In Muslim Africa, he discovered that Muslim West Africans maintained African sociocultural practices even as they accepted Islam. In this method, Blyden found a formula to maintain his African identity even as he embraced the progressive elements of his Euro-Christian training.

In his final metamorphosis, Blyden was now no longer uneasy about African life and customs. In fact, he embarked on a conscientious or systematic study of "unmixed [African] culture, to himself, through a study of the customs of his fathers."[89] Blyden's inchoateness, incomplete ideas, and contradictions, therefore, need to be measured against these transformative moments that led him to an embrace and understanding of Africa as the center. His writing of *African Life and Customs*, then, was Blyden's final escape from the culture of mimicking European culture in the same way that the plantation intellectuals of the Americas rejected the racially organized system of plantation agriculture.

Through *African Life and Customs*, Blyden bequeathed to the next generation of black intellectuals his place of escape and belonging—the *African Personality*, as the first systematic articulation of Pan-Africanism. Due to his Afro-positivist scholarship, which sought to glorify Africa and African-descended peoples, Blyden influenced the next generation of African and African diasporan nationalists, like Du Bois and Nkrumah. Nkrumah, who convened the 1945 Pan-African Congress with Du Bois, was the first president of the modern nation of Ghana, which became the first black African country to gain independence, in 1957. After independence, Nkrumah, with the help of his West Indian friend George Padmore, rearticulated Blyden's African Personality to mean a proclamation of the African Personality and leadership on the world stage, a worldwide liberation of African-descended peoples, the integrity of African and Afro-diasporic cultures, and solidarity between continental Africans and diasporic Africans.[90]

So what exactly were Blyden's contributions to Pan-Africanism? Blyden is distinguished by his unique penetrating analytic gaze and salient consideration of Africa's global encounters, in particular, its trans-Saharan encounter with the world as well as its transatlantic meeting with Europe and the Americas. Blyden's abandonment of some of the Christian bias of his youth and his embrace of the intellectual value of Islam is indicative of his unique reflective abilities. The impersonation in rural Arkansas demonstrates that through his public intellectualism, rootedness in the African historical experience, advocacy of the African personality, and use of Afro-positivism, Blyden had become popular among both urban and rural black communities and groups. His renown among black clergy and black intellectuals and his continued influence over at least two generations of African intellectuals and nationalists further entrenches him as the most influential black intellectual of the nineteenth and early twentieth centuries.

Epilogue

> If you can't have a local centre, then you can't have a claim to a global position. Even Jesus was born in Bethlehem of Judea and people knew him as the son of Joseph of Nazareth. In my thinking, I am international, but when it comes to doing something for the betterment of the people, I go to the local place.
>
> —Taban Makotiyang Lo Liyong, *Daily Nation*, September 13, 2013

Following Taiye Sellasie's articulation of the term *Afropolitanism* in "Bye-Bye BarBar," and its subsequent explication by Achille Mbembe, it has thrived in academic discourse, music, and popular culture. In 2014, Ghanaian-born American artist, Blitz the Ambassador, named his third Studio album *Afropolitan Dreams*. Afropolitan scenes, start-ups, networks, think-tanks, and fads have emerged in the United States, notably Afropolitan SF, Afropolitan D.C., Afropolitan L.A., Afropolitan N.Y., and Afropolitan Atlanta all under the banner of *Afropolitan Cities*. The Afropolitan Movement in the United States is described as "currently the largest diaspora movement of its kind attracting over 3500 young professionals across 8 cities each month."[1] This author also belongs to a Northern California, Bay Area "Afropolitan" think-tank, Launchpad Africa, which is made up of blacks of American, Caribbean, and African heritage. This group comprises professionals, intellectuals, filmmakers, chefs, DJs, and community organizers, whose mission is to connect people to create, own, and drive sustainable economic and intellectual capital in Africa and beyond.

In the academic field, theories, analyses, and conceptualizations about the meaning and significance of Afropolitanism have burgeoned in various journals, art museums, and conferences.[2] As some of these articles demonstrate, a standard definition of Afropolitanism has remained elusive. As Blitz the Ambassador's statement demonstrates, the term is

> defined by everybody differently, but for me . . . Afropolitan Dream is a new definition of who we are . . . And I feel like we've gotten to a point where we young Africans, even some old Africans are thinking a lot more Diaspora, rather than what can I do in my small corner, thinking about how can I link it all up. Because if you think about it our struggles are the same, our joys are the same, no matter where you find us. So that to me is the important part of what it means to be an Afropolitan, but at the end of the day taking it all back home. Because that's where it began and that's where it ends.[3]

The Afropolitan Cities network also describes Afropolitans as "progressive and culturally savvy young urban professionals of various races, but typically of African descent, living in metropolitan cities around the world and identify with Afro-Caribbean culture."[4] While the term remains tenuous, some like Binyavanga Wainana have rejected the term, preferring to be Pan-Africanist than Afropolitan.[5] Emma Dabiri seeks to be part of a "more radical, counter-cultural movement, and to reinvest Afropolitanism (if we are to keep the term) with progressive activism."[6] Nigerian author Chimamanda Ngozi Adichie is weary of been called Afropolitan and prefers African. She questions "are Africans so outside of the general history of humanity that they must be designated by a particular name when they travel or are found in capitals of the world? The second thing, is that history (sadly not well) shows that [African] cosmopolitanism doesn't date from yesterday."[7]

At the heart of this discourse about Afropolitanism are three issues that Edward Blyden's intellectual career can help us resolve. First, the term *Afropolitan*, as it is currently conceptualized, is hegemonic favoring the diaspora. It excludes cosmopolitan spaces, organizing, and networking on the African continent and is also limited to mobile elite groups and individuals. Blyden's career in Monrovia, Liberia, and Freetown, Sierra Leone, and his influences in public spheres in Lagos and Accra as well as in rustic locales in the Greater Senegambia show, as Adichie reiterates, that cosmopolitanism is not novel to the African continent or African intellectuals. Afropolitanism, as presently articulated, does not include contemporary scenes in African cities like Abuja, Accra, Cape Town, Dar es Salaam, Dakar, Johannesburg, and Zanzibar.

Secondly, Blyden's articulation of an Afro-positivist perspective in his discourse with different public spheres demonstrates that moving in and out Africa as well as having knowledge and ease in multiple spaces do not preclude the need to be centered in a specific place. Blyden was born in the Danish West Indies, lived and traveled in the United States, emigrated to Monrovia and then to Freetown. He was not only familiar with the cosmopolitan centers of the global west but also trekked, lived, and held discourse from his centeredness in the African historical experience of the Greater Senegambia region. As South Sudanese poet Tabo Liyong argues, having a transnational perspective, multiple belongings, or departures does not diminish the need for centeredness in a specific place.

> If you can't have a local centre, then you can't have a claim to a global position. Even Jesus was born in Bethlehem of Judea and people knew him as the son of Joseph of Nazareth. In my thinking, I am international, but when it comes to doing something for the betterment of the people, I go to the local place.[8]

The idea of networking and celebrating Afro-Caribbean cultures, in particular cities among Afropolitans in the United States, further demonstrates the importance of being anchored in a specific Afro-place.

Finally, attempts to network black or Africa-descended professionals or to celebrate Africa-derived cultures—as seen in the case of Afropolitan Cities—or to create black-owned entities as is evident with the Launchpad Africa group is not new to Diasporic African spaces. Such organizing and networking predate Afropolitanism. The one difference is that numbers of (new Afropolitans) recent African immigrants to the West since, at least the 1960s, seems to suggest that they represent a more critical mass, around which black publics have emerged. The black cosmopoles in Blyden's day may not have been as large as the kinds of cohorts that we currently find among the "new" African/Black elite or Afropolitans. The contemporary demographic ascendancies are therefore critical to our understanding of Afropolitan as something different. However, a thorough examination of nineteenth century West African intellectual life shows that there are figures like Blyden and intellectual movements that portended the current Afropolitan movement and its linked circuits of knowledge, creativity, trade, and mobility. Blyden and his peers are therefore pioneers of the artistic and intellectual currents now labeled Afropolitan.

Acknowledgments

Without the support and encouragement of my wife and partner, Clementine Naa Kowa Odamtten, this work would not have been possible at all. Her sacrifices and care for our three children—Simon Jr., Sadie-Janelle, and Simone-Jada—have been immaculate. My parents, Simon and Regina Odamtten, as well as siblings, Christine and Geena, anchor me by reminding me who I am and the depths from which I have come as a person. I am also grateful to the creator and master of the universe and all servants who have grounded me spiritually and fueled my spiritual resurgence in the last ten years.

I owe tons of appreciation to many teachers, scholars, schools of thought, and intellectual genealogies. At Ridge Church School, I remember Mrs. Blege and Miss Djabatey and at Ghanacoll, Mrs. Abrokwa and Mr. Hughes. At Labone Secondary School, I recall the help of Mr. Ahiati and Mr. Bedman Nartey (Tito). At the University of Ghana, Robert Addo-Fening, Kofi Baku, S. S. Quarcoopome, and Irene Quaye were influential. I am also grateful to Jualynne E. Dodson for the time I spent with the African Atlantic Research Team at Michigan State University (MSU).

For this book, special thanks go to the pioneering scholarship of Hollis

Lynch, Robert July, and Peter Esedebe. Without them, this study would have been considerably more difficult. Studying *The Origins of Modern African Thought* first got me interested in African intellectual history and eventually led me to Lynch's seminal biography and other writings on Blyden. Esedebe's book *Pan-Africanism: The Idea and Movement, 1776–1963* still stands as the cornerstone of scholarship on Pan-Africanism.

I am equally indebted to Nwando Achebe and Pero Dagbovie at MSU, who are stuck with me because I refuse to let go of their mentoring strings. Nwando has influenced me in so many ways I cannot recount here, but for which I only give thanks. *Daalu rinne ezigbo nwannem nwanyi.* I continue to admire Pero for his honesty, passion, scholarship, and sterling example as an intellectual historian, *akpe ka ka ka*. Together with Laurent Dubois and Folu Ogundimu, their probing questions have continually forced me to rethink and reshape my work.

I want to express sincere gratitude to colleagues Naomi Andrews, Emmanuel Asiedu-Acquah, Kwame Essien, Kwasi Konadu, Leonard Ndubueze, Joseph Oduro-Frimpong, and Nancy Unger, who took time to read proposals or chapters and offered substantial critique that made this work expressively better. I am equally appreciative of David Skinner for reading the chapter on Islam and for sharing with me his Church Missionary Service archival notes.

I am indebted to Michaela Ahlstrom, the history department's student assistant, and Mrs. Gifty Saddique-Hammond their work on the graphs based on data from the Trans-Atlantic Slave Trade Database, and to Mr. Donald Thorpe for his assistance with the cover's art. Thanks also to Dr. Charles Yorke for creating all but one of the maps at short notice. Thanks to my mentees Herman von Hesse and Eric Kesse who delivered on short notice to all my research checks requests.

I am thankful to series coeditors, Glenn Chambers and Quito Swan, as well as the blind reviewers whose comments have made this work significantly better. Immeasurable thanks to Anastasia Wraight and all the editors who worked on this manuscript in diverse ways.

Merci beaucoup to my uncle and aunt Thomas Nicholson Laryea Odamtten and Patricia Odamtten and the whole family at No. 1 Orchard Way for their generosity. Same appreciations go to Clement Sowa, Randy Semenhyia, and the entire Pirin Court family for their fraternity while researching at SOAS and Kew Gardens. Thanks as well to Henry Nyakpo for the hospitality he showed me at his residence during a brief stopover at the University of Birmingham.

Thanks to my friends and colleagues in graduate school: Carlos Enrique Aleman, Crystal Eddins, Baranda Fermin, Alexandra Gelbard, Darcia Grant, Leslie Hadfield, Rashida L. Harrison, Bayyinah Jeffries, Sonya Maria Johnson, Sowande Mustakeen, Candace Parker, Matthew Pettway, Bala Saho, Assan Sarr, Lumumba Shabakar, Walter Sistrunk, Andrew Woodson, Ashley Woodson, and Shanti Ali Zaid, who influenced my life and scholarship in diverse ways at MSU. Same appreciation goes to Samuel Ntewusu and Edem Adotey of the University of Ghana. Without the support and care of my aunty, Mrs. Felicia Ankrah, and family in Virginia, graduate school would have been much tougher. I acknowledge Rev. Henry Asare-Duah's influence, and thank Dr. Akwasi Frimpong-Mensah for possessing the "key" that unsealed this book.

Initial support for this work came from the MSU Research Abroad and Dissertation Fellowships, which enabled me to access archival holdings in Birmingham and London in 2009. I utilized the American Colonization Papers collection while serving as visiting professor at the University of Central Arkansas in 2010–2011. A 2012 dean's grant from the College of Arts and Sciences at Santa Clara University also allowed me to travel to the Enid M. Baa Public Library in St. Thomas, Virgin Islands, to access the Von Scholten Collection and other materials.

Notes

INTRODUCTION

1. Kwame Anthony Appiah, *In My Father's House: Africa in the Philosophy of Culture* (London: Methuen, 1992), 21.
2. Edward Blyden, *Christianity, Islam and the Negro Race* (Edinburgh: Edinburgh University Press, 1967), 272–73.
3. Edward Curtis IV, *Black Muslim Religion in the Nation of Islam 1960–1975* (Chapel Hill: University of North Carolina Press, 2006); Michael A. Gomez, *Black Crescent: The Experience and Legacy of African Muslims in the Americas* (Cambridge: Cambridge University Press, 2005), 257–58; Samory Rashid, *Black Muslims in the US: History, Politics, and the Struggle of a Community* (New York: Palgrave Macmillan, 2013).
4. Hollis R. Lynch, *Edward Wilmot Blyden: Pan-Negro Patriot, 1832–1912* (Oxford: Oxford University Press, 1970), vii–viii; Thomas Livingston, *Education and Race: A Biography of Edward Wilmot Blyden* (San Francisco: Glendessary Press, 1975), 206–23.
5. Edith Holden, *Blyden of Liberia: An Account of the Life and Labors of Edward Wilmot Blyden, LL.D. As Recorded in Life and in Print* (New York: Vantage Press, 1966), 19. This book is not a historical account but a compendium of Blyden's letter correspondence and travels. It is therefore a useful sourcebook of primary documents for Blyden scholars.

6. Ibid., 19–20.
7. Ibid., 11, 20.
8. Edward W. Blyden to William Coppinger, September 13, 1884, "American Colonization Papers (A.C.S.) vol. 21," Library of Congress, Washington, DC.
9. Blyden to Coppinger; Edward W. Blyden, quoted in Lynch, *Edward Wilmot Blyden*, 4.
10. See Holden, *Blyden of Liberia*, appendix 2, 1025–29.
11. Gregory Mann, "Afropositivism," *Cultural Anthropology Online*, June 10, 2013, http://culanth.org.
12. Carl C. Reindorf, *The History of the Gold Coast and Asante: Based on Tradition and Historical Facts Comprising a Period of More Than Three Centuries from about 1500–1860*, 2nd ed. (Basel: Basel Mission Depot, 1895). For other discussions on Reindorf see Paul Jenkins, ed., *The Recovery of the West African Past: African Pastors and African History in the Nineteenth Century; C. C. Reindorf & Samuel Johnson: Papers from an International Seminar held in Basel, Switzerland, 25–28th October 1995 to Celebrate the Centenary of the Publication of C. C. Reindorf's* History of the Gold Coast and Asante (Basel: Basler Afrika Bibliographien, 1998). For further information about Bishop Samuel Ajayi Crowther, see July, *Origins of Modern African Thought: Its Development in West Africa during the Nineteenth and Twentieth Centuries* (New York: Praeger, 1967), 143, 177–207. James Africanus Horton, *West African Countries and Peoples: A Vindication of the Negro Race* (Edinburgh: Edinburgh University Press, 1969). J. E. C. Hayford, *Ethiopia Unbound: Studies in Race Emancipation* (London: Cass, 1970). For a collective discussion, see July, *Origins of Modern African Thought.*
13. Valentine Mudimbe, *The Invention of Africa: Gnosis, Philosophy, and the Order of Knowledge* (Bloomington: Indiana University Press), 105–19, 124–30.
14. Harry N. K. Odamtten, "A History of Ideas: West Africa, the 'Black Atlantic,' and Pan-Africanism" (PhD diss., Michigan State University, 2010), 262–66; Holden, *Blyden of Liberia*, 902–15.
15. *Consolidated Final Report: Truth and Reconciliation Commission of Liberia* (Monrovia: Republic of Monrovia, 2009), 68.
16. Ibid., 68–70.
17. Ibid., esp. 68.
18. Paul Gilroy, *The Black Atlantic: Modernity and Double Consciousness* (Cambridge, MA: Harvard University Press, 1993); other texts dealing with the Black Atlantic include John K. Thornton, *Africa and Africans in the Making of the Atlantic World, 1400–1800* (Cambridge: Cambridge University Press, 1998); and J. Lorand Matory, *Black Atlantic Religion: Tradition, Transnationalism, and Matriarchy in the Afro-Brazilian Candomblé* (Princeton, NJ: Princeton University Press, 2005).

19. Gilroy, *Black Atlantic*, 205–23.
20. Pieter Boele van Hensbroek used the term *import thesis* in "The 'Import Thesis' about African Political Thought," *Journal of African Philosophy* 2 (2003): 1–39. See also Pieter Boele van Hensbroek, *Political Discourses in African Thought: 1860 to the Present* (Westport, CT: Palgrave, 1999), 1–22.
21. Robert Farris Thompson, *Flash of the Spirit: African and Afro-American Art and Philosophy* (New York: Random House, 1984), xiii–xvii.
22. Gilroy, *Black Atlantic*, 2–40.
23. Ruth Simms Hamilton, *Routes of Passage: Rethinking the African Diaspora* (East Lansing: Michigan State University Press, 2007).
24. Kwaku Larbi Korang, *Writing Ghana, Imagining Africa: Nation and African Modernity* (Rochester, NY: University of Rochester Press, 2003).
25. For these mutually exclusive positions, see the exclusion of Africa from the Black Atlantic in the work of Gilroy, *Black Atlantic*. For racialist discourse and Pan-Africanism, see Kwame Anthony Appiah, *In My Father's House: Africa in the Philosophy of Culture* (London: Methuen, 1992).
26. For current texts, see Neville A. T. Hall, *Slave Society in the Danish West Indies: St. Thomas, St. John and St. Croix*, ed. B. W. Higman (Baltimore: Johns Hopkins University Press, 1992); Ole Justesen, ed., *Danish Sources for the History of the Ghana, 1657–1754* (Copenhagen: Royal Danish Academy of Sciences and Letters, 2005); and John Sensbach, *Rebecca's Revival: Creating Black Christianity in the Atlantic World* (Cambridge, MA: Harvard University Press, 2005). For older texts see, for example, Francois de Paris, *Voyage of the Coast of Africa, Named Guinea, and to the Isles of America, Made in the Years 1682 and 1683*, trans. Aimery Caron (Madison: University of Wisconsin, African Studies Program, 2001).
27. By Greater Senegambia, I am referring to the region between the Senegal and Gambia Rivers described in Boubacar Barry, *Senegal and the Atlantic Slave Trade* (Cambridge: Cambridge University Press, 1998), xv.
28. The discussion of Orientalism as it pertains to Blyden does not refer to the critique of Oriental scholarship as an academic tradition, which is also used as a tool of political domination as argued in the writings of Edward Said. On the contrary, this book argues that Blyden's African centered analytical approach to the societies, cultures, and peoples of West Africa, North Africa, and the Middle East was different from his peers.
29. Gomez, *Black Crescent*, 257–58.

CHAPTER 1. AFROPUBLICAN COMMONS: CONCEPTUAL GROUNDINGS

1. Neville A. T. Hall, *Slave Society in the Danish West Indies: St. Thomas, St. John and St. Croix*, ed. B. W. Higman (Baltimore: Johns Hopkins University Press, 1992), 146–49.
2. *Sanct. Thomae Tidende* (hereafter *STT*), July 5, 1848, vol. 2, no. 157; and *STT*, July 19, 1848, vol. 2, no. 159; or *St. Croix Avis* (hereafter *SCA*), July 3, 1848, 3^{die} Quartal, no. 471; and *SCA* September 25, 1848, 3^{die} Quartal, no. 495.
3. I use Afro-Danish in this text not as a marker of linguistic ability or national association, but to indicate the extent to which the Danish colonial enterprise in Danish West Africa, the Danish West Indies, and Denmark influenced the lives of African-descended peoples within its orbit. Afro-Danish is therefore distinct in that it encompasses slaves, subjects, as well as free black Danes who tended to either speak some Danish and/or were biracial. I sometimes use Afro-Danish subject to encompass all of these identities.
4. Ruth Simms Hamilton, *Routes of Passage: Rethinking the African Diaspora* (East Lansing: Michigan State University Press, 2007), 1.
5. Michael Gomez, ed., *Diasporic Africa: A Reader* (New York: New York University Press, 2006), 4.
6. I have coined *Afropublicanism* in this book to distinguish it from the term *Afropolitanism*, popularized in academic discourse by Achille Mbembe. The latter term encompasses the flow of ideas and cultural aesthetics of contemporary global Africans through their migration or movement, and cosmopolitanism or multisitedness as African intellectuals, litterateurs, artists, business professionals, and—more recently—as cyberpolitans: Africans with cyber and social media presence in multiple cosmopolitan locations. Mbembe emphasizes the long history of human movement and cross-cultural interactions within the African continent itself as well as the mutual process of global inflows (Asian, Arabic, European) into Africa and African outflows across the Sahara and the Indian and Atlantic Oceans into the wider world. Afropolitanism was offered in public culture through the writings of Taiye Tuakli-Wosornu (Taiye Sellasi). Tuakli-Wosornu's literary explanation is focused on immigrant and foreign-born Africans who celebrate their multiple places of belonging (rootlessness) and concomitant myriad identities, but also express a nonapologetic commitment to living a cosmopolitan African way of life abroad. See Achille Mbembe, "Afropolitanism," in *Africa Remix: Contemporary Art of a Continent*, ed. Njami Simon and Lucy Durán (Johannesburg: Johannesburg Art Gallery, 2007), 26–30; Taiye Tuakli-Wosornu, "Bye-Bye BarBar," *Lip Magazine*, March 3, 2005.

7. Edward Blyden, *Christianity, Islam and the Negro Race* (Edinburgh: Edinburgh University Press, 1967), 265.
8. Jürgen Habermas, "The Public Sphere: An Encyclopedia Article" (1964), in *The Idea of the Public Sphere*, ed. Jostein Gripsrud et al. (Lanham, MD: Lexington Books, 2010), 114–20. Thanks to Emmanuel Asiedu-Acquah for helping provide an interpretive understanding of the "expansive/capacious" meaning of public culture as compared to popular culture as well as its relatedness to the public sphere.
9. Mary Kupiec Cayton, "What Is Public Culture? Agency and Contested Meaning in American Culture; An Introduction," in *Public Culture: Diversity, Democracy, and Community in the United States*, ed. Marguerite S. Shaffer, 1–25 (Philadelphia: University of Pennsylvania Press, 2008); Arjun Appadurai and Carol Breckenridge, "Debates and Controversies: Why Public Culture?," *Public Culture* 1, no. 1 (1988): 5–9.
10. Michael Warner, *Publics and Counterpublics* (New York: Zone Books, 2002).
11. Ibid., 122.
12. V. Y. Mudimbe, *The Invention of Africa: Gnosis, Philosophy, and Order of Knowledge* (Bloomington: Indiana University Press, 1988), 98–134.
13. Apparudai and Breckenridge, "Debates and Controversies," 7.
14. Harry N. K. Odamtten, "History of Ideas: 'The Black Atlantic' West Africa, and Pan-Africanism" (PhD diss. Michigan State University, 2010), 140–57.
15. Cayton, "What Is Public Culture?," 16.
16. Robert July, *The Origins of Modern African Thought: Its Development in West Africa during the Nineteenth and Twentieth Centuries* (New York: Praegar), 196–207.
17. Olaudah Equiano, *The Interesting Narrative of the Life of Olaudah Equiano, or Gustavus Vassa, the African* (London, published by author, 1791); Ottobah Cugoano, *Thoughts and Sentiments on the Evil of Slavery* (London, published by author, 1787); Ottobah Cugoano, *Narrative of the Enslavement of Ottobah Cuguano, a Native of Africa* (London, published by author, 1825).
18. For an example of African philosophical thought, see Kwame Gyekye, *An Essay on African Philosophical Thought: The Akan Conceptual Scheme* (Cambridge: Cambridge University Press, 1990); for African Islamic thought, see Souleymane Bachir Diagne, "Toward an Intellectual History of West Africa: The Meaning of Timbuktu," in *The Meanings of Timbuktu*, ed. Shamil Jeppie and Souleymane Bachir Diagne (Cape Town: HSRC Press/CODESRIA, 2008), 19–27; for modern African thought, see July, *Origins of Modern African Thought*; for literary and cultural criticism, see Kwame A. Appiah, *In My Father's House: Africa in the Philosophy of Culture* (London: Metheun, 1992), and Kwaku L. Korang, *Writing Ghana, Imagining Africa: Nation and African Modernity* (Rochester, NY: University

of Rochester Press, 2003). For a foundational text on African religious thought, see John Mbiti, *African Religions and Philosophy* (Oxford: Heinemann, 1990); for African political thought, see Pieter Boele van Hensbroek, *Political Discourses in African Thought: 1860 to the Present* (Westport, CT: Praeger, 1999).

19. See, for example, Per O. Hernaes, *Slaves, Danes, and African Society: The Danish Slave Trade from West Africa and Afro-Danish Relations on the Eighteenth-Century Gold Coast* (Trondheim, NO: University of Trondheim, 1995); Ivor Wilks, *Akwamu 1640–1750: The Rise and Fall of a West African Empire* (Trondheim, NO: University of Trondheim, 2001); Robert Addo-Fening, *Akyem Abuakwa, 1700–1943: From Ofori Panyin to Sir Ofori Atta* (Trondheim, NO: Norwegian University of Science and Technology, Department of History, 1997); David Henderson-Quartey, *The Ga of Ghana: The History and Culture of a West African People* (London: Self-published, 2001).
20. Agreement between Okai Kwei, King of Accra, and Jost Cramer, Commandant of Fredricksburgh, in Guinea, August 18, 1661. Furley Collection (hereafter cited as FC), Balme Library, University of Ghana, Legon, V.G.K. 77, Breve og Ugaede 1624, 1659–1680.
21. For information on ships, see Thorkhild Hansen, *Ships of Slaves*, trans. Kari Dako (Accra: Sub-Saharan Publishers, 2007), 14–15.
22. Translation of the pamphlets *Tegen Bericht*, October 18, 1664, 17, D.2, FC; Thorkhild Hansen, *Island of Slaves*, trans. Kari Dako (Accra: Sub-Saharan Publishers, 2004), 19; Selena Axelrod Winsnes, *Letters on West Africa and the Slave Trade: Paul Erdmann Isert's Journey to Guinea and the Caribbean Islands in Columbia* (1788) (Oxford: Oxford University Press for the British Academy, 1992).
23. With an understanding of the Volta River as bridge rather than a divide, together with the different trade exchanges, cross-migrations, and other interactions between the peoples on all sides of the Volta, I use "Volta Basin diaspora" here to complicate the distinction made between the Gold Coast and the Bight of Benin as two separate cultural areas.
24. For the earlier literature, see Pierre Verger, *Flux et reflux de la traite des negres entre le Golfe de Benin et Bahia de Todos os Santos, du 17 au 19 siecle* (Paris, 1968); Raimundo Nina Rodriguez, *Os africanos no Brasil* (Rio de Janeiro: Centro-Edelstein de Pesquisa Social, 2010); Fernando Ortiz, *Etnia y sociedad* (Havana: Editorial de Ciencias Sociales, 1993); Fernando Ortiz, *Los negros esclavos* (Havana: Editorial de Ciencias Sociales, 1987); Melville J. Herskovits, "On the Provenience of New World Negroes," *Social Forces* 12 (1933): 247–62; Melville J. Herskovits, "A Preliminary Consideration of the Culture Areas of Africa," *American Anthropologist* 26 (1924): 50–63; Gonzalo Aguirre Beltran, "Tribal Origins of Slaves in Mexico," *Journal of Negro History* 31 (1946), 269–352; Daryll Forde,

"The Cultural Map of West Africa: Successive Adaptations to Tropical Forests and Grassland," in *Cultures and Societies of Africa*, ed. Simon Ottenberg and Phoebe Ottenberg (New York: Random House, 1960); Daryll Forde, ed., *African Worlds: Studies in the Cosmological and Social Values of African Peoples* (Oxford: Oxford University Press, 1954); Fernando Ortiz, *Cuban Counterpoint: Tobacco and Sugar* (New York: A. A. Knopf, 1947). For the debates, see Melville J. Herskovits, *Myth of the Negro Past* (New York: Harper and Brothers, 1941); E. Franklin Frazier, *The Negro Family in the United States* (Chicago: University of Chicago Press, 1939); Sydney Mintz and Richard Price, *The Birth of African-American Culture: An Anthropological Perspective* (Boston: Beacon Press, 1992); and John K. Thornton, *Africa and Africans in the Making of the Atlantic World, 1400–1800* (Cambridge: Cambridge University Press, 1992), 206–79.

25. For new literature on transatlantic ethnicities, see Paul E. Lovejoy and David V. Trotman, eds., *Trans-Atlantic Dimensions of Ethnicity in the African Diaspora* (London: Continuum, 2003). For ethnic clusters, see Gwendolyn Midlo Hall, *Slavery and African Ethnicities in the Americas: Restoring the Links* (Chapel Hill: University of North Carolina Press, 2005). For current literature on ethnic diasporas, see Kwasi Konadu, *The Akan Diaspora in the Americas* (Oxford: Oxford University Press, 2010); Joel E. Tishken, Toyin Falola, and Akíntúndé Akínyẹmí, *Sàngó in Africa and the African Diaspora* (Bloomington: Indiana University Press, 2009); and Matt Childs and Toyin Falola, *The Yoruba Diaspora in the Atlantic World* (Bloomington: Indiana University Press, 2005).

26. For the rebellion of enslaved Gold Coast peoples in the Danish West Indies, see examples in Pierre J. Pannet, *Report on the Execrable Conspiracy Carried Out by the Amina Negroes on the Danish Island of St. Jan in America, 1733*, trans. and ed. Aimery P. Caron and Arnold R. Highfield (Christiansted, St. Croix: Antilles Press, 1984); Waldemar Westergaard, "Account of the Negro Rebellion on St. Croix, Danish West Indies 1759," *Journal of Negro History* 11, no. 1 (1926): 50–61. David Barry Gaspar also writes about Gold Coast natives' rebellion in Antigua influenced by their kin in St. Croix in "The Antigua Slave Conspiracy of 1736: A Case Study of the Origins of Collective Resistance," *William and Mary Quarterly* 35, no. 2 (1978): 308–23; see also, Ray A. Kea, "'When I Die I Shall Return to My Own Land': An 'Amina' Slave Rebellion in the Danish West Indies," in *The Cloth of Many Colored Silks: Papers on History and Society, Ghanaian and Islamic in Honor of Ivor Wilks*, ed. John Hunwick and Nancy Lawler (Evanston, IL: Northwestern University Press, 1996).

27. A great deal of controversy surrounds the caravel ship—its exact discovery, etymology, and archetype. For a discussion on the caravel see B. W. Diffie and George D. Winius, *Foundations of the Portuguese Empire, 1415–1580* (Minneapolis:

University of Minnesota Press, 1977), 28.

28. Robert H. Thurston, *A History of the Growth of the Steam-Engine* (Ithaca, NY: Cornell University Press, 1939); Elizabeth L. Eisenstein, *The Printing Press as an Agent of Change: Communications and Cultural Transformations in Early Modern Europe* (New York: Cambridge University Press, 1979); Marshall McLuhan, *The Global Village: Transformations in World Life and History in the 21st Century* (New York: Oxford University Press, 1989); Peter Stearns, ed., *Encyclopedia of World History: Ancient, Medieval, and Modern, Chronologically Arranged*, 6th ed. (Boston: Houghton Mifflin, 2001).
29. Edith Holden, *Blyden of Liberia: An Account of the Life and Labors of Edward Wilmot Blyden, LL.D As Recorded in Letters and in Print* (New York: Vantage Press, 1966), 1025–29.
30. James L. Matory, *Black Atlantic Religion: Tradition, Transnationalism, and Matriarchy in the Afro-Brazilian Candomblé* (Princeton, NJ: Princeton University Press, 2005), 291.
31. Ibid., 35–40, 60–67.
32. See Thomas H. Henriksen, "African Intellectual Influences on Black Americans: The Role of Edward Blyden," *Phylon* 36 (1960): 279–90; Ralph L. Crowder, *John Edward Bruce: Politician, Journalist, and Self-Trained Historian of the African Diaspora* (New York: New York University Press, 2004); John E. Bruce Papers, Schomburg Collection, New York Public Library.
33. G. W. F. Hegel, *The Philosophy of History*, trans. J. Sibree (New York: Dover Publications, 1956).
34. July, *Origins of Modern African Thought*, 22–50.
35. Hugh Trevor-Roper, *Rise of Christian Europe* (New York: Harcourt, Brace & World, 1965), 9.
36. Immanuel Geiss, *The Pan-African Movement: A History of Pan-Africanism in America, Europe, and Africa* (New York: African Publishing Co., 1974), 424–32.
37. Cyril L. R. James, *Black Jacobins: Toussaint L'Ouverture and the San Domingo Revolution* (New York: Vintage Books, 1963). *David Walker's Appeal, Together with Four Articles and a Preamble to the Colored Citizens of the World* (Baltimore: Black Classics Press, 1993).
38. David Eltis, James Walvin, and Sven Green-Pederson, eds., *The Abolition of the Atlantic Slave Trade: Origins and Effects in Europe, Africa, and the Americas* (Madison: University of Wisconsin Press, 1981).
39. Edward W. Blyden, quoted in Hollis R. Lynch, ed., *Black Spokesman: Selected Published Writings of Edward Wilmot Blyden* (London: Frank Cass, 1971), 327.
40. Edward W. Blyden, *West Africa Before Europe and Other Addresses Delivered in England in 1901* (London: C.M. Phillips, 1902), 73.

41. Blyden, *Christianity, Islam*, 426.
42. Ethiopia was the other independent African nation, whilst Black American emigrants founded Liberia in 1847 with backing from the American Colonization Society. For African resistance to European Imperialism, see Robert I. Rothberg and Ali Mazrui, *Protest and Power in Black Africa* (New York: Oxford University Press, 1970); and Albert A. Boahen, *African Perspectives on Colonialism* (Baltimore: Johns Hopkins University Press, 1987).
43. Holden, *Blyden of Liberia*, 11, 20–23.
44. Ibid., 21.
45. See discussion of Blyden's language skills in ibid., 11–16; Lynch, *Black Spokesman*; and Hollis Lynch, *Selected letters of Edward Wilmot Blyden*, ed. Hollis R. Lynch (Millwood, NY: KTO Press, 1978).
46. A.V. Adams, introduction to Hansen, *Island of Slaves*, 11.
47. Ibid. Adams dates the extinction of Negerhollands or Dutch Creole on St. Thomas to the 1970s. For more information on Dutch Creole, see also C. G. A. Oldendorp, *History of the Mission of the Evangelical Brethren on the Caribbean Islands of St. Thomas, St. Croix, and St. John*, trans. Arnold R. Highfield and Vladimir Borac, ed. Johan Jakob Bossard (Ann Arbor: Karoma Publishers, 1987), 251–65.
48. Holden, *Blyden of Liberia*, 19–20.
49. Ibid., 11–16.
50. Blyden, *Christianity, Islam*, xiv; Lynch, *Black Spokesman*, xii.
51. Maureen W. Lewis, *Notes to Masks* (Benin City, NG: Ethiope Publishing Corporation, 1977), 2.
52. Hamilton, *Routes of Passage*, 11–12.
53. Lewis, *Notes to Masks*, 2.

CHAPTER 2. REPRESENTATIONS OF THE FATHER OF PAN-AFRICANISM

1. "Man of the Month," *The Crisis: A Record of the Darker Races* (hereafter cited as *Crisis*), January 3, 1912, 103.
2. Mark C. Hayford, prefatory remarks to Edward Blyden, *Africa and Africans, Proceedings on the Occasion of a Banquet, Given at the Holborn Restaurant to Edward W. Blyden, August 15th, 1903, by West Africans in London* (London: C. M. Phillips, 1903), 1.
3. See, for example, Edward Blyden, *The African Problem and Other Discourses Delivered in America in 1890* (London: W. B. Withingham, 1890), 105. See also Edward Blyden, "The Call of Providence to the Descendants of Africa in America," in *Liberia's Offering: Being Addresses, Sermons, Etc.* (New York: J. A. Gray, 1862),

67–91; and many other writings published in Hollis R. Lynch, *Black Spokesman: Selected Published Writings of Edward Wilmot Blyden* (New York: Humanities Press, 1971); and Hollis R. Lynch, ed., *Selected Letters of Edward Wilmot Blyden* (Millwood, NY: KTO Press, 1978).

4. Blyden, *African Problem*, 105; Edith Holden, *Blyden of Liberia: An Account of the Life and Labors of Edward Wilmot Blyden, LL.D As Recorded in Letters and in Print* (New York: Vantage Press, 1966), 1019–23.
5. Blyden, *African Problem*, 105.
6. Edward Gladstone, quoted in Holden, *Blyden of Liberia*, 65.
7. Edward W. Blyden, quoted in ibid., 66.
8. Ibid., 67.
9. Ibid., 67–68.
10. Edward W. Blyden, quoted in Lynch, *Selected Letters*, 18–19, 43.
11. Holden, *Blyden of Liberia*, 36–37.
12. Ibid., 50.
13. Ibid., 52.
14. Ibid., 52–63.
15. Ibid., 54.
16. Ibid., 82–87.
17. Ibid., 87.
18. Lynch, *Selected Letters*, 54.
19. Holden, *Blyden of Liberia*, 127–28, 130, 488.
20. "Along the Color Line," *Crisis* 3, no. 3 (March 1912): 187; American Colonization Society, *African Repository* 45 (1869): 298; Lynch, *Black Spokesman*, xxxii; Holden, *Blyden of Liberia*, 165, 284; Edward W. Blyden, *Christianity, Islam and the Negro Race* (Edinburgh: Edinburgh University Press, 1967), ix.
21. "Edward Blyden to William Coppinger," August 9, 1878, in Lynch, *Selected Letters*, 274–76.
22. *London Star*, May 19, 1892; *Lagos Weekly Record*, 3, August 20, 1892; Blyden, *Christianity, Islam*, ix.
23. C. Collyer, "Edward Wilmot Blyden, a Correspondent of William Ewart Gladstone," *Journal of Negro History* 35, no. 1 (1950): 75–78.
24. Wilbur Deveraux Jones, "Blyden, Gladstone and the War," *Journal of Negro History* 49, no. 1 (1964): 56–58.
25. Ibid.
26. "Obituary Notice," *Journal of the African Society* 1 (1911–12): 362.
27. Stephen Gwynn, *The Life of Mary Kingsley* (London: MacMillan, 1932), 254.
28. Tracy K. Flemming, "Negro Travel and the Pan-African Imagination during the Nineteenth Century" (PhD diss., University of Michigan, 2010), 1–7; Simon

Gikandi, *Maps of Englishness: Writing Identity in the Culture of Colonialism* (New York: Columbia University Press, 1996).

29. Edward W. Blyden, *From West Africa to Palestine* (London: T. J. Sawyer, 1873), 76–77.
30. Blyden, *Christianity, Islam*, 265.
31. Gregory Mann, "Afropositivism," *Cultural Anthropology Online*, June 10, 2013, https://culanth.org.
32. Edward W. Blyden, *The Jewish Question* (Liverpool: Lionel Hart, 1898).
33. Edward W. Blyden, quoted in Lynch, *Black Spokesman*, 209; Daniel Brook, "The Forgotten Confederate Jew: How History Lost Judah P. Benjamin, the Most Prominent American Jew of the 19th Century," *Tablet*, July 17, 2012,
34. Michael J. C. Echeruo, "Edward W. Blyden, 'The Jewish Question,' and the Diaspora Theory and Practice," *Journal of Black Studies* 40, no. 4 (2010): 544.
35. Blyden, quoted in Lynch, *Black Spokesman*, 210.
36. Lloyd D. Easton and Kurt H. Guddat, eds., *Writings of the Young Marx on Philosophy and Society* (New York: Doubleday, 1967), 216–48.
37. For more details on the intellectuals, see Blyden, *Jewish Question*; and Blyden, quoted in Lynch, *Black Spokesman*, 209–14.
38. Blyden, *Jewish Question*, quoted in Lynch, *Black Spokesman*, 210–11.
39. I show that Blyden was first introduced to Islamic and Orientalist literature by West African Muslim intellectuals. After this initial encounter, Blyden traveled to North Africa and the Middle East to acquaint himself with the Arabic language and Orientalism as a field of study. Blyden balanced this later training with his experiences among Muslim West Africans, hence my use of *Africa-centered Orientalism*. For more details, see chap. 4 and esp. chap. 5.
40. *Southwestern Christian Advocate*, quoted in Blyden, *African Problem*, 105.
41. Blyden, quoted in Lynch, *Selected Letters*, 486. See also Wilson J. Moses, "The Lost World of the Negro, 1895–1919: Black Literary and Intellectual Life before the 'Renaissance,'" *Black American Literature Forum* 21, nos. 1–2 (1987): 61–84.
42. Holden, *Blyden of Liberia*, 275–96, 615–24, 648–68.
43. Ralph L. Crowder, *John Edward Bruce: Politician, Journalist, and Self-Trained Historian of the African Diaspora* (New York: New York University Press, 2004).
44. Alice Moore Dunbar-Nelson, ed., *Masterpieces of Negro Eloquence* (New York: The Bookery, 1914), 263–64; Raymond L. Buell, *The Native Problem in Africa*, vol. 2, (London: MacMillan, 1928); Georgina A. Gollock, *Sons of Africa* (London: Student Christian Movement, 1928); Davidson Nichol, "Great Sons of Africa," *Africana* 1, no. 2 (1949): 19–20.
45. Dunbar-Nelson, *Masterpieces of Negro Eloquence*, 263.
46. W. E. B. Du Bois to Edward Blyden, 1905, in *The Correspondence of W. E. B Du Bois*, (Amherst: University of Massachusetts Press, 1973), 199–200.

47. Ibid., 146.
48. "Along the Color Line," *Crisis* 6, no. 1 (May 1913): 13.
49. "Man of the Month," 103.
50. Robert Trenton Vinson III, *The Americans Are Coming: Dreams of African-American Liberation in Segregationist South Africa* (Athens: Ohio University Press, 2012), 1–10.
51. Moses, "Lost World of the Negro," 61–84.
52. Edward Blyden, "The Negro in Ancient History," *Methodist Quarterly Review* (1869): 71–93; Lynch, *Black Spokesman*, 141.
53. Lynch, *Black Spokesman*, xxv.
54. Blyden, *Christianity, Islam*, 9n12, 98n2.
55. William Seraile, *Fire in His Heart: Bishop Benjamin Tucker Tanner and the A.M.E. Church* (Knoxville: University of Tennessee Press, 1998), 70–72.
56. *New York Daily Tribune*, February 9, 1912; *Despatch from Sierra Leone*, February 9, 1912; "Dr. Edward W. Blyden, the Famous Negro Lecturer and Author Died Today," *New York Times*, February 9, 1912. See also Holden, *Blyden of Liberia*, 862, 865.
57. *Sierra Leone Weekly News*, March 2, 1912; *London Times*, May 24, 1912, 33; Holden, *Blyden of Liberia*, 862–65.
58. V. P. Franklin and Betty Collier-Thomas, "Race Vindication, and African-American Intellectuals," *Journal of Negro History* 81, no. 1 (1996): 7.
59. Blyden, *Christianity, Islam*, vii–ix.
60. J. E. Casely Hayford, *Ethiopia Unbound: Studies in Race Emancipation* (London: Frank Cass, 1969), 163–65.
61. "Along the Color Line," 187.
62. "The Horizon," *Crisis* 16, no. 5 (September 1918): 242.
63. Abiola Irele, *The African Experience in Literature and Ideology* (Bloomington: Indiana University Press, 1981), 97.
64. Flemming, "Negro Travel and Pan-African Imagination," 1–7.
65. Gilroy, *Black Atlantic*, 3–19.
66. Ibid., 19–40, 58, 112–208.
67. Ibid., 1–19.
68. Ibid., 15–19.
69. Ibid., 58, 112, 193, 208–11.
70. Emphasis mine; Hayford, *Ethiopia Unbound*, 163.
71. Emphasis mine; ibid.
72. Edward Blyden, "Islam in the Western Soudan," *Journal of the African Society* 5 (1902): 11–37.
73. Alfred A. Moss Jr., *The American Negro Academy: Voice of the Talented Tenth* (Baton Rouge: Louisiana State University Press, 1981), 79.

74. Ibid., 127–29.
75. Edward Blyden, *A Vindication of the African Race* (Monrovia, LR: G. Killian, 1857); Appeared in *Liberia's Offering*, 55–62.
76. Ibid.
77. Lynch, *Selected Letters*, 486.
78. W. E. B. Du Bois, *The Negro* (New York: Cosimo Classics, 1915), 41.
79. For other definitions and the historiography on Ethiopianism, see Charles S. Morris, "A Work for American Negroes," in *Ecumenical Missionary Conference, New York: Report of the Ecumenical Conference on Foreign Missions* (New York: American Tract Society, 1900), 1:469–71; George A. Shepperson, "Ethiopianism and African Nationalism," *Phylon* 14, no. 1 (1953): 9–18; George A. Shepperson, "Notes on Negro American Influences on African Nationalism," *Journal of African History* 1, no. 2 (1960): 299–312; George A. Shepperson, "Pan-Africanism and 'Pan-Africanism': Some Historical Notes," *Phylon* 23, no. 4 (1962): 346–58; James Campbell, *Middle Passages: African American Journeys to Africa, 1787–2005* (New York: Penguin), 2006; and Vinson, *Americans Are Coming*, 2012.
80. John C. Shields, *The Collected Works of Phyllis Wheatley* (New York: Oxford University Press, 1988); Vinson, *Americans Are Coming*; Nathaniel Samuel Murrell, William David Spencer, and Adrian Anthony McFarlane, eds., *The Rastafari Reader: Chanting Down Babylon*, (Philadelphia: Temple University Press, 1998). Monique A. Bedasse, *Jah Kingdom: Rastafarians, Tanzania and Pan-Africanism in the Age of Decolonization* (Chapel Hill: University of North Carolina, 2017).
81. Murrell, *Chanting Down Babylon*, 145–216.
82. Campbell, *Middle Passages*, 16–21.
83. A. B. C. Sibthorpe, *The History of Sierra Leone* (London, 1881); Reginald Coupland, *The British Anti-Slavery Movement* (London: Frank Cass, 1969); Leo Spitzer, *The Creoles of Sierra Leone* (Madison: University of Wisconsin Press, 1974); Gibril Cole, *The Krio of West Africa: Islam, Culture, Creolization, and Colonialism in the Nineteenth Century* (Athens: Ohio University Press, 2013).
84. Campbell, *Middle Passages*, 39–46.
85. Ibid., 44, 40–46.
86. Shepperson, "Ethiopianism and African Nationalism," 9–13.
87. Ibid., 9.
88. For the formation of independent Black communities in Pennsylvania, see W. E. B. Du Bois, *The Philadelphia Negro: A Social Study* (Philadelphia: University of Pennsylvania Press, 1996), 20–24.
89. Shepperson, "Ethiopianism and African Nationalism," 10. For South Africa, specifically see Vinson, *Americans Are Coming*.
90. Shepperson, "Ethiopianism and African Nationalism," 9.

91. Ibid., 9–18; Shepperson, "Notes on Negro American Influences on African Nationalism," 299–312; Shepperson, "Pan-Africanism and 'Pan-Africanism,'" 346–58.
92. Bruce Dorsey, "A Gendered History of African Colonization in the Antebellum United States," *Journal of Social History* 34, no. 1 (2003): 77–103.
93. For a history of these emigration movements, see with accompanying citations, Richard Blackett, "Martin R. Delany and Robert Campbell: Black Americans in Search of an African Colony," *Journal of Negro History* 62, no. 1 (1977): 1–25.
94. See Blyden's correspondence with these organizations in Lynch, *Selected Letters*, 3–28.
95. Holden, *Blyden of Liberia*, 28–29.
96. Morris, *Ecumenical Missionary Conference*, 469–71.
97. Blyden, quoted in Holden, *Blyden of Liberia*, 226–27.
98. Ibid., 29.
99. Ibid., 26.
100. Ibid., 33–34.
101. Ibid., 41–44.
102. Ibid.
103. Ibid., 58.
104. Holden, *Blyden of Liberia*, 926, see fn 16.
105. Lynch, *Selected letters*, 273–307.
106. Walter L. Williams, "Nineteenth Pan-Africanist: John Henry Smyth, United States Minister to Liberia, 1878–1885," *Journal of Negro History* 63, no. 1 (1978): 18–25.
107. Gilroy, *Black Atlantic*, 112–212.
108. Holden, *Blyden of Liberia*, 275–96, 626–68.
109. Martin R. Delany, *The Condition, Elevation, Emigration, and Destiny of the Colored People of the United States* (New York: Arno Press, 1968), 31.
110. Ibid., 171–89; See also, Martin R. Delany, *Blake; or, The Huts of America, a Novel* (Boston: Beacon Press, 1970); and *Proceedings of the National Emigration Convention of the Colored People, Held at Cleveland, Ohio, August 24 and 26, 1854* (Pittsburgh: A. A. Anderson, 1854).
111. Martin R. Delany, *Official Report of the Niger Valley Exploration Party* (New York: Niger Valley Exploration Party, 1861); for Delany's enlistment, see Vincent Harding's interpretation in *There Is a River: The Black Struggle for Freedom in America* (New York: Harcourt Brace Jovanovich, 1981).
112. Edward Blyden, "The Call for Providence to the Descendants of Africa in America," in Lynch, *Black Spokesman*, 25–26, 29.
113. Edward Blyden, "The Origin and Purpose of African Colonization," in Lynch, *Black Spokesman*, 43.

CHAPTER 3. THE AFRO-POSITIVIST FOUNDATIONS OF PAN-AFRICANISM: PLANTATION INTELLECTUALS AND AFRICA'S ATLANTIC SCHOLARS

1. Harry N. K. Odamtten, "A History of Ideas: 'The Black Atlantic' West Africa, and Pan-Africanism" (PhD diss. Michigan State University, 2010), 238–45.
2. "Christian Protten—Missionary to the Gold Coast of Africa," *This Month in Moravian History* 74, June 2012, 1; Peter Sebald, "Christian Jacob Protten Africanus (1715–1769) Erster Missionar Einer Deutschen Missionsgelleschaft in Schwarzafrika," in *Kolonien und Missionen Referate des 3: Internationalen Kolonialgeschictlichen Symposiums 1993*, ed. Wilfred Wagner (Münster: LIT Verlag, 1994), 117–18.
3. Sebald, "Christian Jacob Protten," 117–18.
4. C. G. A. Oldendorp, *History of the Mission of the Evangelical Brethren on the Caribbean Islands of St. Thomas, St. Croix, and St. John*, trans. Arnold R. Highfield and Vladimir Borac, ed. Johan Jakob Bossard (Ann Arbor: Karoma Publishers, 1985), 358–74.
5. Ray A. Kea, "'When I Die, I Shall Return to My Own Land': An 'Amina' Slave Rebellion in the Danish West Indies, 1733–1734," in *The Cloth of Many Colored Silks: Papers on History and Society, Ghanaian and Islamic in Honor of Ivor Wilks*, ed. John Hunwick and Nancy Lawler (Evanston, IL: Northwestern University Press, 1996), 159.
6. Michael Gomez, *Exchanging Our Country Marks: The Transformation of African Identities in the Colonial Antebellum South* (Chapel Hill: University of North Carolina Press, 1998), 8–11, identifies these two realms as elements of acculturation in the American South. I have resignified these terms as part of plantation public culture.
7. Some of the earlier works that focus on cultural processes include the classical anthropological texts Sydney Mintz and Richard Price, *The Birth of African American Culture: An Anthropological Perspective* (Boston: Beacon Press, 1992); and Melville J. Herskovits, *The Myth of the Negro Past* (Boston: Beacon Press 1958). Some of the exceptions that show the enslaved as thinkers include C. L. R. James, *Black Jacobins: Toussaint L'Ouverture and the San Domingo Revolution* (New York: Vintage Books, 1963); John Thornton, "'I Am the Subject of the King of Congo': African Political Ideology and the Haitian Revolution," *Journal of World History* 4, no. 2 (1993): 181–214; James Sweet, *Domingos Álvares, African Healing, and the Intellectual History of the Atlantic World* (Chapel Hill: University of North Carolina. Press, 2011).
8. Joseph. K. Adjaye, "Pan-Africanism," in *Survey of Social Science: Government and*

Politics, ed. Frank N. Magill (Englewood Cliffs, NJ: Salem Press, 1995), 1369–70.

9. Wilson Armistead, *A Tribute for the Negro: Being a Vindication of the Moral, Intellectual, and Moral Capabilities of the Colored Portion of Mankind; With Particular Reference to the African Race* (Manchester: William Irwin, 1848), 265–67.
10. *David Walker's Appeal, Together with Four Articles and a Preamble to the Colored Citizens of the World* (Baltimore: Black Classics Press, 1983); Edward W. Blyden, *A Voice from Bleeding Africa on Behalf of Her Exiled Children* (Monrovia: G. Killian, 1856), 21; Edward W. Blyden, *A Vindication of the African Race: Being a Brief Examination of the Arguments in Favor of African Inferiority* (Monrovia, LR: G. Killian, 1857).
11. Oldendorp, *History of the Mission*, 236.
12. Ibid., 235–36; Pierre J. Pannet, *Report on the Execrable Conspiracy Carried Out by the Amina Negroes on the Danish Island of St. Jan in America, 1733*, trans. and ed. Aimery P. Caron and Arnold R. Highfield (Christiansted, St. Croix: Antilles Press, 1984), 1–18.
13. Oldendorp, *History of the Mission*, 199.
14. Pannet, *Report on the Execrable Conspiracy*, 1–18.
15. Oldendorp, *History of the Mission*, 220.
16. Guerin C. Montilus, "Guinea versus Congo Lands: Aspects of the Collective Memory in Haiti," in *Global Dimensions of the African Diaspora*, ed. Joseph Harris (Washington, DC: Howard University Press, 1982), 163–69.
17. Gomez, *Exchanging Our Country Marks*, 118–20, 121–34.
18. Olaudah Equiano, *The Interesting Narrative of the Life of Olaudah Equiano, or Gustavus Vassa, the African* (London: Self-Published, 1789); Cugoano, *Thoughts and Sentiments on the Evil of Slavery and Commerce of the Human Species* (London: Self-Published, 1787); H. M. J. Trutenau, ed., *Christian Protten's 1764 Introduction to the Fante and Accra (Ga) Languages* (London, 1971).
19. Emphasis mine; Henry Louis Gates Jr. and William L. Andrews, eds., *Pioneers of the Black Atlantic: Five Slave Narratives from the Enlightenment* (Washington, DC: Civitas Counterpoint, 1998).
20. For Protten, see "Useful Grammatical Introduction"; for Amo, see William E. Abraham, "Anton Wilhelm Amo," in *A Companion to African Philosophy*, ed. Kwasi Wiredu (Oxford: Blackwell, 2004), 191–99; Equiano, *Interesting Narrative*; Cugoano, *Thoughts and Sentiments*; Jacobus Elisha Capitein, *The Agony of Asar: A Thesis on Slavery by a Former Slave*, trans. and ed. Grant Parker (Princeton, NJ: Markus Wiener, 2001).
21. For such a perspective, see Paul Gilroy, *The Black Atlantic, Modernity and Double Consciousness* (Cambridge, MA: Harvard University Press, 1993).
22. Abraham, "Anton Wilhelm Amo," 191; William E. Abraham, "The Life and Times of

Anton Wilhelm Amo," *Transactions of the Historical Society of Ghana* 7 (1964): 61.

23. For Blyden's challenge of the Presbyterian culture and conservatism, see Moses N. Moore Jr., "Edward Blyden and the Liberian Mission in Liberia," *Union Seminary Quarterly Review* 48 (1994): 59–114.
24. Abraham, "Anton Wilhelm Amo," 191–92; Abraham, "Life and Times of Anton Wilhelm Amo," 64–65.
25. Abraham, "Anton Wilhelm Amo," 192.
26. Ibid., 192–93.
27. Abraham, "Life and Times of Anton Wilhelm Amo," 72–73.
28. Blyden, *Christianity, Islam*, xi–ix.
29. Ibid., 77.
30. Ibid., 73–74, 76–77.
31. Ibid., 78.
32. Ibid., 79.
33. Hollis R. Lynch, *Selected Letters of Edward Wilmot Blyden* (Millwood, NY: KTO Press, 1978), 4.
34. Ibid., 69–70.
35. Ibid., 70–71.
36. Ibid., 69.
37. Kwasi Wiredu, "Amo's Critique of Descartes' Philosophy of Mind," in *A Companion to African Philosophy*, ed. Kwasi Wiredu (Oxford: Blackwell, 2004), 200–206.
38. Abraham, "Life and Times of Anton Wilhelm Amo," 73–74.
39. Ibid., 75.
40. See Amo's influence in Paulin Hountodji, *African Philosophy: Myth and Reality* (Bloomington: Indiana University Press, 1983), 114; Armistead, *Tribute for the Negro*, 265–67; W. E. B. Du Bois, *Black Folk: Then and Now: An Essay in the History and Sociology of the Negro Race* (New York: H. Holt and Company, 1939) , 87.
41. *African Mail*, February 16, 1912, 191.
42. Lady Elinor F. Bosworth Smith Grogan, *Reginald Bosworth Smith: A Memoir* (London: James Nisket, 1909), 76–77.
43. Hollis R. Lynch, *Edward Wilmot Blyden: Pan-Negro Patriot 1832–1912* (London: Oxford University Press, 1967), 59; see also *Journal of the Anthropological Society of London*, 8 vols. (1863–1870).
44. Lynch, *Edward Wilmot Blyden*, 59.
45. Edward W. Blyden, *African Life and Customs* (London, 1908), 7–12; see also M. Yu. Frenkel, "Edward Blyden and the Concept of African Personality," *African Affairs* 73 (1974): 277–89; Robert W. July, "Nineteenth-Century Negritude: Edward Wilmot Blyden," *Journal of African History* 5 (1964): 73–86.
46. Blyden, *African Life and Customs*, 7–12.

47. Ibid., 8.
48. Ibid., 8–90; Frenkel, "Edward Blyden," 277–89; July, "Nineteenth-Century Negritude," 73–86.
49. *Washington Post*, October 14, 1895, Also quoted in Edith Holden, *Blyden of Liberia: An Account of the Life and Labors of Edward Wilmot Blyden, LL.D. As Recorded in Letters and in Print* (New York: Vantage Press, 1966), 658.
50. Harry N. K. Odamtten, "Dode Akabi: A Reexamination of the Oral and Textual Narrative of a 'Wicked' Female King," *Journal of Women's History* 27, no. 3 (2015): 61–85.
51. Ole Justesen, *Danish Sources for the History of Ghana 1657–1754, vol. 1: 1657–1735, vol. 2: 1735–1754* (Copenhagen: Royal Danish Academy of Sciences and Letters, 2005), 302, 727.
52. Selena Axelrod Winsnes, ed., *Letters of West Africa and the Slave Trade: Paul Erdman Isert's Journey to Guinea and the Caribbean Islands in Columbia* (London: Oxford University Press, 1992), 1; Translation of the Pamphlets "Tegen Bericht," October 18, 1664, 17, D.2, FC; V.G.K. 77, Breve og Ugaede 1624, 1659–1680. Agreement between Okai Kwei, king of Accra, and Jost Cramer, commandant of Fredricksburgh in Guinea, August 18, 1661; Irene Quaye, "The Ga and Their Neighbors, 1600–1742" (PhD diss., University of Ghana–Legon, 1972), 51; Georg N. Nørregaard, *Danish Settlements in West Africa, 1658–1850* (Boston: Boston University Press. 1966), 42–43; J. Reindorf, *Scandinavians in Africa: Guide Relating to Ghana in the Danish National Archives*, ed. J. Simensen (Oslo: Universitetsforlaget, 1980), 1–4.
53. John Parker, *Making the Town: Ga State and Society in Early Colonial Accra* (Portsmouth, NH: Heinemann, 2000), 1–10.
54. Ibid., 33.
55. Ibid.; Nii Kwabena Bonne III, *Milestones in the History of the Gold Coast: Autobiography of Nii Kwabena Bone III Osu Alata Mantse, also Nana Owusu Akenten III Oyokohene of Techiman, Ashanti* (London: Diplomatist Publications, 1953).
56. David Kimble, *A Political History of Ghana: The Rise of Gold Coast Nationalism, 1850–1928* (Oxford: Clarendon Press, 1963), 65.
57. Reindorf, *Scandinavians in Africa*, 1.
58. Ibid., 3–6.
59. David N. A. Kpobi, *Mission in Chains: The Life, Theology, and Ministry of the Ex-Slave Jacobus E.J. Capitein (1717–1747); with a Translation of His Major Publications* (Zoetermeer: Boekencentrum, 1993), 163.
60. Protten likely spent a year in the village of Sorterup with Elias Svane preparing for the university, similar to when Amo received pansophic (general knowledge)

training before attending the university. (See Christian Protten, "Des Malatten C. J. Prottens Schrieben um die Aufnahme in die Evange: Mährische Brüder-Gemeine" [The Mullato C. J. Protten's Description of His Admission to the Evangelical Moravian Brethren's Congregation"], in Nikolaus Ludwig von Zinzendorf, *Ergänzungsband VII* [Hildesheim, 1965]: 4:418–19); Gunvor Simonsen, "Belonging in Africa: Frederik Svane and Christian Protten on the Gold Coast in the Eighteenth Century," *Itinerario* 31, no. 1 (2015): 93.

61. Edward W. Blyden, quoted in Hollis R. Lynch, *Black Spokesman: Selected Published Writings of Edward Wilmot Blyden* (London: Frank Cass, 1971), 211. Also see Blyden, *African Life and Customs.*
62. Trutenau, *Christian Protten's 1764 Introduction*; Simonsen, "Belonging in Africa," 104.
63. Simonsen, "Belonging in Africa," 105.
64. J. A. Zimmerman, *Grammatical Sketch and Vocabulary of the Akra or Ga-Language with an Appendix on the Adanme-Dialect*, vol. 2 (Stuttgart, 1858); Thomas Bearth, "J. G. Christaller: A Holistic View of Language and Culture—and C. C. Reindorf's History," in *The Recovery of the West African Past: African Pastors and African History in the Nineteenth Century; C.C. Reindorf & Samuel Johnson; Papers from an International Seminar Held in Basel, Switzerland, 25–28th October 1995 to Celebrate the Centenary of the Publication of C.C. Reindorf's* History of the Gold Coast and Asante, ed. Paul Jenkins (Basel: Basler Afrika Bibliographien, 1986); Johann Gottlieb Christaller, *A Grammar of the Asante and Fante Language Called Tsi (Chwee, Twi)* (Basel, 1875). Christaller's other works include *Twi Mmebusem Mpensa-Ahansia Mmoano: A Collection of Three Thousand and Six Hundred Tshi Proverbs* (Basel, 1879) and *Dictionary of the Asante and Fante Language* (Basel, 1881). J. E. Capitein, another Gold Coast–born intellectual, had also earlier translated the Catechism into Fante. See F. L. Bartels, "Jacobus Eliza Capitein, 1717–47," *Transactions of the Historical Society of Ghana* 4, no. 1 (1959).
65. Holden, *Blyden of Liberia*, 584.
66. Simonsen, "Belonging in Africa," 102–3.
67. Ibid.; Oldendorp, *History of the Mission*; Hans W. Debrunner, *A History of Christianity in Ghana* (Accra: Waterville, 1967), 62–63.
68. John F. Sensbach, *Rebecca's Revival: Creating Black Christianity in the Atlantic World* (Cambridge, MA: Harvard University Press, 2005), 191.
69. Protten, "Des Malatten C. J. Prottens Schrieben," 419–21.
70. Sensbach, *Rebecca's Revival*, 202.
71. Ibid., 216.
72. Ibid., 226.
73. Blyden, *Voice from Bleeding Africa*, 19–21.

74. Amo wrote on the "rights of Africans in Europe." For detailed discussion, see Abraham, "Anton Wilhelm Amo"; and John H. McClendon III, "Introduction to Drs. Anton Wilhelm Amo and Charles Leander Hill with Select Bibliography," *American Philosophical Association Newsletter on Philosophy and the Black Experience* 2, no. 2 (2003): 42–50. See also "Useful Grammatical Introduction"; Trutenau, *Christian Protten's 1764 Introduction*; and Capitein, *Agony of Asar*.
75. Gilroy's *Black Atlantic* curiously excludes the entire African continent in the making of a "Black Atlantic."
76. *African Mail*, February 16, 1912, 191.
77. Edward W. Blyden to the Presbytery of West Africa, December 8, 1886, quoted in Holden, *Blyden of Liberia*, 573.
78. Ibid., 575–79.
79. Ibid., 612–13. For more in-depth analysis of the theological disagreements, see Moses N. Moore Jr., "Edward Blyden and the Presbyterian Mission in Liberia," 48 (1994): 59–114.
80. *Sierra Leone Weekly News*, June 28, 1902; Holden, *Blyden of Liberia*, 776.
81. Blyden, *Christianity, Islam*, 71–93.
82. Lynch, *Black Spokesman*, 205–8.
83. Lynch, *Selected Letters*, 489.
84. Ibid.
85. Edward W. Blyden, *African Problem, Proceedings on the Occasion of a Banquet Given at the Holborn Restaurant to Edward W. Blyden, August 15th, 1903, by West Africans in London* (London: C. M Phillips, 1903); J. E. C. Hayford, *Ethiopia Unbound: Studies in Race Emancipation* (London: Frank Cass, 1969).
86. Other texts include Robert Alexander Young, *Ethiopian Manifesto* (New York, 1829), in *The Ideological Origins of Black Nationalism*, ed. Sterling Stuckey (Boston: Beacon Press, 1972), 30–38.
87. George Padmore, *Pan-Africanism or Communism?* (Garden City, NY: Anchor, 1972), 30–53; Peter Esedebe, *Pan-Africanism: The Idea and Movement, 1776–1963* (Washington, DC: Howard University Press, 1982), 29–40.
88. Alfred A. Moss Jr., *The American Negro Academy* (Baton Rouge: Louisiana State University Press, 1981), 79.
89. Ibid., 1.
90. Lynch, *Black Spokesman*, 131.
91. John Gibbs St. Claire Drake, *Black Folk Here and There: An Essay in History and Anthropology* (Los Angeles: University of California, Center for Afro-American Studies, 1987), xvii.
92. Ibid.
93. Ibid.

94. Manning Marable, "Black Studies and the Black Intellectual Tradition," *Race & Reason* 4 (1997–1998): 3–8.
95. I use Africans—that is, Africa-born enslaved—here following the ideas expressed in Gomez, *Exchanging Our Country Marks*, 9, 1–16.
96. Esedebe, *Pan-Africanism*, 7.
97. Sylviane Diouf, ed., *Fighting the Slave Trade: West African Strategies* (Athens: Ohio University Press, 2003); Harding, *There Is a River: The Black Struggle for Freedom in the United States* (New York: Harcourt Brace Jovanovich, 1981), 3–4, 20–23.
98. For identity formation in the United States, see Gomez, *Exchanging Our Country Marks*; for the entire Atlantic, see Paul E. Lovejoy and David V. Trotman, *Trans-Atlantic Dimensions of Ethnicity in the African Diaspora* (London: Continuum, 2003); Linda M. Heywood, *Central Africans and Cultural Transformations in the American Diaspora* (Cambridge: Cambridge University Press, 2002).
99. Matt Childs, *The 1812 Aponte Rebellion in Cuba and the Struggle against Atlantic Slavery* (Chapel Hill: University of North Carolina Press, 2006).
100. See Harry N. K. Odamtten, "Critical Departures in the Practice of Pan-Africanism in the New Millennium," in *Pan-Africanism, and the Politics of African Citizenship and Identity*, Toyin Falola and Kwame Essien (New York: Routledge, 2014), 172–86; Horace Campbell, B. F. Bankie, and S. Sibanda, eds., *Pan Africanism and African Liberation in the 21st century* (Windhoek, Namibia: Pan African Centre of Namibia, 2000); Ibbo Mandaza and Dani Wadada Nabudere, eds., *Pan-Africanism and Integration in Africa* (Harare, Zimbabwe: SAPES Books, 2002).
101. Paul T. Zeleza, *Manufacturing African Studies* (Dakar: CODESRIA, 1997), 512.
102. Gilroy, *Black Atlantic*; Kwame A. Appiah, *In My Father's House: Africa in the Philosophy of Culture* (London: Metheun, 1992).
103. Wilson Jeremiah Moses, *Classical Black Nationalism: From the American Revolution to Marcus Garvey* (New York: New York University Press, 1996), 3; Wilson Jeremiah Moses, *Afrotopia: The Roots of African American Popular Culture* (New York: Cambridge University Press), 131.

CHAPTER 4. EDWARD BLYDEN'S ETHNOSCAPES: IGBO, AFRO-DANISH, AND JEWISH

1. For the debates on African Diaspora see for example Elliot P. Skinner, "The Dialectic between Diaspora and Homelands," in *Global Dimensions of the African Diaspora*, ed. Joseph Harris (Washington, DC: Howard University, 1982); Vincent Bakpetu Thompson, *The Making of the African Diaspora in the Americas 1441–1990* (New York: Longman, 1987), 1; William Safran, "Diasporas in Modern

Societies: Myths of Homeland and Return," *Diaspora* 1, no. 1 (1991): 83–99. For more of the contestations, see Joseph Harris, ed., *Global Dimensions of the African Diaspora* (Washington, DC: Howard University Press, 1982), esp. p. 6; James Clifford, "Diasporas," *Cultural Anthropology* 9, no. 3 (1994): 305–6; Robin Cohen, "Diasporas and the Nation-State: From Victims to Challengers," *International Affairs* 72, no. 3 (1996): 507–20; Tiffany Ruby Patterson and Robin D. G. Kelley, "Unfinished Migrations," *African Studies Review* 43, no. 1 (2000): 11–45; Brent Hayes Edwards et al., "'Unfinished Migrations': Commentary and Response," *African Studies Review* 43, no. 1 (2000): 47–68; Brent Hayes Edwards, "The Uses of Diaspora," *Social Text* 19, no. 1 (2001): 45–73.

2. Edward W. Blyden, *The Jewish Question*, quoted in Hollis R. Lynch, ed., *Selected Letters of Edward Wilmot Blyden* (Millwood, NY: KTO Press, 1978), 210–11.
3. I use "process and condition" here drawing on the use of the terms in Edwards et al., "'Unfinished Migrations': Commentary and Response," 65. In "Unfinished Migrations," Patterson and Kelley explain that the diaspora is both process and condition. As a process, it is always in the making, and as a condition, it is situated within global race and gender hierarchies.
4. John Hunwick, *Jews of a Saharan Oasis: The Elimination of the Tamantif Community* (Princeton, NJ: Markus Wiener, 2006); William F. Miles, *Jews of Nigeria: An Afro-Judaic Odyssey* (Princeton, NJ: Markus Wiener, 2013); John Hunwick, *Afro-Jewish Encounters from Timbuktu to the Indian Ocean and Beyond* (Princeton, NJ: Markus Wiener, 2014); Peter Mark and Jose da Silva Horta, *The Forgotten Diaspora: Jewish Communities in West Africa and the Making of the Atlantic World* (New York: Cambridge University Press, 2011); Tudor Parfitt, *Black Jews in Africa and the Americas* (Cambridge, MA: Harvard University Press, 2013); Edith Bruder and Tudor Parfitt, eds., *African Zion: Studies in Black Judaism* (Newcastle-upon-Tyne: Cambridge Scholars Press, 2012); Edith Bruder, *The Black Jews of Africa: History, Religion, Identity* (New York: Oxford University Press, 2008).
5. Blyden is likely to have read about the events of the rebellion and Peter von Scholten's proclamation of emancipation in the *Sanct. Thomae Tidende*, July 5–19, 1848, or in the *St. Croix Avis*, July 3–September 25, 1848.
6. Churches in the Danish West Indies in this period owned enslaved blacks like Maria Rosina. Like Maria, see the example of "A Negro woman, Sylvia, a good cook, with her three children, a boy and two girls, belong[ed] to the Danish Church" in *RDAG* 5, November 14/16, 1774.
7. *STT*, July 5, 1848, vol. 2, no. 157; and *STT*, July 19, 1848, vol. 2, no. 159; *SCA* July 3, 1848, 3die Quartal, no. 471; and *SCA* September 25, 1848, 3die Quartal, no. 495; Thorkhild Hansen, *Island of Slaves*, trans. Kari Dako (Accra: Sub-Saharan

Publishers, 2004), 370–425.

8. Isaac Dookhan, *A History of the Virgin Islands of the United States* (St. Thomas: Caribbean Universities Press, 1974), 175–78; Hansen, *Island of Slaves*, 21.
9. For previous revolts, see Pierre J. Pannet, *Report on the Execrable Conspiracy Carried Out by the Amina Negroes on the Danish Island of St. Jan in America, 1733*, trans. and ed. Aimery P. Caron and Arnold R. Highfield (Christiansted, St. Croix: Antilles Press, 1984); Waldemar Westergaard, "Account of the Negro Rebellion on St. Croix, Danish West Indies 1759," *The Journal of Negro History* 11, no. 1 (1926): 50–61; David Barry Gaspar, "The Antigua Slave Conspiracy of 1736: A Case Study of the Origins of Collective Resistance," *William and Mary Quarterly* 35, no. 2 (1978): 308–23; Ray A. Kea, "'When I Die, I Shall Return to My Own Land': An 'Amina' Slave Rebellion in the Danish West Indies, 1733–1734," in *The Cloth of Many Colored Silks: Papers on History and Society, Ghanaian and Islamic in Honor of Ivor Wilks*, ed. John Hunwick and Nancy Lawler (Evanston, IL: Northwestern University Press, 1996), 159–67.
10. *Sanct. Thomae Tidende* and *St. Croix Avis*, September 25, 1846; Dookhan, *History of the Virgin Islands*, 175–78; Hansen, *Island of Slaves*, 21.
11. Lewis Tappan, "Correspondence of Lewis Tappan and Others with the British and Foreign Anti-Slavery Society [Part 8]," *Journal of Negro History* 13, no. 3 (July 1927): 413–36, 433; Hansen, *Islands of Slaves*, 424.
12. Tappan, "Correspondence of Lewis Tappan," 433.
13. Hansen, *Island of Slaves*; and Dookhan, *History of the Virgin Islands.*
14. *Sanct. Thomae Tidende*, no. 140. May 6, 1848.
15. Rosanne M. Adderley, *New Negroes from Africa: Slave Trade Abolition and Free African Settlements in the Nineteenth Century Caribbean* (Bloomington: Indiana University Press, 2007), 51–103; Reginald Coupland, *The British Anti-Slavery Movement* (London: Frank Cass, 1969), 163. See also, Miranda Frances Spieler, *Empire and Underworld: Captivity in French Guyana* (Cambridge, MA: Harvard University Press, 2012).
16. Solomon Northup, *Twelve Years a Slave* (New York: Penguin, 2012).
17. Edward W. Blyden, quoted in Edith Holden, *Blyden of Liberia: An Account of the Life and Labors of Edward Wilmot Blyden, LL.D. As Recorded in Letters and in Print* (New York: Vantage Press, 1966), 25.
18. Holden, *Blyden of Liberia*, 19.
19. Judah Cohen, *Through the Sands of Time* (Waltham, MA: Brandeis University Press, 2004); J. Hartog, *The Jews and St. Eustatius* (St. Martin: Windward Islands Bank, 1976).
20. Advertisements of Danish newspapers I examined at the Enid M. Baa Public Library in St. Thomas, Virgin Islands, in fact show that the enslaved blacks in the

Danish West Indies were often multilingual. Several advertisements explain that most of the "runaways" were familiar with Dutch, Creole-Dutch, Danish, English, and Spanish. See also, C. G. A. Oldendorp, *History of the Mission of the Evangelical Brethren on the Caribbean Islands of St. Thomas, St. Croix, and St. John*, trans. Arnold R. Highfield and Vladimir Borac, ed. Johan Jakob Bossard (Ann Arbor: Karoma Publishers, 1985), 251–60.

21. Blyden, quoted in Holden, *Blyden of Liberia*, 20.
22. Ibid., 19.
23. See ibid., 20.
24. Ibid.
25. Edward Blyden, *From West Africa to Palestine* (London: T. J. Sawyer, 1873), iii.
26. *Sanct. Thomae Tidende*, May 6, 1848, no. 140; Holden, *Blyden of Liberia*, 11, 20.
27. Holden, *Blyden of Liberia*, 11.
28. Ibid., 26–28.
29. Ibid.
30. See also *Sierra Leone Weekly News*, February 10, 1912, 6; Holden, *Blyden of Liberia*, 19; P. Olisanwuche Esedebe, *Pan-Africanism: The Idea and Movement, 1776–1963* (Washington, DC: Howard University Press, 1982), 30.
31. Edward W. Blyden, *Christianity, Islam and the Negro Race* (Edinburgh: Edinburgh University Press, 1967), viii.
32. Vincent Harding, *There Is a River: The Black Struggle for Freedom in America* (New York: Harcourt Brace Jovanovich, 1981), 56; Douglas R. Egerton, *He Shall Go Out Free: The Lives of Denmark Vesey* (Madison, WI: Madison House, 1999); Robert L. Paquette, "Jacobins of the Lowcountry: The Vesey Plot on Trial," *William and Mary Quarterly* 59, no. 1 (2002), 185–92.
33. Harding, *There Is a River*, 66–70.
34. Ibid., 78.
35. Karla Gottlieb, *The Mother of Us All: A History of Queen Nanny, Leader of the Windward Jamaican Maroons* (Trenton, NJ: Africa World Press, 2000).
36. Selwyn Cudjoe, *Resistance and Caribbean Literature* (Athens: Ohio University Press, 1980).
37. Pannet, *Report on the Execrable Conspiracy*; Westergaard, "Account of the Negro Rebellion"; Gaspar, "Antigua Slave Conspiracy of 1736," 3.
38. Laurent Dubois, *Avengers of the New World: The Story of the Haitian Revolution* (Cambridge, MA: Harvard University Press, 2004), 99–100.
39. Matt D. Childs, *The 1812 Aponte Rebellion in Cuba and the Struggle against Atlantic Slavery* (Chapel Hill: University of North Carolina Press).
40. Harding, *There Is a River*, 129; Anna J. Cooper, *A Voice from the South by a Black Woman of the South* (New York: Oxford University Press, 1988), 30. For early

biographies of Delany, see Dorothy Sterling, *The Making of an Afro-American: Martin Robison Delany 1812–1885* (New York: Doubleday, 1971); and Victor Ullman, *Martin R. Delany: The Beginnings of Black Nationalism* (Boston: Beacon Press, 1971).

41. James Campbell, *Middle Passages: African American Journeys to Africa, 1787–2005* (New York: Penguin, 2007), 104; Stephen Ward Angell, *Bishop Henry McNeal Turner and African American Religion in the South* (Knoxville: University of Tennessee Press, 1992), 7.
42. W. E. B. Du Bois, *Souls of Black Folk* (Chicago: Lushena Books, 2000), 180.
43. Michael Gomez, *Exchanging Our Country Marks: The Transformations of African Identities in the Colonial and Antebellum South* (Chapel Hill: University of North Carolina Press, 1998), 9.
44. For debates, see Adiele E. Afigbo, *Ropes of Sand: Studies in Igbo History and Culture* (Ibadan, NG: University Press,1981); David Northrup, "Igbo and Myth Igbo: Culture and Ethnicity in the Atlantic World," *Slavery and Abolition* 21, no. 3 (2000): 1–20; Douglas B. Chambers, "The Significance of the Igbo in the Bight of Biafra Slave Trade: A Rejoinder to Northrup's 'Myth Igbo,'" *Slavery and Abolition* 23, no. 1 (2002): 101–20; Phillip D. Morgan, "Becoming African: Identity Formation among Liberated Slaves in Nineteenth-Century Sierra Leone," *Slavery and Abolition* 27, no. 1 (2006): 1–21; Chima J. Korieh, "African Ethnicity as Mirage? Historicizing the Essence of the Igbo in Africa and the Atlantic Diaspora," *Dialectical Anthropology* 30, no. 1 (2006): 91–118.
45. Afigbo, *Ropes of Sand*; Chinua Achebe, *Home and Exile* (Oxford: Oxford University Press, 2000), 1–19; Gomez, *Exchanging Our Country Marks*, 114–34; Gwendolyn M. Hall, *Slavery and African Ethnicities in the Americas: Restoring the Links* (Chapel Hill: University of North Carolina Press, 2005), 126–43.
46. Kamene Okonjo, "The Dual Sex Political System in Operation: Igbo Women and Community Politics in Midwestern Nigeria," in *Women in Africa: Studies in Social and Economic Change*, ed. Edna G. Bay and Nancy J. Hafkin (Stanford: Stanford University Press, 1976), 45–58; G. Ugo Nwokeji, *The Slave Trade and Culture in the Bight of Biafra: An African Society in the Atlantic World* (New York: Cambridge University Press, 2010), xv–xvi; Gomez, *Exchanging Our Country Marks*, 125–31.
47. Myron Jackson, personal conversation with author, Charlotte Amalie, St. Thomas, June 29, 2012.
48. For a discussion of oral evidence in African historiography, see Luis White, Stephan E. Meischer, and David William Cohen, eds., *African Words, African Voices: Critical Practices in Oral History* (Bloomington: Indiana University Press, 2001).
49. Vincent Carretta, *Equiano, the African: Biography of a Self-Made Man* (Athens: University of Georgia Press, 2005); Paul E. Lovejoy, "Autobiography and Memory:

Gustavus Vassa, Alias Olaudah Equiano, the African," *Slavery and Abolition* 27, no. 3 (2006): 317–47; Paul E. Lovejoy, "Issues of Motivation—Vassa/Equiano and Carretta's Critique of the Evidence," *Slavery and Abolition* 28, no. 1 (2007): 121–25; Catherine Acholonu, *The Igbo Roots of Olaudah Equiano* (Owerri, NG: AFA Publications, 1989); S. E. Ogude, "No Roots Here: On the Igbo Roots of Olaudah Equiano," *RELS Monographs* no. 5 (Ibadan, NG: Bookman Educational and Communication Services, 1989), 1–16; O. S. Ogede, "'The Igbo Roots of Olaudah Equiano' by Catherine Acholonu," *Africa: Journal of the International African Institute* 61, no. 1 (1991): 138–41; Ugo Nwojkeji, "Colloquy with the Author: Vincent Carretta and 'Equiano, the African,'" *Studies in Eighteenth-Century Culture* 38 (2009): 1–14; James H. Sweet, "Mistaken Identities? Olaudah Equiano, Domingos Álvares, and the Methodological Challenges of Studying the African Diaspora," *American Historical Review* 114, no. 2 (2009): 279–306; Douglas B. Chambers, "'Almost an Englishman': Carretta's Equiano," review of *Equiano the African: Biography of a Self-Made Man*, by Vincent Carretta, H-Atlantic, H-Net Reviews, November 2007.

50. Data from the Trans-Atlantic Slave Trade Database, http://www.slavevoyages.org/.
51. *RDAG* 4, no. 81, October 11, 1775.
52. *RDAG* 4, no. 81, July 28, 1770.
53. *RDAG* 4, no. 81, August 1, 1770; October 6, 1770.
54. *RDAG* 4, no. 81, November 28, 1770; August 7, 1772.
55. *RDAG* 4, no. 81, August 22, 1770; August 29, 1770; February 20, 1773.
56. *RDAG* 3, no. 290, April 17, 1773.
57. *RDAG* 3, no. 233, September 30, 1772.
58. *RDAG* 6, no. 81, November 4, 1775.
59. Italics mine; Blyden, quoted in Hollis R. Lynch, *Black Spokesman: Selected Published Writings of Edward Wilmot Blyden* (London: Frank Cass, 1971), 55.
60. Achebe, *Home and Exile*, 14; Blyden, quoted in Lynch, *Black Spokesman*, 55.
61. Achebe, *Home and Exile*, 17.
62. Blyden, quoted in Lynch, *Black Spokesman*, 55.
63. Achebe, *Home and Exile*, 7, 18.
64. Blyden, quoted in Lynch, *Black Spokesman*, 55.
65. Achebe, *Home and Exile*, 1–18; Gomez, *Exchanging Our Country Marks*, 114–34; Hall, *Slavery and African Ethnicities*, 126–43; Paul E. Lovejoy and David V. Trotman, eds., *Trans-Atlantic Dimensions of Ethnicity in the African Diaspora* (London: Continuum, 20030; Douglas Chambers, *Murder at Montpelier: Igbo Africans in Virginia* (Jackson: University Press of Mississippi, 2005).
66. Oldendorp, *History of the Mission*; Soi-Daniel W. Brown, "From the Tongues of Africa: A Partial Translation of Oldendorp's Interviews," *Plantation Society in the*

Americas 2, no. 1 (1983): 37–61.

67. For ideas on ethnogenesis, see Stephen Palmirer, "Ethnogenetic Processes and Cultural Transfer in Caribbean Slave Populations," in *Slavery in the Americas*, ed. W. Binder (Würzburg: Königshauser & Neumann, 1993), 337–64; S. Palmié, "Introduction: On Predications of Africanity," in *Africas of the Americas: Beyond the Search for Origins in the Study of Afro-Atlantic Religions*, ed. S. Palmié (Leiden: Brill, 2008), 1–37.
68. Lovejoy and Trotman, *Trans-Atlantic Dimensions of Ethnicity*; Hall, *Slavery and African Ethnicities*; Toyin Falola and Matt Childs, *The Yoruba Diaspora in the Atlantic World* (Bloomington: Indiana University Press. 2004); Kwasi Konadu, *The Akan Diaspora in the Americas* (Oxford: Oxford University Press, 2010); Douglas B. Chambers, *Igbo Diaspora in the Era of the Slave Trade: An Introductory History* (Enugu, Nigeria: Jemezie Associates, 2013).
69. Edward W. Blyden, *The Jewish Question* (Liverpool: Lionel Hart, 1898), 5–6.
70. Blyden, *West Africa to Palestine*, 92.
71. Ibid., 169.
72. Blyden, *The Jewish Question*, 6.
73. *St. Thomae Tidende*, July 26, 1862; August 5, 1862; August 9, 1862; August 23, 1862; August 27, 1862; September 3, 1862.
74. Blyden, *West Africa to Palestine*, 170.
75. *Daily News* (St. Thomas, Virgin Islands), no. 11502, July 26, 1976, no. 5: 17.
76. Rabbi Moch, personal conversation with author, Charlotte Amalie, St. Thomas, June 28, 2012.
77. Blyden, *Jewish Question*, 5.
78. Blyden, in Lynch, *Black Spokesman*, 209–10; *Daily News* (St. Thomas), no. 11506, July 30, 1976, 18.
79. Blyden, *Jewish Question*, 6.
80. See Lynch, *Black Spokesman*, 210.
81. James Dorman, "Lifted out of the Commonplace Grandeur of Modern Times: Reappraising Edward Wilmot Blyden's Views of Islam in Light of His Scholarly Black Christian Orientalism," *Souls: A Critical Journal of Black Politics, Culture and Society* 12, no. 4 (2010): 398–418.
82. To see Blyden's approach read Edward W. Blyden, *The Arabic Bible in the Soudan: A Plea for Transliteration* (London: C. M. Phillips, 1910).
83. Blyden, quoted in Lynch, *Black Spokesman*, 210–11; see also Michael J. C. Echeruo, "Edward Blyden, 'The Jewish Question,' and the Diaspora Theory and Practice," *Journal of Black Studies* 40, no. 4 (2010): 544–65.
84. Blyden, quoted in Lynch, *Black Spokesman*, 209.
85. Benjamin Neuberger, "Early African Nationalism, Judaism and Zionism," *Jewish*

Social Studies 47, no. 2 (1985): 155.

86. Blyden, quoted in Lynch, *Black Spokesman*, 210–11.
87. See Hollis R. Lynch, *Edward Wilmot Blyden, Pan-Negro Patriot 1832–1912* (London: Oxford University Press, 1967); M. Y. Frenkel, "Edward Blyden and the African Personality," *African Affairs* 73 (1974): 277; and Blyden, quoted in Holden, *Blyden of Liberia*, 19.
88. Holden, *Blyden of Liberia*, 19, 923.
89. Heinrich W. Guggenheimer and Eva H. Guggenheimer, *Jewish Family Names and Their Origins: An Etymological Dictionary* (Hoboken, NJ: KTAV Publishing House, 1992), 111.
90. Isaac S. Emmanuel and Suzanne A. Emmanuel, *History of the Jews of the Netherlands Antilles* (Cincinnati: American Jewish Archives, 1970); Hartog, *Jews and St. Eustatius*; Norman F. Barka, "Archaeology of the Jewish Synagogue Honen Dalim, St. Eustacius, Netherlands Antilles," *Archeological Research Series* 4 (1988).
91. Holden notes that Blyden took his middle name, Wilmot, from his uncle Wilmot Nicholson, his mother's brother. See Holden, *Blyden of Liberia*, 926.
92. Hartog, *Jews and St. Eustatius*; S. T. Relkin and M. Abrams, *A Short History of the Hebrew Congregation of St. Thomas* (St. Thomas, 1983); E. Baa, "Historical News and Comments: The Preservation of the Sephardic Records of the Island of St. Thomas, Virgin Islands," *Publications of the American Jewish Historical Society* 44, no. 2 (1954): 114–19. Isidor Paiewonsky, *Jewish Historical Development in the Virgin Islands 1665–1959* (St. Thomas, published by author, 1959).
93. I. S. Emanuel, *The Jews of Coro, Venezuela* (Cincinnati: American Jewish Archive, Hebrew Union College, Jewish institute of Religion, 1973).
94. Blyden, *Jewish Question*.
95. Paiewonsky, *Jewish Historical Development in the Virgin Islands*, 12–13.
96. Parfitt, *Black Jews*, xii, 1–23.
97. Blyden, quoted in Lynch, *Black Spokesman*, 209.
98. See Charles Verlinden, *L'esclavage dans l'Europe médiévale* (Ghent: Rijksuniversiteit te Gent, 1977), 2: 141–55, 217, 353–54; and David Northrup, *Africa's Discovery of Europe, 1450–1850* (New York: Oxford University Press 2014), 6.
99. Parfitt, *Black Jews*, 1.
100. D. T. Niane, "Relationships and Exchanges among the Different Regions," in *UNESCO General History of Africa*, vol.4, *Africa from the Twelfth to the Sixteenth Centuries* (Berkeley: University of California Press, 1984), 614–34.
101. T. Insoll, *The Archeology of Islam in Sub-Saharan Africa* (Cambridge: Cambridge University Press, 2003); Paul Lovejoy, *Salt of the Desert Sun* (Cambridge: Cambridge University Press, 1986); E. Savage, *The Human Commodity: Perspectives on the Trans-Saharan Slave Trade* (London: Frank Cass, 1992); Hall, *Slavery and*

African Ethnicities, 1–8.

102. Philip Curtin, *The Rise and Fall of the Atlantic Complex: Essays in Atlantic History* (New York: Cambridge University Press, 1998).
103. John William Blake, trans and ed., "Rui de Pina, *Chronica d'El Rey Dom João II (c. 1500)*," in *Europeans in West Africa, 1450–1560*, 2 vols. (London: Hakluyt Society, 1942), 70–86.
104. Northrup, *Africa's Discovery of Europe*, 7.
105. James Sweet, *Domingos Álavares, African Healing, and the Intellectual History of the Atlantic World* (Chapel Hill: University of North Carolina. Press, 2011), 159.
106. Mark and da Silva Horta, *Forgotten Diaspora*, 8.
107. Ibid., 1–38.
108. Parfitt, *Black Jews*, 3.
109. Richard L. Kagan and Phillip D. Morgan, eds., *Atlantic Diasporas: Jews, Conversos, and Crypto-Jews in the Age of Mercantilism 1500–1800* (Baltimore: Johns Hopkins University Press, 2009).
110. Wim Klooster, "Networks of Colonial Entrepreneurs: The Founders of the Jewish Settlements in Dutch Americas," in Kagan and Morgan, *Atlantic Diasporas*, 33–49.
111. Emmanuel and Emmanuel, *Jews of the Netherlands Antilles*; Hartog, *Jews and St. Eustatius*; J. Hartog, "The Honen Daliem Congregation of St. Eustatius," *American Jewish Archives* 19 (1967): 60–77; Barka, "Archaeology of the Jewish Synagogue Honen Dalim"; Mordecai Arbell, *The Jewish Nation of the Caribbean: The Spanish-Portuguese Jewish Settlements in the Caribbean and the Guianas* (Jerusalem: Geffen Press, 2002); J. Franklin Jamison, "St. Eustatius in the American Revolution," *American Historical Review* 8, no. 4 (July 1903): 683–708.
112. Blyden, quoted in Lynch, *Black Spokesman*, 211.
113. Robin Cohen, *The Global Diasporas: An Introduction* (Seattle: University of Washington Press, 1997).
114. Blyden, quoted in Lynch, *Black Spokesman*, 211.
115. Edwards et al., "'Unfinished Migrations': Commentary and Response," 65; Ruth Simms Hamilton, *Routes of Passage: Rethinking the African Diaspora* (East Lansing: Michigan State University Press, 2007), 11–12; Kwame Essien, "A Abentura Da Casa Brasil: History of the Tabom People, Part I," in *Back to Africa: Afro-Brazilian Returnees and Their Communities*, by Kwesi Kwah Prah (Cape Town: Centre for Advanced Studies of African Society, 2009): 173–92; Kwame Essien, *Brazilian-African Diaspora in Ghana: The Tabom, Slavery, Dissonance of Memory, Identity, and Locating Home* (East Lansing: Michigan State University Press, 2016).

CHAPTER 5. EDWARD WILMOT BLYDEN AND THE "AFRICANIZATION OF ISLAM" IN WEST AFRICA

1. "Edward Blyden to Henry Venn," September 6, 1871, CA 1/047, Church Missionary Society Archives, London (hereafter cited as CMS). The Muslims Blyden encountered named him Mukhtar (the chosen one), and Abd-al-Kerim; see Edith Holden, *Blyden of Liberia: An Account of the Life and Labors of Edward Wilmot Blyden, LL.D. As Recorded in Letters and in Print* (New York: Vantage Press, 1966), 189.
2. For some of these discussions on intellectual history, see Robert W. July, *The Origins of Modern African Thought: Its Development in West Africa during the Nineteenth and Twentieth Centuries* (New York: Praegar, 1967); Deborah Shapple Spillman, *British Colonial Realism in Africa: Inalienable Objects, Contested Domains* (New York: Palgrave Macmillan, 2012); Teshale Tibebu, *Edward Blyden and the Racial Nationalist Imagination* (Rochester, NY: University of Rochester Press, 2012).
3. Edward W. Blyden, *Christianity, Islam and the Negro Race* (Edinburgh: Edinburgh University Press, 1967), 12.
4. David E. Skinner, "Islam in the Northern Hinterland and Its Influence in the Development of the Sierra Leone Colony," in *Islam and Trade in Sierra Leone*, ed. Alusine Jalloh and David E. Skinner (Trenton, NJ: Africa World Press, 1997), 1–20.
5. "Blyden to Venn," September 6, 1871, CMS.
6. Bruce Dorsey, "A Gendered History of African Colonization in the Antebellum United States," *Journal of Social History* 34, no.1 (2003): 77–103.
7. For a history of these emigration movements, see Richard Blackett, "Martin R. Delany, and Robert Campbell: Black Americans in Search of an African Colony," *Journal of Negro History* 62, no. 1 (1977): 1–25.
8. Charles S. Morris, *Ecumenical Missionary Conference.* (New York: American Tract Society, 1900), 469–71.
9. "Blyden to Venn," August 24, 1871, CMS.
10. "Blyden to Venn," October 10, 1871, CMS.
11. For an example of the impact West African Muslim intellectuals had on Blyden, see Sean Hanretta, "The River of Salvation Flows through Africa: Blyden, Armattoe, and the Redemption of the Culture Concept," in *Indigenous Visions: Rediscovering the World of Franz Boas*, ed. Ned Blackhawk and Isaiah Lorado Wilner (New Haven: Yale University Press, 2018).
12. "Blyden to Venn," August 24, 1871, CMS. See other correspondence with Coppinger in Blyden's letters in Hollis R. Lynch, *Black Spokesman: Selected Published Writings*

of Edward Wilmot Blyden (London: Frank Cass, 1971).

13. Blyden, quoted in Holden, *Blyden of Liberia*, 369.
14. Blyden, *Christianity, Islam*; Blyden, quoted in Lynch, *Black Spokesman*.
15. Blyden, *Christianity, Islam*, xi.
16. David E. Skinner, "Conversion to Islam and the Promotion of 'Modern' Islamic Schools in Ghana," *Journal of Religion in Africa* 43 (2013): 426–50.
17. See, for example, ibid.; Skinner, "Islam and Education in the Colony and Hinterland of Sierra Leone (1750–1914)," *Canadian Journal of African Studies* 10, no. 3 (1976): 499–520.
18. Charles Ambler, "'A School in the Interior': African Studies; Engagement and Interdisciplinary," *African Studies Review* 54, no. 1 (2011): 1–17.
19. Kwame Nkrumah, *Consciencism: Philosophy and Ideology for Decolonization* (Accra: Panaf, 1964).
20. Blyden, *Christianity, Islam*, 4–24.
21. On the concept of the African Personality, see *Sierra Leone Times*, May 27, 1893. Blyden's subsequent writings on the African Personality were serialized in the *Sierra Leone Weekly News* but appeared as a book, *African Life and Customs*.
22. Blyden, *Christianity, Islam*, 1–24, 46–70, 173–88.
23. Ibid., 9–13.
24. Hollis R. Lynch, *Edward Wilmot Blyden, Pan-Negro Patriot 1832–1912* (London: Oxford University Press, 1967), 238–39; E. A. Ayandele, *Holy Johnson: Pioneer of African Nationalism 1836–1917* (London: Frank Cass, 1970).
25. Lynch, *Edward Wilmot Blyden*, 238–39; Ayandele, *Holy Johnson*.
26. Ali A. Mazrui, *The Africans: A Triple Heritage* (New York: Little Brown, 1986); Ali A. Mazrui, "Pan-Africanism and the Origins of Globalization" and "Pan-Africanism and the Globalization of Africa: A Triple Process," in *W. E. B. Dubois–George Padmore–Kwame Nkrumah Lecture Series* (Accra: DuBois Center, 2001).
27. E. G. Parrinder, "Islam in West African Indigenous Religion," *Numen* 6, no. 1 (1959): 130–41; Lamin Sanneh, "The Domestication of Islam and Christianity in African Societies: A Methodological Exploration," *Journal of Religion in Africa* 11, no. 1 (1980): 1–12.
28. Edward Curtis IV, *Black Muslim Religion in the Nation of Islam 1960–1975* (Chapel Hill: University of North Carolina Press, 2006), 91; Edward Curtis IV, "Edward Wilmot Blyden (1832–1912) and the Paradox of Islam," in *Islam in Black America: Identity Liberation and Difference in African-American Islamic Thought* (Albany: State University of New York Press, 2002), 21–43; Michael Gomez, *Black Crescent: The Experience and Legacy of African Muslims in the Americas* (Cambridge: Cambridge University Press, 2005); Michael Gomez, "Muslims in Early America," *Journal of Southern History* 60, no. 4 (1994): 671–710.

29. Habibul Haque Khondker, "Glocalization as Globalization: Evolution of a Sociological Concept," *Bangladesh e-Journal of Sociology* 1, no. 2 (2004): 1–9; M. M. Kraidy, "The Local, the Global and the Hybrid: A Native Ethnography of Glocalization," *Critical Studies in Media Communication* 16, no. 4 (1999): 456–77; Joseph Oduro-Frimpong, "Glocalization Trends: The Case of Hiplife Music in Contemporary Ghana," *International Journal of Communication* 3 (2009): 1085–1106.
30. Blyden, *Christianity, Islam*, 10.
31. Ibid., 11–12.
32. Nehemiah Levtzion, *Ancient Ghana and Mali* (London: Methuen, 1973), 183–99; Nehemiah Levtzion, *Islam in West Africa: Religion, Society, and Politics to 1800* (Norfolk, UK: Variorum, 1994), 208.
33. David Robinson, *Muslim Societies in African History* (Cambridge: Cambridge University Press, 2004), 42–59.
34. John Hunwick, *Africa, Islam, and the Arab World: Studies in Honor of Basil Davidson* (Princeton, NJ: Markus Wiener, 2003), 92–93.
35. Edward W. Blyden, *From West Africa to Palestine* (London: T. J. Sawyer, 1873); Blyden, quoted in Holden, *Blyden of Liberia*, 141.
36. Blyden, quoted in Holden, *Blyden of Liberia*, 141.
37. Ibid.
38. Ibid., 142.
39. Gov. Pope Hennessy, September 1, 1872, encl. "Report of the Expedition to Falaba, Jan.–March 1872," E. W. Blyden, March 26, 1872, CO 267/316, NA, Kew Gardens.
40. ACS, *African Repository* 43 (1867): 127; Blyden, quoted in Holden, *Blyden of Liberia*, 156.
41. Barbara E. Harrell-Bond, Allen M. Howard, and David E. Skinner, *Community, Leadership, and the Transformation, of Freetown, (1801–1976): Change and Continuity in Africa* (The Hague: Mouton, 1978), 134.
42. Blyden, quoted in Holden, *Blyden of Liberia*, 182.
43. Ibid., 190–93.
44. "Interesting Letter from West Africa," *Crescent*, October 21, 1896, 1093; Brent Singleton, "'That Ye May Know Each Other': Late Victorian Interactions between West African and British Muslims," *Journal of Muslim Minority Affairs* 29, no. 3 (2009): 369–85.
45. Edward Blyden, "Mohammedanism in Western Africa," *Methodist Quarterly Review* (1871): 133–48.
46. Blyden, *Christianity, Islam*; see entire book for Blyden's citations and debates with these scholars. See also, Lady Elinor F. Bosworth Smith Grogan, *Reginald Bosworth Smith: A Memoir* (London: James Nisket, 1909), 76–77.

47. Lynch, *Edward Wilmot Blyden*, 69–70.
48. *Methodist Quarterly Review* (January 1871); *Fraser's Magazine* (1875): 598–615; Blyden, *Christianity, Islam*, 306–36.
49. Edward Blyden, "Islam in the Western Soudan," *Journal of the African Society* 5 (1902): 11–37; Blyden, in Lynch, *Black Spokesman*, 271–311.
50. Blyden, *Christianity, Islam*, 173–88.
51. Blyden, *Fraser's Magazine* (1875): 598–615; Blyden, quoted in Lynch, *Black Spokesman*, 274.
52. Blyden, *Christianity, Islam*, 4.
53. Ibid., 4–6.
54. Ibid., 4–5.
55. Blyden, "Mohammedanism and the Negro Race," *Methodist Quarterly Review*, 133–48.
56. Ibid.; Lynch, *Black Spokesman*, 275.
57. Robinson, *Muslim Societies in African History*, 44–57.
58. Blyden, "Islam in the Western Soudan," 11–37; Edward Blyden, "The Koran in Africa," *Journal of the African Society* (1905): 157–71; Blyden, quoted in Lynch, *Black Spokesman*, 296–301.
59. Blyden, *Christianity, Islam*, 16; Blyden, "Islam in the Western Soudan," 11–37; Blyden, "Koran in Africa," 157–71.
60. H. M. Schieffelin, ed., *The People of Africa: A Series of Papers on Their Character, Conditions and Future* (New York: Anson D. R. Randolph, 1871), 1–34.
61. Blyden, quoted in Holden, *Blyden of Liberia*, 173.
62. Moulaye Hassane, "Ajami in Africa: The Use of Arabic Script in the Transcription of African Languages," in *The Meanings of Timbuktu*, ed. Shamil Jeppie and Souleymane Bachir Diagne (Cape Town: Human Sciences Research Council Press/CODESRIA), 109–22.
63. Ibid., 109.
64. Blyden, quoted in Holden, *Blyden of Liberia*, 195.
65. Blyden, *Christianity, Islam*, 186.
66. Blyden, "Mohammedanism in Western Africa"; Blyden, quoted in Lynch, *Black Spokesman*, 279.
67. Blyden, *Christianity, Islam*, 9.
68. Blyden, quoted in Holden, *Blyden of Liberia*, 161–64.
69. Ibid., 162–63.
70. Ibid., 166.
71. Ibid., 167.
72. For further commentary on Kankan as an African city of Islamic learning, see Nehemiah Levtzion and Randall Pouwels, *The History of Islam in Africa* (Athens:

Ohio University Press, 2000).
73. Singleton, "'That Ye May Know Each Other,'" 381.
74. My statement here is a pun and a disagreement with Lynch, in *Edward Wilmot Blyden*, vii–viii; Lynch writes that "Blyden was a failure as a leader and practical man of affairs: he possessed little organizing ability."
75. Blyden, quoted in Holden, *Blyden of Liberia*, 161, 163.
76. Ibid., 192.
77. Ibid.
78. Ibid., 162.
79. Ibid., 205.
80. Edward Blyden, "Report on the Expedition to Falaba," 1872; Edward Blyden to Alexander Bravo, "Expedition to Timbo," 1873—267/316, NA.
81. Blyden, quoted in Holden, *Blyden of Liberia*, 167.
82. Ibid., 169.
83. Map of Blyden's Route 1872, M.P.GG 102, NA.
84. "Edward Blyden to Kendall, Garyah," February 1, 1872, CA 1/047, CMS.
85. Governor Pope Hennessy, September 1, 1872, encl. E. W. Blyden, "Report on the Expedition to Falaba, Jan.–March, 1872," March 26, 1872, CO 267/316, NA. See also "Blyden to Venn," January 19, 1872, CA 1/047, CMS.
86. Harrell-Bond, Howard, and Skinner, *Community, Leadership, and Transformation*, 117–18.
87. E. W. Blyden, "Report on the Expedition to Falaba," CO 267/316, NA; Edward Blyden, "Falaba Expedition," Edward Blyden to Kendall, Kukuna, January 26, 1872, CA 1/047, CMS.
88. Edward Blyden, "Report on the Expedition, to Falaba" Edward Blyden to Kendall, Kukuna, January 26, 1872, CA 1/047, CMS.
89. Blyden's Report, Kennedy to Granville, March 10, 1873, CO 267/320, NA.
90. David Skinner, *Thomas George Lawson: African Historian and Administrator in Sierra Leone* (Stanford, CA: Hoover Institution Press, Stanford University, 1980), 60, see fn. 21, 60–80.
91. Falaba Expedition, Edward Blyden to Kendall, Kukuna, January 26, 1872, CA 1/047, CMS.
92. "Report of Expedition to Falaba, Jan.–March, 1872," CO 267/316, NA.
93. Blyden, *Christianity, Islam*, 46–70.
94. Blyden, *West Africa to Palestine*, 88.
95. Blyden, quoted in Lynch, *Black Spokesman*, 11–20, 25–33.
96. Ibid., 43, 46.
97. Ibid., 191–94.
98. Ibid., 193.

CHAPTER 6. DR. EDWARD BLYDEN, THEY KNOW YOUR NAME: BLYDEN AND WEST AFRICAN ETHIOPIANISM

1. *Lagos Times*, December 10, 1890, 4. These words were written on a lantern produced by an Afro-Brazilian mechanic repatriate to Lagos. to the inscription marked Blyden's arrival in Lagos, Nigeria. See *Lagos Times*, 4, December 10, 1890.
2. See Bruce Dorsey, "A Gendered History of African Colonization in the Antebellum United States," *Journal of Social History* 34, no. 1 (2003): 77–103; Richard Blackett, ""Martin R. Delany and Robert Campbell: Black Americans in Search of an African Colony," *Journal of Negro History* 62, no. 1 (1977): 1–25.
3. Blyden, quoted in Edith Holden, *Blyden of Liberia: An Account of the Life and Labors of Edward Wilmot Blyden, LL.D. As Recorded in Letters and in Print* (New York: Vantage Press, 1966), 96.
4. Ibid., 102; see 100–114 for all travels.
5. Azariah S. Root to Coppinger, August 25, 1891, ACS Reel 138; Cornelius McKare to Coppinger, August 22, 1891, ACS Reel 138. American Colonization Society Papers, Special Collections University of Central Arkansas.
6. D. G. Hendricks to Coppinger, August 14, 1891, ACS Reel 138.
7. Horace George to Coppinger, August 16, 1891, ACS Reel 138.
8. William Gale to Coppinger, August 14, 1891, ACS Reel 138.
9. Rev. R L. Davies to Coppinger, August 31, 1891, ACS Reel 138.
10. John Allington to Coppinger, August 6, 1891; and J. W. Williams to Coppinger, August 9, 1891, ACS Reel 138.
11. Blyden, quoted in Holden, *Blyden of Liberia*, 615–16.
12. Ibid., 620–21.
13. Moses King to Coppinger, August 27, 1891; and J. W. Turner to Coppinger, August 24, 1891, ACS Reel 138.
14. Moses King to Coppinger, August 27, 1891, ACS Reel 138.
15. G. W. Lowe to Coppinger, August 26, 1891, ACS Reel 138.
16. For nicknames and historiographical literature on William Wade Harris, see Watson A. O. Omulokoli, "William Wade Harris: Premier African Evangelist," *African Journal of Evangelical Theology* 21, no. 1 (2002): 3–11; David Shank, "The Prophet Harris: A Historiographical and Bibliographical Survey," *Journal of Religion in Africa* 14, no. 2 (1983): 130–60; David Shank, *Prophet Harris, "The Black Elijah" of West Africa* (New York: Brill, 1994).
17. Shank, "Prophet Harris," 72–80, 102.
18. Ibid., 92–96, 102.
19. Edward W. Blyden, *Christianity, Islam and the Negro Race* (Edinburgh: Edinburgh

University Press, 1967), 231–48; Hollis R. Lynch, *Edward Wilmot Blyden, Pan-Negro Patriot 1832–1912* (London: Oxford University Press, 1967), 214.

20. Edward W. Blyden, *African Life and Customs* (London, 1908), 33.
21. Lynch, *Edward Wilmot Blyden*, 85–86.
22. Ibid., 84–88.
23. CO 267/324, No. 978, Enclosure: *The Negro*, 2, April 16, 1873. NA.
24. For Blyden's influence and beginnings of West African Ethiopianism in Sierra Leone, see CO 267/316, CO 267/320, and CO 806/46, for governor's dispatches from Sierra Leone and other correspondence that concerns Blyden, in NA. See also Blyden, quoted in Hollis R. Lynch, *Selected Letters of Edward Wilmot Blyden* (Millwood, NY: KTO Press, 1978), 82–147; and Blyden, quoted in Holden, *Blyden of Liberia*, 216–74.
25. Blyden, quoted in *Proceedings of the Banquet in London*, 52–53; Blyden, quoted in Lynch, *Edward Wilmot Blyden*, 94.
26. Colonial Office Minutes, July 18, 1873, CO 267/321, NA.
27. No. 6209: Report on the Timbo Expedition, CO 267/320, NA; see also Lynch, *Edward Wilmot Blyden*, 96–97.
28. Blyden, in Hollis R. Lynch, *Black Spokesman: Selected Published Writings of Edward Wilmot Blyden* (London: Frank Cass, 1971), 210–14.
29. Casely Hayford, quoted in Blyden, *African Life and Customs*, Appendix A.
30. As shown at the beginning of this chapter, Casely Hayford's brother and known Blyden mentee, Rev. Mark Hayford, also established the Native Baptist Church in the Gold Coast. See also Clifton R. Clarke, "African Indigenous Churches in Ghana—Past, Present and Future," *Journal of African Instituted Church Theology* 2, no. 1 (2006): 1–28.
31. Blyden, quoted in Casely Hayford, *West African Land Question*, 113.
32. Casely Hayford, *William Waddy Harris: The West African Reformer* (London: C. M. Phillips, 1915); Shank, "Prophet Harris," 11, 107–10, 128.
33. John Zarwan, "William Wade Harris: The Genesis of an African Religious Movement," *Missiology: An International Review* 3, no. 4 (1975): 431–50.
34. E. A. Ayandele, *Holy Johnson: Pioneer of African Nationalism 1836–1917* (London: Frank Cass, 1970), 285–308.
35. *Lagos Times*, 4, January 10, 1891. For Afro-Brazilian connections in Lagos see James L. Matory, *Black Atlantic Religion: Tradition, Transnationalism, and Matriarchy in the Afro-Brazilian Candomblé* (Princeton, NJ: Princeton University Press, 2005), 1–38.
36. See Lynch, *Black Spokesman*, 191–94. Holden, *Blyden of Liberia*, 630.
37. Lynch, *Edward Wilmot Blyden*, 98, 221–26.
38. Holden, *Blyden of Liberia*, 630.

39. Blyden, *African Life and Customs*, 4.
40. Ibid., 8.
41. Blyden, quoted in Lynch, *Selected Letters*, 54.
42. Holden, *Blyden of Liberia*, 52, 901; Lynch, *Edward Wilmot Blydens*, 38.
43. Holden, *Blyden of Liberia*, 64, 146, 188, 360, 463.
44. Blyden, quoted in ibid., 902.
45. Ibid.
46. Ibid., 902–5.
47. Ibid., 903–4.
48. Ibid., 906–7.
49. Blyden, quoted in ibid., 157.
50. Ibid., 912–13.
51. Ibid., 912.
52. Ibid., 914–15. For more on Anna Erskine, see Nemata Blyden, "The Search for Anna Erskine: African American Women in Nineteenth Century Liberia," in *Stepping Forward: Black Women in Africa and the Americas*, ed. Catherine Higgs, Barbara A. Moss, and Earline Rae Ferguson (Athens: Ohio University Press, 2002), 31–43.
53. Blyden, quoted in Lynch, *Selected Letters*, 72; emphasis in original.
54. Lynch, *Black Spokesman*, 187–89.
55. Ibid.
56. Blyden, quoted in ibid., 188–89.
57. Blyden, quoted in Lynch, *Edward Wilmot Blyden*, 52–53.
58. Blyden, quoted in Lynch, *Black Spokesman*, 189.
59. Blyden, quoted in Holden, *Blyden of Liberia*, 903–5.
60. Blyden, "The Search for Anna Erskine," 37. *African Repository* 38 (1862): 200; Blyden, quoted in Lynch, *Black Spokesman*, 378.
61. Holden, *Blyden of Liberia*, 905.
62. Ibid., 912.
63. Blyden, quoted in ibid., 576.
64. Blyden, quoted in ibid., 100.
65. Ibid., 576.
66. Lynch, *Selected Letters*, 486.
67. Blyden, quoted in ibid.
68. Blyden, *African Life and Customs*, 11.
69. Ibid., 11, 13.
70. Ibid., 14, 16, 24, 71.
71. Holden, *Blyden of Liberia*, 914.
72. Evelyn Higginbotham, "African American Women's History and the Metalanguage of Race," *Signs* 17, no. 2 (1992): 251–74.

73. Kwaku L. Korang, *Writing Ghana, Imagining Africa: Nation and African Modernity* (Rochester, NY: University of Rochester Press, 2003), 23–24.
74. Blyden, *African Life and Customs*, 10.
75. Ibid., 10, 8–90; M. Yu Frenkel, "Edward Blyden and the Concept of African Personality," *African Affairs* 73 (1974): 277–89.
76. Blyden, *African Life and Customs*, 7–30.
77. See ibid., 30–60.
78. Blyden, quoted in Lynch, *Black Spokesman*, 194.
79. Ibid., 203.
80. Ibid., 194.
81. Ibid., 205–7.
82. Ibid.
83. Ibid., 202.
84. Ibid., 203, 45–52.
85. Blyden, *Christianity, Islam*, 277.
86. Korang, *Writing Ghana, Imagining Africa*, 74–80.
87. For a discussion of duplexive discourse in African philosophy, which in many ways shows why Blyden was a philosophical antecedent to Nkrumah, see John H. McClendon, "Nkrumah's *Consciencism* as Philosophical Text: Matters of Confusion," *Journal of Africa Philosophy* 3 (2003): 25–35.
88. Blyden, quoted in *Lagos Times* 4, February 21, 1891.
89. Blyden, *African Life and Customs*, 3.
90. Kwame Nkrumah, *Consciencism: Philosophy and Ideology for Decolonization* (London: Panaf, 1978), 78–106; George Padmore, *Pan-Africanism or Communism* (New York: Anchor Books, 1972), 30–43, 149–62.

EPILOGUE

1. "The Afropolitan Movement," Afropolitan Cities, https://www.afropolitancities.com/.
2. For some of these articles, see Salah M. Hassan, "Rethinking Cosmopolitanism: Is 'Afropolitanism' the Answer," *Reflections* 5 (2012): 3–29; Stephanie Bosch Santana, "Excorcizing the Future: Afropolitanism's Spectral Origins," *Journal of African Cultural Studies* 28, no. 1 (2016): 120–26; Christopher T. Fan, "Battle Hymn of the Afropolitan: Sino-African Futures in Ghana Must Go and Americanah," *Journal of Asian American Studies* 20, no. 1 (2017): 69–93.
3. Blitz the Ambassador (Samuel Bazawule), Interview with Afrofusion TV, May 6, 2013.

4. "Who Is Afropolitan?" Afropolitan Cities, https://www.afropolitancities.com/about.
5. Stephanie Bosch Santana, "Exorcizing Afropolitanism: Binyavanga Wainaina Explains Why "I Am Pan-Africanist, Not Afropolitan" at ASAUK 2012," *AiW*, February 8, 2013. https://africainwords.com/.
6. Emma Dabiri, ""Why I Am (Still) Not an Afropolitan"" *Journal of Cultural Studies* 28, no. 1 (2016): 104–8, 104.
7. Chimamanda Ngozi Adichie, quoted in Santana, "Exorcizing the Future," 122.
8. Taban Makotiyang Lo Liyong, "Jua kali artisans deserve the Nobel more than Ngugi," *Daily Nation*, September 13, 2013, https://www.nation.co.ke.

Bibliography

ARCHIVAL SOURCES

National Archives Kew Gardens, Surrey, London

Colonial Office CO 267, Original Correspondence, Sierra Leone

CO 806 Africa No. 82 and Africa No. 25, Boundary Negotiations with Liberia

CO 879 Confidential Prints: Africa

Foreign Office FO 84 Edward Blyden Correspondence 1877–1892

Maps M.P. GG 102 Map of Blyden's Route 1872

University of Central Arkansas Library, Archives

The Records of the American Colonization Society (ACS), 1792–1964

Furley Collection, Balme Library, University of Ghana, Legon

D 1 Frederich III to Caerlof

D 2 Translation of the Pamphlets "Tegen Bericht"

D 4 1698–1703 Christiansborg Diary

E 35 Danish Settlements

V.G.K. 77, Breve og Ugaede 1624, 1659–1680

Enid M. Baa Public Library, Charlotte Amalie, St. Thomas, Von Scholten Collection

Sanct. Thomae Tidende 1842–1862
St. Croix Avis, 1846–1848
Royal Danish American Gazette 1770–1775
The Virgin Islands Daily News (St. Thomas, Virgin Islands), 1976

Church Missionary Society Archives (CMS, Salisbury Court, London)

C A1 Sierra Leone Missionary Reports, Diaries, and Letters

University of Massachusetts, Amherst, Special Collections and University Archives

W. E. B. Du Bois Papers (MS 312): Correspondence, 1877–1965. http://credo.library.umass.edu/view/collection/mums312.

INTERVIEWS

Myron Jackson, personal conversation with author, Charlotte Amalie, St. Thomas, June 29, 2012

Rabbi Moch, personal conversation with author, Charlotte Amalie, St. Thomas, June 28, 2012

EDWARD BLYDEN'S PUBLISHED WRITINGS

Blyden, Edward W. *Africa and Africans, Proceedings on the Occasion of a Banquet Given at the Holborn Restaurant to Edward W. Blyden, August 15th, 1903, by West Africans in London.* London: C. M. Phillips, 1903.

———. *African Colonization. Rev. E. W. Blyden's Address at the Annual Meeting of the Maine Colonization Society, June 1862.* N.p., 1862.

———. *African Life and Customs.* London, 1908.

———. *The African Problem, and Other Discourses: Delivered in America in 1890.* London: W. B. Whittingham, 1890.

———. *The African Society and Miss Mary Kingsley.* London: J. Scott, 1901.

———. *The Aims and Methods of a Liberal Education for Africans.* Cambridge, MA: John Wilson and Son, 1882.

———. *The Arabic Bible in the Soudan: A Plea for Transliteration.* London: C. M.

Phillips, 1910.
———. *The Call of Providence to the Descendants of Africa in America.* In *Liberia's Offering: Being Addresses, Sermons, etc.* New York: John A. Gray, 1862.
———. *Christianity, Islam and the Negro Race.* Edinburgh: Edinburgh University Press, 1967.
———. *From West Africa to Palestine.* London: T. J. Sawyer, 1873.
———. *The Jewish Question.* Liverpool: Lionel Hart, 1898.
———. *Liberia's Offering: Being Addresses, Sermons, Etc.* New York: J. A. Gray, 1862.
———. "The Negro in Ancient History." *Methodist Quarterly Review* (1869): 71–93.
———. *A Vindication of the African Race: Being a Brief Examination of the Arguments in Favor of African Inferiority.* Monrovia, LR: G. Killian, 1857.
———. *A Voice from Bleeding Africa on Behalf of Her Exiled Children.* Monrovia, LR: G. Killian, 1856.
———. *West Africa Before Europe and Other Addresses Delivered in England in 1901.* London: C. M. Phillips, 1902.

PUBLISHED BOOKS AND JOURNAL ARTICLES

Abraham, E. W. "Amo." In *A Companion to the Philosophers*, edited by Robert L. Arrington, 191–99. Oxford: Blackwell, 2001.
———. "The Life and Times of Anton Wilhelm Amo." *Transactions of the Historical Society of Ghana* 7 (1964): 60–81.
———. *The Mind of Africa.* Chicago: University of Chicago, 1962.
Achebe, Chinua. *Home and Exile.* Oxford: Oxford University Press, 2000.
Achebe, Nwando. *Farmers, Traders, Warriors, and Kings: Female Power and Authority in Northern Igboland, 1900–1960.* Portsmouth, NH: Heinemann, 2005.
———. "Nwando Achebe—Daughter, Wife, and Guest—A Researcher at the Crossroads." *Journal of Women's History* 14, no. 3 (2002): 9–31.
Acholonu, Catherine. *The Igbo Roots of Olaudah Equiano.* Owerri, NG: AFA Publications, 1989.
Adderley, Rosanne M. *New Negroes from Africa: Slave Trade Abolition and Free African Settlements in the Nineteenth-Century Caribbean.* Bloomington: Indiana University Press, 2007.
Addo-Fening, R. *Akyem Abuakwa 1700–1943: From Ofori Panyin to Sir Ofori Atta.* Trondheim: Department of History, Norwegian University of Science and Technology, 1997.
Adenaike, Carolyn Keyes, and Jan Vansina. *In Pursuit of History.* London: Heinemann, 1996.

Adi, Hakim. "Pan-Africanism and Pan-African Nationalism." *African Studies Review* 43, no. 1, (2000): 69–82.

Adi, Hakim, and Marika Sherwood. *Pan-African History: Political Figures from Africa and the Diaspora since 1787*. London: Routledge, 2003.

Adjaye, Joseph. K. "Pan-Africanism." In *Survey of Social Science: Government and Politics*, edited by Frank N. Magill, 1369–76. Englewood Cliffs, NJ: Salem Press, 1995.

———. "Perspectives on Fifty Years of Ghanaian History." *History in Africa* 35 (2008): 1–24.

Afigbo, A. E. "Colonial Historiography." In *African Historiography: Essays in Honor of Jacob Ade Ajayi*, edited by Toyin Falola, 40–41. Harlow, UK: Longman, 1993.

———. "Oral Tradition and History in Eastern Nigeria: An Essay in Historical Methodology." Research and Documentation Associates, 1983.

———. *Ropes of Sand: Studies in Igbo History and Culture*. Ibadan, NG: University Press, 1981.

Ambler, Charles. "'A School in the Interior': African Studies; Engagement and Interdisciplinary." *African Studies Review* 54, no. 1 (2011): 1–17.

American Society of African Culture. *Pan-Africanism Reconsidered*. Berkeley: University of California Press, 1962.

Amos, Alcione, and Ebenezer Ayesu. "'I Am Brazilian': History of the Tabon, Afro-Brazilians in Accra, Ghana." *Transactions of the Historical Society of Ghana* 6 (2002): 35–58.

Angell, Stephen Ward. *Bishop Henry McNeal Turner and African American Religion in the South*. Knoxville: University of Tennessee Press, 1992.

Anyidoho, Kofi. *Pan-African Ideal in Literatures of the Black World*. Accra: Ghana Universities Press, 1989.

Appadurai, Arjun, and Carol Breckenridge. "Debates and Controversies: Why Public Culture?" *Public Culture* 1, no. 1 (1988): 5–9.

Appiah, Kwame A. "Alexander Crummell and the Invention of Africa." *The Massachusetts Review* 31, no. 3 (1990): 385–406.

———. "The Conservation of 'Race.'" *Black American Literature Forum* 23, no. 1 (1989): 37–60.

———. *In My Father's House: Africa in the Philosophy of Culture*. London: Metheun, 1992.

———. "The Uncompleted Argument: DuBois and the Illusion of Race." *Critical Inquiry* 12, no. 1 (1985): 21–37.

Armistead, Wilson. *A Tribute for the Negro: Being a Vindication of the Moral, Intellectual, and Moral Capabilities of the Colored Portion of Mankind; With Particular Reference to the African Race*. Manchester: William Irwin, 1848.

Armitage, David, and M. J. Braddick. *The British Atlantic World 1500–1800*. New York:

Palgrave, 2002.

Asante, Molefi K. *The Afrocentric Idea*. Philadelphia: Temple University Press, 1987.

———. *Afrocentricity*. Trenton, NJ: Africa World Press, 1988.

———. *Kemet, Afrocentricity and Knowledge*. Trenton, NJ: Africa World Press, 1990.

Ayandele, E. A. *Holy Johnson: Pioneer of African Nationalism 1836–1917*. London: Frank Cass, 1970.

Baa, E. "Historical News and Comments: The Preservation of the Sephardic Records of the Island of St. Thomas, Virgin Islands." *Publications of the American Jewish Historical Society* 44, no. 2 (1954): 114–19.

Banks, Williams M. *Black Intellectuals: Race and Responsibility in America*. New York: Norton & Co., 1998.

Barka, Norman F. *Archaeology of the Jewish Synagogue Honen Dalim, St. Eustacius, Netherlands Antilles*. Williamsburg, VA: Department of Anthropology, College of William and Mary, 1988.

Barnard, Frederick M. *Herder's Social and Political Thought: From Enlightenment to Nationalism*. Oxford: Oxford University Press, 1965.

Barry, Boubacar. *Senegal and the Atlantic Slave Trade*. Cambridge: Cambridge University Press, 1998.

Bay, Edna. *Wives of the Leopard: Gender, Politics, and Culture in the Kingdom of Dahomey*. Charlottesville: University of Virginia Press, 1998.

Bedasse, Monique A. *Jah Kingdom: Rastafarians, Tanzania and Pan-Africanism in the Age of Decolonization*. Chapel Hill: University of North Carolina, 2017.

Bediako, Kwame. "African Theology." In *The Modern Theology*, edited by David Ford, 426–44. Oxford: Blackwell, 1996.

Beltran, Gonzalo A. "Tribal Origins of Slaves in Mexico." *Journal of Negro History* 31 (1946): 269–352.

Blackett, Richard. "Martin R. Delany and Robert Campbell: Black Americans in Search of an African Colony." *Journal of Negro History* 62, no. 1 (1977): 1–25.

Blake, John William, trans and ed. "Rui de Pina, *Chronica d'El Rey Dom João II (c. 1500)*." In *Europeans in West Africa, 1450–1560*, 2 vols., 70–86. London: Hakluyt Society, 1942.

Blyden, Nemata A. "The Search for Anna Erskine: African American Women in Nineteenth Century Liberia." In *Stepping Forward: Black Women in Africa and the Americas*, edited by Catherine Higgs, Barbara Moss, and Earline Rae Ferguson, 31–43. Athens: Ohio University Press, 2002.

———. *West Indians in West Africa, 1808–1880: The African Diaspora in Reverse*. Rochester, NY: University of Rochester Press, 2000.

Boas, Franz. *The Mind of Primitive Man*. New York: Macmillan, 1938.

Boele van Hensbroek, Pieter. "The 'Import Thesis' about African Political Thought."

Journal on African Philosophy 2 (2003): 1–10.

———. *Political Discourses in African Thought: 1860 to the Present.* Westport, CT: Praeger, 1999.

Bossman, William. *A New and Accurate Description of the Coast of Guinea.* London, 1705.

Bosworth Smith Grogan, Lady Elinor F. *Reginald Bosworth Smith: A Memoir.* London: James Nisket, 1909.

Boyer, William W. *Americas Virgin Islands: A History of Human Rights and Wrongs.* Durham: Carolina Academic Press, 1983.

Brandon, George. *Santeria from Africa to the New World: The Dead Sell Memories.* Bloomington: Indiana University Press, 1993.

Brathwaite, Edward Kamau. *Masks.* London: Oxford University Press, 1968.

Brecht, Martin. *Martin Luther: His Road to Reformation 1483–1521.* Translated by James L. Schaaf. Philadelphia: Fortress Press, 1985.

Breman, Paul. *You Better Believe It: Black Verse in English from Africa, the West Indies and the United States.* Baltimore: Penguin Press, 1973.

Brempong, Owusu. "Language as a Factor in Ethnographic Research." *Institute of African Studies Research Review*, n.s., 8 (1992): 55–63.

Brock, Lisa. "Questioning the Diaspora: Hegemony, Black Intellectuals and Doing International History from Below." *ISSUE: A Journal of Opinion* 24, no. 2 (1996): 9–12.

Brook, Daniel. "The Forgotten Confederate Jew: How History Lost Judah P. Benjamin, the Most Prominent American Jew of the 19th Century." *Tablet*, July 17, 2012. http://tabletmag.com.

Brooks, George E. *Euro-Africans in Western Africa: Commerce Social Status, Gender, and Religious Observances from the Sixteenth to the Eighteenth Century.* Athens: Ohio University Press, 2003.

Brown, Soi-Daniel W. "From the Tongues of Africa: A Partial Translation of Oldendorp's Interviews." *Plantation Society in the Americas* 2, no. 1 (1983): 37–61.

Brown University and the University of Tulsa: The Modernist Journals Project. "The Crisis: A Record of the Darker Races, 1912–1918." http://modjourn.org/MJPnewsarchive.html.

Bruder, Edith, and Tudor Parfitt, eds. *African Zion: Studies in Black Judaism.* Newcastle-upon-Tyne: Cambridge Scholars Press, 2012.

Buell, Raymond L. *The Native Problem in Africa.* Vol. 2. New York: Macmillan, 1928.

Butler, Kim. *Freedom Given, Freedoms Won: Afro-Brazilians in Post-Abolition Sao Paulo and Salvador.* New Brunswick, NJ: Rutgers University Press, 1998.

Butt-Thompson, F. W. *West African Secret Societies: Their Organizations, Officials and Teaching.* London: H.F. & G. Witherby, 1929.

Buxton, Victor T. F. "The Creole in West Africa." *Journal of the Royal African Society* 12 (1913): 385–94.

Campbell, Horace., B. F. Bankie, and S. Sibanda, eds. *Pan Africanism and African Liberation in the 21st Century*. Windhoek, NM: Pan African Centre of Namibia, 2000.

Campbell, James. *Middle Passages: African American Journeys to Africa, 1787–2005*. New York: Penguin, 2006.

Capitein, Jacobus Elisha. *The Agony of Asar: A Thesis on Slavery by a Former Slave*. Translated and edited by Grant Parker. Princeton, NJ: Markus Wiener, 2001.

Caron, Aimery P., and Arnold R. Highfield. *St. Croix under French Dominion, 1650–1733*. Christiansted, St. Croix: Antilles Press, 1984.

Carreta, Vincent. *Equiano, the African: Biography of a Self-Made Man*. Athens: University of Georgia Press, 2005.

———. *Unchained Voices: Anthology of Black Authors in the English-Speaking World of the Eighteenth Century*. Lexington: University of Kentucky Press, 1996.

Cesaire, Aime. *Return to My Native Land*. Paris: Presence Africaine, 1968.

Challenor, Herchelle Sullivan. "No Longer at Ease: Confrontation at the 12th Annual African Studies Association Meeting in Montreal." *African Today* 16, no. 5 (1969): 4–7.

Chambers, Douglas B. "'Almost an Englishman': Carretta's Equiano." Review of *Equiano the African: Biography of a Self-Made Man*, by Vincent Carretta, H-Atlantic, H-Net Reviews, November 2007.

———. *Igbo Diaspora in the Era of the Slave Trade: An Introductory History*. Enugu, NG: Jemezie Associates, 2013.

———. "The Significance of the Igbo in the Bight of Biafra Slave Trade: A Rejoinder to Northrup's 'Myth Igbo.'" *Slavery and Abolition* 23, no. 1 (2002): 101–20.

Childs, Matt. *The 1812 Aponte Rebellion in Cuba and the Struggle Against Atlantic Slavery*. Chapel Hill: University of North Carolina Press, 2006.

Chrisman, Robert, ed. "Pan-Africanism II." *The Black Scholar* 2, no. 7 (1971): 1–63.

Christaller, J. G. *Dictionary of the Asante and Fante Language*. Basel, 1881.

———. *A Grammar of the Asante and Fante Language Called Tsi (Chwee, Twi)*. Basel, 1875.

———. *Twi Mmebusem Mpensa-Ahansia Mmoano: A Collection of Three Thousand and Six Hundred Tshi Proverbs*. Basel, 1879.

Clarke, Clifton R. "African Indigenous Churches in Ghana—Past, Present and Future." *Journal of African Instituted Church Theology* 2, no. 1 (2006): 1–28.

Clarke, John Henry. "African Heritage Studies Association (AHSA): Some Notes on the Conflict with the African Studies Association (ASA) and the Fight to Reclaim African History." *A Journal of Opinion* 6, no. 2 (1976): 5–11.

———. "African Studies in the United States, An Afro-American View." *Africa Today* 16, no. 2 (1969): 10–12.

Clarke, Richard. *Against All Enemies: Inside America's War on Terror*. New York: Free Press, 2004.

Clifford, James. "Diasporas." *Cultural Anthropology* 9, no. 3 (1994): 302–38.

———. *Routes: Travel and Translation in the Late Twentieth Century*. Cambridge, MA: Harvard University Press, 1997.

Cohen, Judah. *Through the Sands of Time*. Waltham, MA: Brandeis University Press, 2004.

Cohen, Robin. "Diasporas and the Nation-State: From Victims to Challengers." *International Affairs* 72, no. 3 (1996): 507–20.

———. *The Global Diasporas: An Introduction*. Seattle: University of Washington Press, 1997.

Cole, Douglas. *Franz Boas: The Early Years*. Seattle: University of Washington Press, 1999.

Cole, Gibril. *The Krio of West Africa: Islam, Culture, Creolization, and Colonialism in the Nineteenth Century*. Athens: Ohio University Press, 2013.

Collins, R. O., J. M. Burns, and E. K. Ching. *Historical Problems of Imperial Africa*. Princeton, NJ: Markus Weiner, 1994.

Collyer, C. "Edward W. Blyden, a Correspondent of William Ewart Gladstone." *Journal of Negro History* 35, no. 1 (1950): 75–78.

Comte de Gobineau, Arthur. *Inequality of the Races*. London: Heinemann, 1915.

Connif, Michael, and Thomas Davis. *Africans in the Americas: A History of the Black Diaspora*. New York: St. Martin's Press, 1994.

Consolidated Final Report: Truth and Reconciliation Commission of Liberia. Monrovia: Republic of Monrovia, 2009.

Cooper, Anna J. *A Voice from the South by a Black Woman of the South*. New York: Oxford University Press, 1988.

Coupland, Reginald. *The British Anti-Slavery Movement*. London: Frank Cass, 1969.

Cromwell, Adelaide. *An African Victorian Feminist: Adelaide Casely Hayford 1868–1960*. London: Cass, 1986.

Cromwell, John. *The Negro in American History*. Washington, DC: American Negro Academy, 1914.

Crowder, Michael. "The Second World War: Prelude to Decolonization in Africa." In *The Cambridge History of Africa*, vol. 8, *From c.1940 to c.1975*, edited by Michael Crowder, 8–51. Cambridge: Cambridge University Press.

Crowder, Ralph L. *John Edward Bruce: Politician, Journalist, and Self-Trained Historian of the African Diaspora*. New York: New York University Press, 2004.

Cruse, Harold. *The Crisis of the Negro Intellectual: A Historical Analysis of the Failure of*

Black Leadership. New York: Quill, 1984.

Cudjoe, Selwyn. *Resistance and Caribbean Literature*. Athens: Ohio University Press, 1980.

Cugoano, Ottobah. *Narrative of the Enslavement of Ottobah Cugoano, a Native of Africa*. London: published by author, 1825.

———. *Thoughts and Sentiments on the Evil of Slavery and Commerce of the Human Species*. London: published by author, 1787.

Curtin, Philip D. *The Atlantic Slave Trade: A Census*. Madison: University of Wisconsin Press, 1969.

———. *Cross-Cultural Trade in World History*. Cambridge: Cambridge University Press, 1984.

———. *The Rise and Fall of the Atlantic Complex: Essays in Atlantic History*. New York: Cambridge University Press, 1998.

Curtis, Edward, IV. *Black Muslim Religion in the Nation of Islam 1960–1975*. Chapel Hill: University of North Carolina Press, 2006.

———. *Islam in Black America: Identity Liberation and in African-American Islamic Thought*. Albany: State University of New York Press, 2002.

Dagbovie, Pero G. *The Early Black History Movement, Carter G. Woodson, and Lorenzo Greene*. Urbana: University of Illinois Press, 2007.

Damas, Leon. *Pigments*. Paris: Presence Africaine, 1962.

Darity, William A., Jr., Jason Dietrich, and Darrick Hamilton. "Bleach in the Rainbow: Latin Ethnicity and Preference for Whiteness." *Transforming Anthropology* 13, no. 2 (2005): 103–9.

Davies, Carol Boyce. *Migrations of the Subject: Black Women, Writing and Identity*. London: Routledge, 1994.

Davis, Gregson. *Aime Cesaire*. Cambridge: Cambridge University Press, 1997.

Davis, Ronald W. Review of *Education and Race: A Biography of Edward Wilmot Blyden*, by Thomas W. Livingston. *The International Journal of African Historical Studies* 10, no. 1 (1977): 114–16.

Debrunner, Hans W. *A History of Christianity in Ghana*. Accra: Waterville, 1967.

Delany, Martin R. *Blake: Or, The Huts of America, a Novel*. Boston: Beacon Press, 1970.

———. *The Condition, Elevation, Emigration, and Destiny of the Colored People of the United States*. New York: Arno Press, 1968.

———. *Proceedings of the National Emigration Convention of the Colored People, Held at Cleveland, Ohio, August 24 and 26, 1854*. Pittsburgh: A. A. Anderson, 1854.

Diffie, B. W., and George D. Winius. *Foundations of the Portuguese Empire, 1415–1580*. Minneapolis: University of Minnesota Press, 1977.

Diouf, Sylviane, ed. *Fighting the Slave Trade: West African Strategies*. Athens: Ohio University Press, 2003.

Donham, Donald L. *Marxist Modern: An Ethnographic History of the Ethiopian Revolution*. Berkeley: University of California Press, 1999.

Dookhan, Isaac. *A History of the Virgin Islands of the United States*. St. Thomas: Caribbean Universities Press, 1974.

Dorman, James. "Lifted out of the Commonplace Grandeur of Modern Times: Reappraising Edward Wilmot Blyden's Views of Islam in Light of His Scholarly Black Christian Orientalism." *Souls: A Critical Journal of Black Politics, Culture and Society* 12, no. 4 (2010): 398–418.

Dorsey, Bruce. "A Gendered History of African Colonization in the Antebellum United States." *Journal of Social History* 34, no. 1 (2003): 77–103.

Doyle, Betraam E. *The Etiquette of Race Relations in the South: A Study in Social Control*. Chicago: University of Chicago Press, 1937.

Drake, John Gibbs St. Claire. "The African Diaspora in Pan-African Perspective." *Black Scholar* 7 (1975): 2–14.

———. *Black Folk Here and There: An Essay in History and Anthropology*. Los Angeles: Center for Afro-American Studies, University of California, 1987.

Drake, John Gibbs St. Claire, and Horace R. Cayton. *Black Metropolis: A Study of Negro Life in a Northern City*. New York: Harcourt Brace and Co., 1945.

Dubois, L. *Avengers of the New World: The Story of the Haitian Revolution*. Cambridge, MA: Harvard University Press, 2004.

Du Bois, W. E. B. *Black Folk: Then and Now; An Essay in the History and Sociology of the Negro Race*. New York: H. Holt and Company, 1939.

———. *Conservation of the Races American Negro Academy Occasional Papers*, no. 2, 1897.

———. *The Negro*. Millwood, NY: Kraus-Thomson Organization Ltd., 1975.

———. *The Philadelphia Negro*. Milwood, NY: Kraus-Thomson Organization Ltd., 1974.

———. *Souls of Black Folk*. Chicago: Lushena, 2000.

Duffield, Ian. "Pan-Africanism Rational and Irrational." *Journal of African History* 18 (1977): 570–620.

Dunbar-Nelson, Alice Moore, ed. *Masterpieces of Negro Eloquence*. New York: The Bookery Publishing Co., 1914.

Easton, Lloyd D., and Kurt H. Guddat, eds. *Writings of the Young Marx on Philosophy and Society*. New York: Doubleday, 1967.

Echeruo, Michael J. C. "Edward W. Blyden, 'The Jewish Question,' and the Diaspora Theory and Practice." *Journal of Black Studies* 40, no. 4 (2010): 544–65.

Edwards, Brent Hayes, Cheryl Johnson-Odim, Augustin Lao-Montes, Michael O. West, Tiffany Ruby Patterson and Robin Kelley Brent Hayes Edwards, Cheryl Johnson-Odim, Agustin Lao-Montes, Michael O. West, Tiffany Ruby Patterson, and Robin Kelley. "'Unfinished Migrations': Commentary and Response." *African Studies*

Review 43, no. 1 (2000): 47–68.

———. "The Uses of Diaspora." *Social Text* 19, no. 1 (2001): 45–73.

Egerton, Douglas R. *He Shall Go Out Free: The Lives of Denmark Vesey*. Madison, WI: Madison House, 1999.

Einstein, Elizabeth L. *The Printing Press as an Agent of Change: Communications and Cultural Transformations in Early Modern Europe*. New York: Cambridge University Press, 1979.

Eltis, D., and J. Walvin, eds. *The Abolition of the Atlantic Slave Trade: Origins and Effects in Europe, Africa, and the Americas*. Madison: University of Wisconsin Press, 1981.

Emmanuel, Isaac S., and Suzanne A. Emmanuel. *History of the Jews of the Netherlands Antilles*. Cincinnati: American Jewish Archives, 1970.

———. *The Jews of Coro, Venezuela*. Cincinnati: American Jewish Archives, 1973.

Equiano, Olaudah. *The Interesting Narrative of the Life of Olaudah Equiano, or Gustavus Vassa, the African*. London: published by author, 1791.

Esedebe, P. Olisanwuche. *Pan-Africanism: The Idea and Movement, 1776–1963*. Washington, DC: Howard University Press, 1982.

Essien, Kwame. "A Abentura Da Casa Brasil: History of the Tabom People, Part I." In *Back to Africa: Afro-Brazilian Returnees and Their Communities*, by Kwesi Kwah Prah, 173–92. Cape Town: Centre for Advanced Studies of African Society, 2009.

———. *Brazilian-African Diaspora in Ghana: The Tabom, Slavery, Dissonance of Memory, Identity, and Locating Home*. East Lansing: Michigan State University Press, 2016.

Fage, J. D. "The Development of African Historiography." In *UNESCO General History of Africa*, vol. 1, *Methodology and African Prehistory (Abridged)*, edited by J. Ki-Zerbo, 24–42. Berkeley: University of California Press, 1981.

———. "Some Remarks on Beads and Trade in Lower Guinea in the Sixteenth and Seventeenth Centuries." *Journal of African History* 3, no. 2 (1962): 343–47.

Falola, Toyin, ed. *African Historiography Essays in Honor of Jacob Ade Ajayi*. Harlow, UK: Longman, 1993.

———. *Nationalism and African Intellectuals*. New York: University of Rochester Press, 2001.

Falola, Toyin, and Matt Childs. *The Yoruba Diaspora in the Atlantic World*. Bloomington: Indiana University Press. 2004.

Falola, Toyin, and Paul E. Lovejoy. *Pawnship in Africa: Debt Bondage in Historical Perspective*. Boulder: Westview Press, 1994.

Fanon, Frantz. *Black Skin: White Masks*. Translated by Charles Lam Markmann. New York: Grove Press, 1967.

———. *The Wretched of the Earth*. New York: Grove Press, 1963.

Feracho, Leslie. "The Legacy of Negrismo/Negritud: Inter American Dialogues."

Langston Hughes Review 16, no. 2 (2001): 1–5.

Forde, Darryl, ed. *African Worlds: Studies in the Cosmological Ideas and Social Values of African Peoples*. London: Oxford University Press, 1954.

———. "The Cultural Map of West Africa: Successive Adaptations to Tropical Forests and Grassland." In *Cultures and Societies of Africa*, edited by Simon Ottenberg and Phoebe Ottenberg, 157–67. New York: Random House, 1960.

Franklin, V. P., and Betty Collier-Thomas. "Biography, Race Vindication, and African-American Intellectuals." *Journal of Negro History* 81, no. 1 (1996): 1–16.

Frazier, Franklin E. *Black Bourgeoisie*. Glencoe, IL: Free Press, 1957.

———. *The Free Negro Family: A Study of Family Origins before the Civil War*. Nashville: Fisk University Press, 1932.

———. *The Negro Church in America*. New York: Schocken Books, 1964.

———. *The Negro Family in the United States*. Chicago: University of Chicago Press, 1939.

Freeman, Edward A. *The Epoch of Negro Baptists and the Foreign Mission Board*. New York: Arno Press, 1980.

Frenkel, M. Yu. "Edward Blyden and the Concept of African Personality." *African Affairs* 73 (1974): 277–89.

Fyfe, Christopher. *Africanus Horton, 1835–1883, West African Scientist and Patriot*. Aldershot, UK: Gregg Revivals, 1972.

Gaines, Kevin. *American Africans in Ghana: Black Expatriates during the Civil Rights Era*. Chapel Hill: University of North Carolina Press, 2006.

Gates, Henry Louis, and William L. Andrews, eds. *Pioneers of the Black Atlantic: Five Slave Narratives from the Enlightenment 1772–1815*. Washington, DC: Civitas Counterpoint, 1998.

———. "A Preliminary Response to Ali Mazrui's Preliminary Critique of Wonders of the African World." *West African Review* 1, no. 2 (2000): 10–14.

Garvey, Marcus. *The Philosophy and Opinions of Marcus Garvey: Or Africa for the Africans*. Compiled by Amy Jacques Garvey. Dover, NY: The Majority Press, 1986.

Gaspar, David Barry. "The Antigua Slave Conspiracy of 1736: A Case Study of the Origins of Collective Resistance." *William and Mary Quarterly* 35, no. 2 (1978): 308–23.

Geiss, Immanuel. *The Pan-African Movement: A History of Pan-Africanism in America, Europe and Africa*. New York: African Publishing Co., 1974.

Gilroy, Paul. *The Black Atlantic, Modernity and Double Consciousness*. Cambridge, MA: Harvard University Press, 1993.

Gocking, Roger. "Creole Society and the Revival of Traditional Culture in Cape Coast during the Colonial Period." *The International Journal of African Historical Studies* 17 (1984): 601–22.

———. *Facing Two Ways: Ghana's Coastal Communities Under Colonial Rule*. Lanham,

MD: University Press of America, 1999.

Gollock, Georgina A. *Sons of Africa.* London: Student Christian Movement, 1928.

Gomez, Michael. *Black Crescent: The Experience and Legacy of African Muslims in the Americas.* Cambridge: Cambridge University Press, 2005.

———. *Diasporic Africa: A Reader.* New York: New York University Press, 2006.

———. *Exchanging Our Country Marks: The Transformations of African Identities in the Colonial and Antebellum South.* Chapel Hill: University of North Carolina Press, 1998.

———. *Reversing Sail: A History of the African Diaspora.* Cambridge: Cambridge University Press, 2005.

Gottlieb, Karla. *The Mother of Us All: A History of Queen Nanny, Leader of the Windward Jamaican Maroons.* Trenton, NJ: Africa World Press, 2000.

Greenberg, Joseph. *Studies in African Linguistic Classification.* New Haven, CT: Yale University Press, 1955.

Guggenheimer, Heinrich W., and Eva H. Guggenheimer. *Jewish Family Names and Their Origins: An Etymological Dictionary.* Hoboken, NJ: KTAV Publishing House, 1992.

Gyekye, Kwame. *African Philosophical Thought: Akan Conceptual Scheme.* Cambridge: Cambridge University Press, 1987.

Gwynn, Stephen. *The Life of Mary Kingsley.* London: MacMillan, 1932.

Habermas, Jürgen. "The Public Sphere: An Encyclopedia Article" (1964). In *The Idea of the Public Sphere*, edited by Jostein Gripsrud, Hallvard Moe, Anders Molander, and Graham Murdock, 114–26. Lanham, MD: Lexington Books, 2010.

Hair, P. E. H. "Africanism: The Freetown Contribution." *The Journal of Modern African Studies* 5 (1967): 521–39.

Hall, Gwendolyn M. *Africans in Colonial Louisiana: The Development of Afro-Creole Society in the Eighteenth Century.* Baton Rouge: Louisiana State University, 1992.

———. *Slavery and African Ethnicities in the Americas: Restoring the Links.* Chapel Hill: University of North Carolina Press, 2005.

Hall, Neville A. T. *Slave Society in the Danish West Indies: St. Thomas, St. John and St. Croix.* Edited by B. W. Higman. Baltimore: Johns Hopkins University Press, 1992.

Hamilton, Ruth Simms. *Routes of Passage: Rethinking the African Diaspora.* East Lansing: Michigan State University Press, 2007.

Hammond, Dorothy, and Alta Jablow. *The Africa That Never Was: Four Centuries of British Writing on Africa.* Long Grove, IL: Waveland Press, 1992.

Hanchard, Michael. *Orpheus and Power: The Movimento Negro of Rio de Janeiro and Sao Paulo, Brazil 1945–1988.* Princeton: Princeton University Press, 1994.

Hanretta, Sean. "The River of Salvation Flows through Africa: Blyden, Armattoe, and the Redemption of the Culture Concept." In *Indigenous Visions: Rediscovering the World of Franz Boas*, edited by Ned Blackhawk and Isaiah Lorado Wilner, 279–315.

New Haven: Yale University Press, 2018.

Hansen, Thorkhild. *Island of Slaves*. Translated by Kari Dako. Accra: Sub-Saharan Publishers, 2004.

———. *Ships of Slaves*. Translated by Kari Dako. Accra: Sub-Saharan Publishers, 2007.

Harding, Vincent. *There Is a River: The Black Struggle for Freedom in America*. New York: Harcourt Brace Jovanovich, 1981.

———. "Vocation of the Black Scholar." *Harvard Educational Review* (1974): 3–29.

Harrell-Bond, Barbara E., Allen M. Howard, and David E. Skinner. *Community, Leadership, and the Transformation, of Freetown, (1801–1976): Change and Continuity in Africa*. The Hague: Mouton, 1978.

Harris, Joseph, ed. *Global Dimensions of the African Diaspora*. Washington, DC: Howard University Press, 1982.

Hartog, J. "The Honen Daliem Congregation of St. Eustatius." *American Jewish Archives* 19 (1967): 60–77.

———. *The Jews and St. Eustatius*. St. Martin: Windward Islands Bank, 1976.

Hayford, J. E. C. *Ethiopia Unbound: Studies in Race Emancipation*. London: Frank Cass, 1969.

———. *Gold Coast Native Institutions: With Thoughts upon a Healthy Imperial Policy for the Gold Coast and Ashanti*. London: Frank Cass, 1970.

———. *William Waddy Harris: The West African Reformer*. London: C. M. Phillips, 1915.

Headland, Thomas, Kenneth Pike, and Marvin Harris, eds. *Emics and Etics: The Insider/Outsider Debate*. Thousand Oaks, CA: Sage Publications, 1990.

Hegel, G. W. F. *The Philosophy of History*. Translated by J. Sibree. New York: Dover Publications, 1956.

Henige, David, and T. C. McCaskie, eds. *West Africa Economic and Social History: Studies in Memory of Marion Johnson*. Madison: African Studies Program, University of Wisconsin, 1990.

Henriksen, Thomas H. "African Intellectual Influences on Black Americans: The Role of Edward Blyden." *Phylon* 36 (1960): 279–90.

Herder, Johan Gottfried. *Ideas for the Philosophy of the History of Humanity* (1784–1791). In *J.G. Herder on Social and Political Culture*, translated and edited by F. M. Barnard. Cambridge: Cambridge University Press, 1969.

Hernaes, Per. O. *Slaves, Danes, and African Society: The Danish Slave Trade from West Africa and Afro-Danish Relations on the Eighteenth Century Gold Coast*. Trondheim: University of Trondheim, 1995.

Herskovits, Melville J. *The Myth of the Negro Past*. Boston: Beacon Press, 1958.

———. "On the Provenience of New World Negroes." *Social Forces* 12 (1933): 247–62.

———. "A Preliminary Consideration of the Culture Areas of Africa." *American Anthropologist* 26 (1924): 50–63.

Herskovits, Melville J., Frances S. Herskovits, and Mieczyslaw Kolinski. *Suriname Folklore.* New York: Columbia University Press, 1936.

Heywood, Linda M. *Central Africans and Cultural Transformations in the American Diaspora.* Cambridge: Cambridge University, 2002.

———. *Central Africans, Atlantic Creoles, and the Foundations of the Americas 1585–1660.* Cambridge: Cambridge University Press, 2007.

Hill, Robert, ed. *Pan-African Biography.* Los Angeles: African Studies Center, University of California, Los Angeles, 1987.

Hine, Darlene Clarke, Wilma King, and Linda Reed, eds. *"We Specialize in the Wholly Impossible": A Reader in Black Women's History.* Brooklyn, NY: Carlson Pub., 1995.

Holden, Edith. *Blyden of Liberia: An Account of the Life and Labors of Edward Wilmot Blyden, LL.D. As Recorded in Letters and in Print.* New York: Vantage Press, 1966.

Hooker, J. R. *The Pan-African Conference 1900.* Transition no. 46 (1974): 1–6.

Horton, James Africanus. *The Dawn of Nationalism in Modern Africa: Extracts from the Political, Educational, Scientific and Medical Writings of J. A. B. Horton.* Edited by Davidson Nicol. London: Harlow, Longmans, 1969.

———. *West African Countries and Peoples: A Vindication of the Negro Race.* Edinburgh: Edinburgh University Press, 1969.

Hountodji, Paulin. *African Philosophy: Myth and Reality.* Bloomington: Indiana University Press, 1983.

Hrbek, I. "Written Sources from the Fifteenth Century Onwards." In *UNESCO General History of Africa*, vol.1, *Methodology and African Prehistory (Abridged)*, edited by J. Ki-Zerbo, 114–41. Berkeley: University of California Press, 1981.

Hunt, James. *The Negro's Place in Nature: A Paper Read before the London Anthropological Society.* New York: Van Evrie, Horton & Co., 1864.

Hunwick John. *Africa, Islam, and the Arab World: Studies in Honor of Basil Davidson.* Princeton, NJ: Markus Wiener, 2003.

Hunwick, John, and Nancy Lawler. *Afro-Jewish Encounters from Timbuktu to the Indian Ocean and Beyond.* Princeton, NJ: Markus Wiener, 2014.

———, eds. *The Cloth of Many Colored Silks: Papers on History and Society, Ghanaian and Islamic in Honor of Ivor Wilks.* Evanston, IL: Northwestern University Press, 1996.

———. *Jews of a Saharan Oasis: The Elimination of the Tamantif Community.* Princeton, NJ: Markus Wiener, 2006.

Insoll, T. *The Archeology of Islam in Sub-Saharan Africa.* Cambridge: Cambridge University Press, 2003.

Irele, Abiola. *The African Experience in Literature and Ideology.* Bloomington: Indiana University Press, 1981.

Jacobs, Sylvia M., ed. *Black Americans and the Missionary Movement in Africa.* Westport,

CT: Greenwood Press, 1982.

———. "'Say Africa When You Pray': The Activities of Early Black Baptist Women Missionaries Among Liberian Women and Children." *Sage* 3 (Fall 1986): 16–21.

Jalloh, Alusine, and David E. Skinner, eds. *Islam and Trade in Sierra Leone.* Trenton, NJ: Africa World Press, 1997.

James, C. L. R. *Black Jacobins: Toussaint L'Ouverture and the San Domingo Revolution.* New York: Vintage Books, 1963.

Jenkins, Paul, ed. *The Recovery of the West African Past: African Pastors and African History in the Nineteenth Century; C.C. Reindorf & Samuel Johnson; Papers from an International Seminar Held in Basel, Switzerland, 25–28th October 1995 to Celebrate the Centenary of the Publication of C.C. Reindorf's* History of the Gold Coast and Asante. Basel: Basler Afrika Bibliographien, 1986.

Jeppie, Shamil, and Souleymane Bachir Diagne, eds. *The Meanings of Timbuktu.* Cape Town: HSRC Press/CODESRIA, 2008.

Johnson-Odim, Cheryl, and Nina Emma Mba. *For Women and the Nation: Funmilayo Ransome-Kuti.* Urbana: University of Illinois Press, 1997.

Jones, Wilbur Deveraux. "Blyden, Gladstone and the War." *Journal of Negro History* 49, no. 1 (1964): 56–58.

Jones-Quartey, K. A. B. *The Problems of the Press, in West African Affairs.* London: Bureau of Current Affairs, 1950.

July, Robert W. *A History of the African People.* New York: Charles Scribner's Sons, 1970.

———. "Nineteenth-Century Negritude: Edward Wilmot Blyden." *The Journal of African History* 5 (1964): 73–86.

———. *The Origins of Modern African Thought: Its Development in West Africa during the Nineteenth and Twentieth Centuries.* New York: Praegar, 1967.

Justesen, Ole. *Danish Sources for the History of Ghana 1657–1754, vol. 1: 1657–1735, vol. 2: 1735–1754.* Copenhagen: Royal Danish Academy Sciences and Letters, 2005.

———. "Henrich Richter 1785–1849: Trader and Politician in the Danish Settlements on the Gold Coast." *Transactions of the Historical Society of Ghana*, n.s., 7 (2003): 93–192.

Kaba, Lansine. "The Atlantic Slave Trade Was Not a 'Black-on-Black Holocaust.'" *African Studies Review* 44 (2001): 1–20.

Kagan, Richard L., and Phillip D. Morgan, eds. *Atlantic Diasporas: Jews, Conversos, and Crypto-Jews in the Age of Mercantilism 1500–1800.* Baltimore: Johns Hopkins University Press, 2009.

Kaplan, Flora, ed. *Queens, Queen Mothers, Priestesses, and Power: Case Studies in African Gender.* New York Academy of Sciences, 1997.

Karp, Ivan., and D. A. Masolo, eds. *African Philosophy as Cultural Inquiry.* Bloomington, Indiana University Press, 2000.

Kea, Ray. "'I Am Here to Plunder on the General Road' Bandits and Banditry in Pre-Nineteenth Century Gold Coast." In *Banditry, Rebellion and Social Protest in Africa*, edited by Donald Crummey. London: James Currey, 1986.

———. "'When I Die, I Shall Return to My Own Land': An 'Amina' Slave Rebellion in the Danish West Indies, 1733–1734." In *The Cloth of Many Colored Silks: Papers on History and Society, Ghanaian and Islamic in Honor of Ivor Wilks*, edited by John Hunwick and Nancy Lawler (Evanston, IL: Northwestern University Press, 1996).

Kelley, Robin D. "How the West Was One: On the Uses and Limitations of the Diaspora." *Black Scholar* 30, no. 3 (2000): 31–37.

Khondker, Habibul Haque. "Glocalization as Globalization: Evolution of a Sociological Concept." *Bangladesh e-Journal of Sociology* 1, no. 2 (2004): 12–20.

Ki-Zerbo, Joseph, ed. *UNESCO General History of Africa*. Vol. 1, *Methodology and African Prehistory (Abridged)*. Berkeley: University of California Press, 1981.

Knox, Robert. *The Races of Men*. London, 1850.

Konadu, Kwasi. *The Akan Diaspora in the Americas*. Oxford: Oxford University Press, 2010.

Korang, Kwaku L. *Writing Ghana, Imagining Africa: Nation and African Modernity*. Rochester, NY: University of Rochester Press, 2003.

Korieh, J. Chima. "African Ethnicity as Mirage? Historicizing the Essence of the Igbo in Africa and the Atlantic Diaspora." *Dialectical Anthropology* 30, no. 1 (2006): 91–118.

Kpobi, David N. A. *Mission in Chains: The Life, Theology, and Ministry of the Ex-Slave Jacobus E.J. Capitein (1717–1747); With a Translation of His Major Publications*. Zoetermeer: Boekencentrum, 1993.

Kraidy, M. M. "The Local, the Global and the Hybrid: A Native Ethnography of Glocalization." *Critical Studies in Media Communication* 16, no. 4 (1999): 456–77.

Kropp Dakubu, M. E. *Korle Meets the Sea: A Socio-Linguistic View of Accra*. New York: Oxford University Press, 1997.

———. *One Voice: The Linguistic Culture of an Accra Lineage*. Leiden: African Studies Center, 1981.

Langley, J. A. *Pan-Africanism and Nationalism in West Africa, 1900–1945: A Study in Ideology and Social Classes*. Oxford: Clarendon Press, 1973.

Law, Robin. "Ethnicities of Enslaved Africans in the Diaspora: On the Meaning of 'Mina' (Again)." *History of Africa* 32 (2005): 247–67.

Lawrence, A. W. *Trade Castles and Forts of West Africa*. London, 1965.

Levtzion, Nehemiah. *Ancient Ghana and Mali*. London: Methuen, 1973.

———. *Islam in West Africa: Religion, Society, and Politics to 1800*. Norfolk, UK: Variorum, 1994.

Lewis, Maureen W. *Notes to Masks*. Benin City, NG: Ethiope Publishing Corporation,

1977.
Little, K. L. "The Significance of the West African Creole for Africanist and Afro-American Studies." *African Affairs* 49 (1950): 309–19.
Livingston, Thomas W. *Education and Race: A Biography of Edward Wilmot Blyden*. San Francisco: Glendessary Press, 1975.
Long, Charles H. "Transculturation: An Overview." Unpublished manuscript, 2006.
Lovejoy, Paul E. "Autobiography and Memory: Gustavus Vassa, Alias Olaudah Equiano, the African." *Slavery and Abolition* 27, no. 3 (2006), 317–47.
———. "Issues of Motivation—Vassa/Equiano and Carretta's Critique of the Evidence." *Slavery and Abolition* 28, no. 1 (2007): 121–25.
———. *Salt of the Desert Sun*. Cambridge: Cambridge University Press, 1986.
Lovejoy, Paul E., and David V. Trotman, eds. *Trans-Atlantic Dimensions of Ethnicity in the African Diaspora*. London: Continuum, 2003.
Lugard, Frederick J. D. *The Dual Mandate in British Tropical Africa*. Edinburgh: William Blackwood and Sons, 1922.
Lynch, Hollis R. *Black Spokesman: Selected Published Writings of Edward Wilmot Blyden*. London: Frank Cass, 1971.
———. *Edward Wilmot Blyden: Pan-Negro Patriot 1832–1912*. London: Oxford University Press, 1970.
———, ed. *Selected Letters of Edward Wilmot Blyden*. Millwood, NY: KTO Press, 1978.
Lynn, Martin. "Technology, Trade and 'A Race of Native Capitalists': The Krio Diaspora of West Africa and the Steamship, 1852–95." *The Journal of African History* 33, no. 3 (1992): 421–40.
Mandaza, Ibbo, and Dani Wadada Nabudere, eds. *Pan-Africanism and Integration in Africa*. Harare, ZI: SAPES Books, 2002.
Mann, Gregory. "Afropositivism." *Cultural Anthropology Online*, June 10, 2013, https://culanth.org.
Marable, Manning. "Black Studies and the Black Intellectual Tradition." *Race & Reason* 4 (1997–1998): 3–8.
———. *Dispatches from the Ebony Tower: Black Intellectuals Confront the African American Experience*. New York: Columbia University Press, 2000.
Marees, Pieter de, A. van Dantzig, and Adam Jones. *Description and Historical Account of the Gold Kingdom of Guinea (1602)*. Oxford: Oxford University Press, 1987.
Mark, Peter, and Jose da Silva Horta, *The Forgotten Diaspora: Jewish Communities in West Africa and the Making of the Atlantic World*. New York: Cambridge University Press, 2011.
Masolo, D. A. *African Philosophy in Search of Identity*. Bloomington: Indiana Press, 1994.
Matory, James L. *Black Atlantic Religion: Tradition, Transnationalism, and Matriarchy in the Afro-Brazilian Candomblé*. Princeton, NJ: Princeton University Press, 2005.

Mazrui, Ali A. *The Africans: A Triple Heritage.* New York: Little Brown, 1986.

———. "Pan-Africanism and the Globalization of Africa: A Triple Process." In *W. E. B. Dubois–George Padmore–Kwame Nkrumah Lecture Series.* Accra: DuBois Center, 2001.

———. "Pan-Africanism and the Origins of Globalization." In *W. E. B. Dubois–George Padmore–Kwame Nkrumah Lecture Series.* Accra: DuBois Center, 2001.

———. "Preliminary Critique of Gates' African Wonders." *West Africa Review* 1, no. 2 (2000): 5–6.

Mbabuike, Michael C. "Wonders Shall Never Cease: Decoding Henry Louis Gates's Ambiguous Adventure." *Journal of Black Studies* 31 (2000): 232–46.

Mbiti, John S. *African Religions and Philosophy.* Portsmouth, NH: Heinemann, 1990.

McClendon, John H., III. "Introduction to Drs. Anton Wilhelm Amo and Charles Leander Hill with Select Bibliography." *American Philosophical Association Newsletter on Philosophy and the Black Experience* 2, no. 2 (2003): 42–50.

———. "Nkrumah's Consciencism as Philosophical Text: Matter of Confusion." *Journal on African Philosophy* 3 (2003): 1–39.

McLuhan, Marshal. *The Global Village: Transformations in World Life and History in the 21st Century.* New York: Oxford University Press, 1989.

Miles, William F. *Jews of Nigeria: An Afro-Judaic Odyssey.* Princeton, NJ: Markus Wiener, 2013.

Mintz, Sydney, and Richard Price. *The Birth of African American Culture: An Anthropological Perspective.* Boston: Beacon Press, 1992.

Mkandawire, Thandika, ed. *African Intellectuals: Rethinking Politics, Language, Gender and Development.* New York: Zed Books/CODESRIA, 2005.

Moore, Moses N., Jr. "Edward Blyden and the Presbyterian Mission in Liberia." *Union Seminary Quarterly Review* 48 (1994): 59–114.

Moore, Sally F. *Anthropology and Africa: Changing Perspectives on a Changing Scene.* Charlottesville: University Press of Virginia, 1994.

Morgan, Phillip D. "Becoming African: Identity Formation among Liberated Slaves in Nineteenth-Century Sierra Leone." *Slavery and Abolition* 27, no. 1 (2006): 1–21.

Morris, Charles S. *Ecumenical Missionary Conference.* New York: American Tract Society, 1900.

Moses, Wilson J. *Afrotopia: The Roots if African American Popular History.* New York: Cambridge University Press, 1998.

———, ed. *Classical Black Nationalism: From the American Revolution to Marcus.* New York: New York Universities Press, 1996.

———. "The Lost World of the Negro, 1895–1919: Black Literary and Intellectual Life before the 'Renaissance.'" *Black American Literature Forum* 21, nos. 1–2 (1987): 61–84.

Moss, Alfred A. *American Negro Academy.* Baton Rouge: Louisiana State University Press, 1981.

Muchie, Mammo. *The Making of the African Nation: Pan-Africanism and the African Renaissance.* London: Adonis & Abbey, 2003.

Mudimbe, V. Y. *The Invention of Africa: Gnosis, Philosophy, and Order of Knowledge.* Bloomington: Indiana University Press, 1988.

Montilus, Guerin C. "Guinea versus Congo Lands: Aspects of the Collective Memory in Haiti." In *Global Dimensions of the African Diaspora*, edited by Joseph Harris, 163–69. Washington, DC: Howard University Press, 1982.

Murrell, Nathaniel Samuel, William David Spencer, and Adrian Anthony McFarlane, eds. *The Rastafari Reader: Chanting Down Babylon.* Philadelphia, PA: Temple University Press, 1998.

Nantambu, Kwame. "Pan-Africanism Versus Pan-African Nationalism: An Afrocentric Analysis." *Journal of Black Studies* 28 (1998): 561–74.

Nascimento, Abdias D. *Africans in Brazil: A Pan-African Perspective.* Trenton, NJ: Africa World Press, 1989.

Neuberger, Benyamin. "Early African Nationalism, Judaism and Zionism: Edward Wilmot Blyden." *Jewish Social Studies* 47, no. 2 (1985): 151–66.

Nichol, Davidson. "Great Sons of Africa" *Africana* 1, no. 2 (1949): 19–20.

Nketsia, J. H. *Ethnomusicology and African Music Modes of Inquiry and Interpretation.* Vol. 1. Accra: Afram Publications, 2005.

Nkrumah, Kwame. *Consciencism: Philosophy and Ideology for Decolonization.* London: Panaf, 1978.

———. *Ghana: The Autobiography of Kwame Nkrumah.* New York: International Publishers, 1957.

Nørregaard, Georg N. *Danish Settlements in West Africa, 1658–1850.* Translated by Sigurd Mammen. Boston: Boston University Press, 1966.

Northrup, David. *Africa's Discovery of Europe, 1450–1850.* New York: Oxford University Press, 2014.

———. "Igbo and Myth Igbo: Culture and Ethnicity in the Atlantic World." *Slavery and Abolition* 21, no. 3 (2000): 1–20.

Northup, Solomon. *Twelve Years a Slave.* New York: Penguin, 2012.

Nwokeji, Ugo G. "Colloquy with the Author: Vincent Carretta and 'Equiano, the African.'" *Studies in Eighteenth-Century Culture* 38 (2009): 1–14.

———. *The Slave Trade and Culture in the Bight of Biafra: An African Society in the Atlantic World.* New York: Cambridge University Press, 2010.

Odamtten, Harry N. K. "Critical Departures in the Practice of Pan-Africanism in the New Millennium." In *Pan-Africanism, and the Politics of African Citizenship and Identity,* edited by Toyin Falola and Kwame Essien, 172–86. New York: Routledge,

2014.

———. "Dode Akabi: A Reexamination of the Oral and Textual Narrative of a 'Wicked' Female King." *Journal of Women's History* 27, no. 3 (2015): 61–85.

Odamtten, K. Silvanus. *Indigenous and Western Educational Systems in Ghana.* Accra: Ghana Universities Press, 1986.

———. *Indigenous Educational Ideas in Ghana.* Accra: Ghana National Association of Teachers, GNAT, 1995.

———. *Missionary Factor in Ghana's Development up to the 1800's.* Accra: Waterville Publishing, 1978.

Oduro-Frimpong, Joseph. "Glocalization Trends: The Case of Hiplife Music in Contemporary Ghana." *International Journal of Communication* 3 (2009): 1085–106.

Ogede, O. S. "'The Igbo Roots of Olaudah Equiano' by Catherine Acholonu." *Africa: Journal of the International African Institute* 61, no. 1 (1991): 138–41.

Ogot, B. A., ed. *UNESCO General History of Africa.* Vol. 5, *Africa from the Sixteenth to the Eighteenth Century.* Berkeley: University of California Press, 1992.

Ogude, S. E. *No Roots Here: On the Igbo Roots of Olaudah Equiano.* Ibadan, NG: Bookman Educational and Communication Services, 1989.

Okafor, Victor. "An Afrocentric Critique of Appiah's *In My Father's House.*" *Journal of Black Studies* 24 (1993): 196–212.

Okonjo, Kamene. "The Dual Sex Political System in Operation: Igbo Women and Community Politics in Midwestern Nigeria." In *Women in Africa: Studies in Social and Economic Change*, edited by Edna G. Bay and Nancy J. Hafkin. Stanford: Stanford University Press, 1976.

Okonkwo, Rina. "Adelaide Casely Hayford: Cultural Nationalist and Feminist." *Phylon* 42, no. 1 (1981): 41–51.

Oldendorp, C. G. A. *Historie der caribischen Inseln Sanct Thomas, Sanct Crux und Sanct Jan, insbesondere der dasigen Neger und der Mission der evangelischen Brüder-Unität Herrnhut, Erster Teil.* Edited by Gudrun Meier et al. Berlin: Staatliches Museum für Völkerkunde Dresden, 2000.

———. *History of the Mission of the Evangelical Brethren on the Caribbean Islands of St. Thomas, St. Croix, and St. John.* Translated by Arnold R. Highfield and Vladimir Borac. Edited by Johan Jakob Bossard. Ann Arbor: Karoma Publishers, 1987.

Omulokoli, Watson A. O. "William Wade Harris: Premier African Evangelist." *African Journal of Evangelical Theology* 21, no. 1 (2002): 3–11.

Ortiz, Fernando. *Cuban Counterpoint: Tobacco and Sugar.* New York: A. A. Knopf, 1947.

———. *Etnia y sociedad.* Havana: Editorial de Ciencias Sociales, 1993.

———. *Los negros esclavos.* Havana: Editorial de Ciencias Sociales, 1987.

Ottenberg, Simon, and Phoebe Ottenberg, eds. *Cultures and Societies of Africa.* New

York: Random House, 1960.

Owusu, Maxwell. "Ethnography of Africa: The Usefulness of the Useless." *American Anthropologist* 80 (1978): 310–34.

Padmore, George. *Pan-Africanism or Communism.* New York: Anchor Books, 1972.

Paiewonsky, Isidor. *Jewish Historical Development in the Virgin Islands 1665–1959.* St. Thomas: published by author, 1959.

Pannet, Pierre J. *Report on the Execrable Conspiracy Carried Out by the Amina Negroes on the Danish Island of St. Jan in America, 1733.* Translated and edited by Aimery P. Caron and Arnold R. Highfield. Christiansted, St. Croix: Antilles Press, 1984.

Paquette, Robert L. "Jacobins of the Lowcountry: The Vesey Plot on Trial." *William and Mary Quarterly* 59, no. 1 (2002): 185–92.

Parfitt, Tudor. *Black Jews in Africa and the Americas.* Cambridge, MA: Harvard University Press, 2013.

Paris, Francois d. *Voyage of the Coast of Africa, Named Guinea, and to the Isles of America, Made in the Years 1682 and 1683.* Translated by Aimery Caron. Madison: University of Wisconsin, African Studies Program, 2001.

Parker, J. *Making the Town: Ga State and Society in Early Colonial Accra.* Portsmouth: Heinemann, 2000.

Parrinder, E. G. "Islam in West African Indigenous Religion," *Numen* 6, no. 1 (1959): 130–41.

Patterson, Ruby F., and Robin D. G. Kelley. "Unfinished Migrations: Reflections on the African Diaspora and the Making of the New World." *African Studies Review* 43, no. 1 (2000): 11–45.

Patton, June O. "'And the Truth Shall Make You Free': Richard Robert Wright, Sr., Black Intellectual and Iconoclast, 1877–1897." *Journal of Negro History* 81, no. 1 (1996): 17–30.

Pereira, Duarte Pacheco. *Esmeraldo de Situ Orbis: Côte occidentale d'Afrique du Sud Marocain au Gabon.* Translated by R. Mauny. Bissau, 1956.

Piersen, William. "Putting Down Ole Massa: African Satire in the New World." In *African Folklore in the New World*, edited by Daniel J. Crowley. Austin: University of Texas Press, 1977.

Prah, Kwesi Kwah. *Back to Africa: Afro-Brazilian Returnees and Their Communities.* Cape Town: Centre for Advanced Studies of African Society, 2009.

Pratt, Mary Louise. *Imperial Eyes: Travel Writing and Transculturation.* New York: Routledge, 1992.

Priestley, Margaret. *West African Trade and Coast Society: A Family Study.* London: Oxford University Press, 1969.

Protten, Christian. "Des Malatten C. J. Prottens Schrieben um die Aufnahme in die Evange: Mährische Brüder-Gemeine" [The Mullato C. J. Protten's description of his admission to the Evangelical Moravian Brethren's congregation]. In Nikolaus Ludwig von Zinzendorf, *Ergänzungsband VII*. Hildesheim, 1965.

———. *Useful Grammatical Introduction to the Hitherto Completely Unknown Language of Fante and Ga*. Copenhagen: Protten, 1764.

Racine, Daniel L. ed. *Leon-Gotran Damas 1912–1978: Founder of the Negritude Movement, a Memorial Casebook*. Washington, DC: University Press of America, 1979.

Rashid, Samory. *Black Muslims in the US: History, Politics, and the Struggle of a Community* New York: Palgrave Macmillan, 2013.

Rask, Johannes. *Two Views from Christianborg*. Translated from Danish by Selena Winsnes. Legon, Accra, Ghana: Sub-Saharan Publishers, 2009.

Reade, W. Winwood. *Savage Africa*. London, 1964.

Reindorf, Carl C. *The History of the Gold Coast and Asante: Based on Traditions and Historical Facts Comprising a Period of More Than Three Centuries from about 1500–1860*. Basel: Basel Mission Depot, 1895.

Reindorf, Carl D. *Remembering Rev. Carl Reindorf*. Osu, GH: published by author, 1984.

Reindorf, J. *Scandinavians in Africa: Guide Relating to Ghana in the Danish National Archives*. Edited by J. Simensen. Oslo: Universitetsforlaget, 1980.

Reis, Joao Jose. *Slave Rebellion in Brazil: The Muslim Uprising of 1835 in Bahia*. Baltimore: Johns Hopkins University Press, 1993.

Relkin, S. T., and M. Abrams. *A Short History of the Hebrew Congregation of St. Thomas*. St. Thomas, 1983.

Robinson, David. *Muslim Societies in African History*. Cambridge: Cambridge University Press, 2004.

Rodney, Walter. "African Slavery and Other Forms of Social Oppression on the Upper Guinea Coast in the Context of the Atlantic Slave Trade." *Journal of African History* 7 (1966): 431–43.

———. *Groundings with my Brothers*. London: Bogle L'Ouverture, 1969.

———. *A History of the Upper Guinea Coast, 1545–1800*. New York: Monthly Review Press, 1970.

———. *How Europe Underdeveloped Africa*. London: Bogle-L'Ouverture Publications, 1972.

———. *West Africa and the Atlantic Slave Trade*. Nairobi: East African Pub. House, 1967.

Rodriguez, Raimundo N. *Os africanos no Brasil*. Rio de Janeiro: Centro-Edelstein de Pesquisa Social, 2010.

Romer, Ludwig F. *A Reliable Account of the Coast of Guinea (1760)*. Oxford: Oxford University Press, 2000.

Rothberg, Robert I., and Ali A. Mazrui. *Protest and Power in Black Africa*. New York: Oxford University Press, 1970.

Safran, William. "Diasporas in Modern Societies: Myths of Homeland and Return." *Diaspora* 1, no. 1 (1991): 83–99.

Sanneh, Lamin. "The Domestication of Islam and Christianity in African Societies: A Methodological Exploration." *Journal of Religion in Africa* 11, no. 1 (1980): 1–12.

Savage, E. *The Human Commodity: Perspectives on the Trans-Saharan Slave Trade.* London: Frank Cass, 1992.

Schieffelin, H. M., ed. *The People of Africa: A Series of Papers on Their Character, Conditions and Future.* New York: Anson D. R. Randolph, 1871.

Scott, James C. *Domination and the Arts of Resistance.* New Haven, CT: Yale University Press, 1990.

Sebald, Peter. "Christian Jacob Protten Africanus (1715–1769) Erster Missionar Einer Deutschen Missionsgelleschaft in Schwarzafrika." In *Kolonien und Missionen Referate des 3: Internationalen Kolonialgeschictlichen Symposiums 1993*, edited by Wilfred Wagner. Münster: LIT Verlag, 1994.

Senghor, Leopold S. *The Foundations of "Africanité" or "Négritude" and "Arabité."* Translated by Mercer Cook. Paris: Presence Africaine, 1971.

Sensbach, John F. *Rebecca's Revival: Creating Black Christianity in the Atlantic World.* Cambridge, MA: Harvard University Press, 2005.

Seraile, William. *Fire in His Heart: Bishop Benjamin Tucker Tanner and the A.M.E. Church* Knoxville: University of Tennessee Press, 1998.

Serequeberhan, Tsenay. *Contested Memory: The Icons of the Occidental Tradition.* Trenton, NJ: Africa World Press, 2007.

———. *The Hermeneutics of African Philosophy: Horizon and Discourse.* New York: Routledge, 1994.

———. *Our Heritage: The Past in the Present of African-American and African Existence.* Lanham, MD: Rowman and Littlefield, 2000.

Shaffer, Marguerite S., ed. *Public Culture: Diversity, Democracy, and Community in the United States.* Philadelphia: University of Pennsylvania Press, 2008.

Shank, David. "The Prophet Harris: A Historiographical and Bibliographical Survey." *Journal of Religion in Africa* 14, no. 2 (1983): 130–60.

———. *Prophet Harris, "The Black Elijah" of West Africa.* New York: Brill, 1994.

Sharpley-Whiting, T. Denean. *Negritude Women.* Minneapolis: University of Minnesota Press, 2002.

Shepperson, George A. "Ethiopianism and African Nationalism." *Phylon* 14, no. 1 (1953): 9–18.

———. "Notes on Negro American Influences on the Emergence of African Nationalism." *The Journal of African History* 1, no. 2 (1960): 299–312.

———. "Pan-Africanism and 'Pan–Africanism': Some Historical Notes." *Phylon* 23, no. 4 (1962): 346–58.

Shields, John C. *The Collected Works of Phyllis Wheatley.* New York: Oxford University Press, 1988.

Sibthorpe, A. B. C. *The History of Sierra Leone.* London, 1881.

Simon, Njami, and Lucy Durán, eds. *Africa Remix: Contemporary Art of a Continent.* Johannesburg: Johannesburg Art Gallery, 2007.

Simonsen, Gunvor. "Belonging in Africa: Frederik Svane and Christian Protten on the Gold Coast in the Eighteenth Century." *Itinerario* 31, no. 1 (2015): 91–115.

Singleton, Brent. "'That Ye May Know Each Other': Late Victorian Interactions between West African and British Muslims." *Journal of Muslim Minority Affairs* 29, no. 3 (2009): 369–85.

Skinner, David E. "Conversion to Islam and the Promotion of 'Modern' Islamic Schools in Ghana." *Journal of Religion in Africa* 43 (2013): 426–50.

———. "Islam and Education in the Colony and Hinterland of Sierra Leone (1750–1914)." *Canadian Journal of African Studies* 10, no. 3 (1976): 499–520.

Spieler, Miranda F. *Empire and Underworld: Captivity in French Guyana.* Cambridge, MA: Harvard University Press, 2012.

Spillman, Deborah Shapple. *British Colonial Realism in Africa: Inalienable Objects, Contested Domains.* New York: Palgrave Macmillan, 2012.

Stearns, Peter, ed. *Encyclopedia of World History: Ancient, Medieval, and Modern, Chronologically Arranged.* 6th ed. Boston: Houghton Mifflin, 2001.

Sterling, Dorothy. *The Making of an Afro-American: Martin Robison Delany 1812–1885.* New York: Doubleday, 1971.

Stern, Curt. *Principles of Human Genetics.* 3rd ed. San Francisco: W.H. Freeman, 1973.

Stuckey, Sterling, ed. *The Ideological Origins of Black Nationalism.* Boston: Beacon Press, 1972.

Sutton, H. Eldon. *An Introduction to Human Genetics.* Philadelphia: Saunders College, 1980.

Svalesen, Leif. *The Slave Ship Fredensborg.* Translated by Pat Shaw and Selena Axelrod Winsnes. Bloomington: Indiana University Press, 2000.

Sweet, James. *Domingos Álvares, African Healing, and the Intellectual History of the Atlantic World.* Chapel Hill: University of North Carolina. Press, 2011.

———. "Mistaken Identities? Olaudah Equiano, Domingos Álvares, and the Methodological Challenges of Studying the African Diaspora." *American Historical Review* 114, no. 2 (2009): 279–306.

Tappan, Lewis. "Correspondence of Lewis Tappan and Others with the British and Foreign Anti-Slavery Society [Part 8]." *Journal of Negro History* 13, no. 3 (1927): 413–36.

Taylor, Ula Yvette. *The Veiled Garvey: The Life & Times of Amy Jacques Garvey.* Chapel Hill: University of North Carolina Press, 2002.

Thomas, Hugh. *The Slave Trade: The Story of the Atlantic Slave Trade, 1440–1870*. New York: Simon & Schuster, 1997.

Thompson, Robert F. *Flash of the Spirit: African and Afro-American Art and Philosophy*. New York: Vintage Books, 1983.

Thompson, Vincent B. *The Making of the African Diaspora in the Americas 1441–1990*. New York: Longman, 1987.

Thornton, John K. *Africa and Africans in the Making of the Atlantic World, 1400–1680*. Cambridge: Cambridge University Press, 1992.

———. "'I Am the Subject of the King of Congo': African Political Ideology and the Haitian Revolution." *Journal of World History* 4, no. 2 (1993): 181–214.

———. *The Kongolese Saint Anthony: Dona Beatriz Kimpa Vita and the Antonian Movement, 1684–1706*. Edinburgh: Cambridge University Press, 1998.

Thurston, Robert H. *A History of the Growth of the Steam-Engine*. Ithaca, NY: Cornell University Press, 1939.

Tilleman, Erick. *En Kort Og Enfoldig Beretning Om Det Landskab Guinea Og Dets (1697): A Short and Simple Account of the Country Guine and Its Nature*. Translated by Selena Axelrod Winsnes. Madison: African Studies Program, University of Wisconsin-Madison, 1994.

Tishken, Joel E., Toyin Falola, and Akíntúnde Akínye mi . *Sàngo in Africa and the African Diaspora*. Bloomington: Indiana University Press, 2009.

Trutenau, H. M. J., ed. *Christian Protten's 1764 Introduction to the Fante and Accra (Ga) Languages*. London, 1971.

Ullman, Victor. *Martin R. Delany: The Beginnings of Black Nationalism*. Boston: Beacon Press, 1971.

Verger, Pierre. *Flux et reflux de la traite des negres entre le Golfe de Benin et Bahia de Todos os Santos, du 17 au 19 siecle*. Paris, 1968.

Verlinden, Charles. *L'esclavage dans l'Europe médiévale*. Ghent: Rijksuniversiteit te Gent, 1977.

Vinson, Robert Trenton. *The Americans Are Coming: Dreams of African-American Liberation in Segregationist South Africa*. Athens: Ohio University Press, 2012.

Von Eschen, Penny M. *Race Against Empire: Black Americans and Anticolonialism 1937–1957*. Ithaca: Cornell University Press, 1997.

Wagner, Wilfred, ed. *Kolonien und Missionen Referate des 3: Internationalen Kolonialgeschictlichen Symposiums 1993*. Hamburg, 1994.

Walker, David. *David Walker's Appeal, Together with Four Articles and a Preamble to the Colored Citizens of the World*. Baltimore: Black Classics Press, 1993.

Walters, Alexander. *My Life and Work*. New York: Fleming H. Revell Co., 1917.

Walters, Ronald W. *Pan-Africanism in the African Diaspora: An Analysis of Modern Afrocentric Movements*. Detroit: Wayne State University Press, 1993.

Warner, Michael. *Publics and Counterpublics*. New York: Zone Books, 2002.

Wauthier, Claude. *The Literature and Thought of Modern Africa*. London: Pall Mall Press, 1966.

Westergaard, Waldemar. "Account of the Negro Rebellion on St. Croix, Danish West Indies 1759." *The Journal of Negro History* 11, no. 1 (1926): 50–61.

Wilks, Ivor. *Akwamu 1640–1750: The Rise and Fall of a West African Empire*. Trondheim: University of Trondheim, 2001.

Williams, Michael. *Pan-Africanism: An Annotated Bibliography* Pasadena: Salem Press, 1992.

Williams, Walter L. "Nineteenth Century Pan-Africanist: John Henry Smyth, United States Minister to Liberia, 1878–1885." *Journal of Negro History* 63, no. 1 (1978): 18–25.

Wills, David W., and Newman, Richard. eds. *Asante in the Nineteenth Century: The Structure and Evolution of a Political Order*. Cambridge: Cambridge University Press, 1975.

———. *Black Apostles at Home and Abroad: Afro-Americans and the Christian Mission from the Revolution to Reconstruction*. Boston: G.K. Hall, 1982.

———. "The Forest and the Twis." *Transactions of the Historical Society of Ghana*, n.s., 8 (2004): 1–81.

———. "Medieval Trade Route from the Niger to the Gulf of Guinea." *Journal of African History* 3, no. 2 (1962): 337–41.

———. *One Nation Many Histories: Ghana Past and Present*. Accra: Ghana Universities Press, 1996.

———. "Wangara, Akan and Portuguese in the Fifteenth and Sixteenth Centuries. I. The Matter of Bitu." *Journal of African History* 23, no. 3 (1982): 333–49.

———. "Wangara, Akan and Portuguese in the Fifteenth and Sixteenth Centuries. II. The Struggle for Trade." *Journal of African History* 23, no. 4 (1982): 463–72.

Winant, Howard. *Racial Conditions: Politics, Theory and Comparisons*. Minneapolis: University of Minnesota Press, 1994.

Winsnes, Selena Axelrod. *A Danish Jew in West Africa: Wulff Joseph Wulff Biography and Letters 1836–1842*. Trondheim: Faculty of Arts, Norwegian University of Science and Technology, 2004.

———, ed. *Letters of West Africa and the Slave Trade: Paul Erdman Isert's Journey to Guinea and the Caribbean Islands in Columbia (1788)*. London: Oxford University Press, 1992.

Wiredu, Kwasi, ed. *A Companion to African Philosophy*. Oxford: Blackwell, 2004.

———. *Conceptual Decolonization in African Philosophy: Four Essays*. Ibadan, NG: Hope Publications, 1995.

———. *Cultural Universals and Particulars: An African Perspective*. Bloomington:

Indiana University Press, 1996.

Young, Alexander. *Ethiopian Manifesto* (New York, 1829). In *The Ideological Origins of Black Nationalism*, edited by Sterling Stuckey. Boston: Beacon Press, 1972.

Zeleza, Paul T. *Manufacturing African Studies*. Dakar: CODESRIA, 1997.

Zimmerman, J. A. *Grammatical Sketch and Vocabulary of the Akra or Ga-Language with an Appendix on the Adanme-Dialect*. 2 Vols. Stuggart, 1858.

THESES AND DISSERTATIONS

Bredwa-Mensa, Yaw. "Historical-Archeological Investigations at the Frederiksgave Plantation, Ghana: A Case Study of Slavery and Plantation Life on a Nineteenth Century Danish Plantation on the Gold Coast." PhD diss., University of Ghana, Legon, 2002.

Ekwelie, Sylvanus A. "The Press in Gold Coast Nationalism, 1890–1957." PhD diss., University of Wisconsin, 1971.

Flemming, Tracy K. "Negro Travel and the Pan-African Imagination during the Nineteenth Century." PhD diss., University of Michigan, 2010.

Harr, W. C. "The Negro as an American Protestant Missionary in Africa." PhD diss., University of Chicago Divinity School, 1945.

Jenkins, Raymond G. "Gold Coast Historians and their Pursuits of Gold Coast Pasts: 1882–1917." PhD diss., University of Birmingham, 1985.

Odamtten, Harry N. K. "A History of Ideas: 'The Black Atlantic' West Africa, and Pan-Africanism." PhD diss., Michigan State University, 2010.

Quaye, Irene. "The Ga and Their Neighbors 1600–1742." PhD diss., University of Ghana, Legon, 1972.

Rowand, Evelyn. "Press and Opinion in British West Africa, 1855–1900: The Development of a Sense of Identity Among the Educated British West Africans in the Later Nineteenth Century." PhD diss., University of Birmingham, 1972.

Step, Eddie. "Interpreting a Forgotten Mission: African-American Missionaries of the Southern Baptist Convention in Liberia, West Africa 1846–1860." PhD diss., Baylor University, 1999.

Index

U

V

W

Y

Z